CLASS ACTION

A volume in the Series

C O N T E S T A T I O N S

General Editor
WILLIAM E. CONNOLLY

A full list of titles in the series appears at the end of the book.

An outdoor Industrial Workers of the World meeting, c. 1918. Archives of Labor and Union Affairs, Wayne State University.

CLASS ACTION

Reading Labor, Theory, and Value

William Corlett

Cornell University Press

Ithaca and London

First published 1998 by Cornell University Press
First printing, Cornell Paperbacks, 1998
Printed in the United States of America

Cornell University Press strives to use environmentally responsible suppliers and
materials to the fullest extent possible in the publishing of its books. Such materials
include vegetable-based, low-VOC inks and acid-free papers that are also recycled,
totally chlorine-free, or partly composed of nonwood fibers.

Library of Congress Cataloging-in-Publication Data

Corlett, William.
Class action : reading labor, theory, and value / William Corlett.
   p.   cm. — (Contestations)
Includes index.
ISBN 0-8014-3278-2 (alk. paper). — ISBN 0-8014-8355-7 (pbk. : alk. paper)
1. Labor theory of value.   2. Working class.   3. Marxian economics.   I. Title.
II. Series.
HB206.C67   1998
335.4'12—dc21   98-8357

Cloth printing   10   9   8   7   6   5   4   3   2   1

Paperback printing   10   9   8   7   6   5   4   3   2   1

For Carole Anne

Contents

viii   Contents

Preface

While the U.S. corporation was adjusting to its newfound status as a person in the early twentieth century, its government was attempting to place the Industrial Workers of the World under permanent erasure. But the surviving Wobblies continued to struggle against capital's axiomatic rule and allowed me to join the educational industry in their public service department when I was writing this book. Signing on with a labor union that doubles as a social movement for all workers (regardless of employment) required changing the way I presented myself as a college teacher. Aside from learning how to sing again—me gusta cantar canciones del syndicato—and overcoming an initial fear of publicity whenever cameras, microphones, and reporters attended rallies and protests, I began to work more diligently with other unions in support actions and became more active in labor education, especially my own. Shortly after the Teamsters struck the United Parcel Service in August 1997, for example, I realized that teaching my fall semester theory classes at Bates could be tantamount to teaching "struck goods" because a few of the bosses made deliveries to the college despite our picket line at the industrial park in Auburn, Maine. The distance between this relatively trivial dilemma and those faced by early twentieth-century Wobs might lead one to suspect, along with Howard Zinn, that many comfortable academics, such as myself, would not have actually put their lives—as opposed to their textbooks—on the line for social justice. Nothing in my life so far can allay this suspicion; but I seek nonetheless to do my share, to lend a hand, in the struggle for economic democracy.

The work for *Class Action* began ten years ago at the close of *Community without Unity*, when I suggested that the time is ripe for a deconstruction of the capital-labor binary. Hoping to draw the extravagance of such an academic suggestion closer to the defiant spirit of the Wobblies, *Class Action* attempts to find a way around several persistent rifts in contemporary political theory. First and foremost, I am concerned with the level of misunderstanding between "scholars" and "activists." The convenience of terms such as these draws attention away from action plans already initiated by educational workers and obscures the fact that most people outside academe working for progressive change *are* educators. Second, within the academic community as traditionally construed, I am concerned with the bad blood that persists between theorists who identify with poststructural approaches and those who maintain their loyalty to varieties of Marxism. The latter's insistence on determinant activity sometimes contrasts sharply with the former's embrace of indeterminacy. *Class Action* cannot join either side against the other in these debates; the misunderstandings still hurt and the bad blood often boils for very good reasons.

To say that I seek a way around these conflicts is not to announce their dialectical resolution. Meeting such expectations would require addressing the richly contradictory literature on Marxism and poststructuralism much more adequately than I could here, even if this were my objective. There will be no dialectical relief found in these pages. My proposed way around the nagging tensions is really more like a salvaging operation. Taking what I find useful in the ruins of late twentieth century capitalism, I ask readers to entertain the possibility that several patterns of poststructural thinking are already cut out to address problems of formulating and executing direct action plans. That the most rarefied theoretical maneuvers might help educational workers appreciate the most economically devalued aspects of everyday life remains the paradox that inspired this work. The indeterminacy permitted by poststructural approaches offers new spaces within which we might displace the tired oppositions that keep us from working with one another.

The danger of approaching the scholar-activist and poststructuralist-Marxist tensions in this fashion is that of losing all possible audiences at precisely the moment one aims to multiply them. Scholars will demand more scholarship than I can provide, activists more plans. Poststructuralists will miss their favorite texts; Marxists will find the master texts grossly underread. To guard against these dangers I have taken two precautions. First, although *Class Action* can be read continuously and perhaps should be—with each successive section of the book posing problems, developing models, and resolving those problems—it is also designed to operate as three parallel arguments on the following topics: labor (the first chapters of each section), theory (the middle chapters of each section), and value (the final chapters of each section). Readers might try, then, reading vertically if the usual horizontal approach fails; these twin axes also serve to remind unsympathetic critics that my poststructuralism supplements structure without abandoning it altogether. Second, regardless of the approach readers take to my arguments, I have attempted to explain in great detail how I read the salvaged passages. In this way, if readers disagree with my reading, they will see precisely where I go astray and we can begin to appreciate our differences, instead of merely dropping names and multiplying confusions.

Any book is a collaborative exercise and I want here to acknowledge at least a few of people who helped bring this one to a close. From publishing arguments or translations I could borrow to providing encouragement or criticism to facilitating the actual work of production, many people were involved.

Although we have never met, I relied heavily on the published work and translations of Gayatri Spivak, Judith Butler, and Terrell Carver. Their various works carry a constant reminder that careful scholarship can form the basis of the most tantalizing arguments.

My union activity in Maine became an important part of writing this book and forced me to keep the significance of such an academic exercise in perspective. Fellow Wobblies in my neck of the woods—including Barbara Briggs, Roger Carpentter, Claire Gelinas, Julian Holmes, Tom Johnson, Chris MacKinnon, Audrey Marrá, John Newton, Ray Polley, and Carole Anne Taylor—never let me forget that direct action gets the goods.

Such fine colleagues in social and political theory as Eloise Buker, William Chaloupka, Rom Coles, Christine Di Stefano, Kathy Ferguson, Dennis Fischman, Mary Hawkesworth, Leslie Hill, Mark Kessler, Bradley MacDonald, Bill Martin, John Nelson, Shane Phelan, Diane Rubenstein, Tracy Strong, Carole Anne Taylor, and Kathi Weeks offered encouragement, often accompanied by criticism of various drafts of these chapters.

William Connolly and Linda Zerilli, the two theorists who worked with me most intensely, provided such excellent criticism of the penultimate version of this book that I had to take an extra year or so to finish. I hope they know that my gratitude outdistances even the length of that "year or so."

Cornell University Press provided an excellent copy editor, John LeRoy, whose enviable work combines skill and intelligence. Carol Betsch and Roger Haydon, my principal contacts at the press, always made it possible to take the extra time I needed. I am also grateful that sections of my "Lispector Haunting Marxism," *Strategies* 9/10:69–93, and "Containing

Indeterminacy," *Political Theory* 24:464-92 were permitted to reappear in Chapters 1 and 5, respectively.

Near the end of an exhausting process, several friends and members of my community group, Community E.R.A. (Education, Resources, Action)—Larry Dansinger, Peter Kellman, Audrey Marrá, Cheryl Shaw, Carole Anne Taylor, and Julian Holmes—helped in specific ways with the many final details.

For most of the past decade at Bates I have enjoyed the continual, patient, and quiet support of President Donald Harward, whose good offices helped with the production costs of this book. Others in my workplace who helped me meet the various deadlines include these co-workers: Jan Bureau, Clementine Brasier, Sallie Hackett, Eric Thoreson, and Beverly Carver.

Finally, I dedicate this book to my partner and sister worker, Carole Anne Taylor. Our time together has convinced me that one can sometimes share, though never deserve, a life enriched by the commingling of wild respect and honest love.

Sabattus, Maine   WILLIAM CORLETT

PART ONE

DESIRE AND REPRESENTATION

CHAPTER ONE

Lispector Haunting Marxism

What are the words you do not yet have? What do you need to say? What are the tyrannies you swallow day by day and attempt to make your own, until you will sicken and die of them, still in silence?

—Audre Lorde, *Sister Outsider*

Labor seems not to signify, as Marx once anticipated, the "living, form-giving fire" that discovers "the manifold uses of things." In bourgeois society Labor is a possibility, not a subject. But one must either write about Labor as if it were a subject or perpetuate its silence. Capital, on the other hand, enjoys the very subjectivity that eludes Labor. Such dreams as the I.W.W.'s "one big union" fall prey to the impossible belief that Labor is a subject; and yet dreaming these dreams sometimes kindles the solidarity we need to contest capital's subjectivity. *Class Action* explores the possibility of Labor as subject without succumbing to the belief that this is what it is.

Even though Marx shares a commitment to Labor as the actual subject, calling it "the transience of things," he had no choice but to make capital the subject of his major written work. Given that both owners of labor-power and owners of money are equally free to enter into contracts or to walk away, how (Marx asks) can one explain the resultant asymmetry of power relations when labor-power becomes the object of capital? Any answers require taking seriously how money gains subjectivity (becoming socialized capital) and Labor loses subjectivity (becoming objectified labor-power) in bourgeois society.

Distinguishing ownership of money from the amounts of money spent hiring people is rather like distinguishing Labor from "labor-power," Marx's name for "the aggregate of those mental and physical capabilities existing in . . . human beings . . . which they set in motion whenever they produce a use-value of any kind" (1976a:270). One can approach Labor, the impossible subject, as the (human) state of possessing labor-power. These distinctions make it easier to appreciate the equivalence involved in the buying and selling of labor-power: although money can move from owner to owner with lightning speed, it cannot grow without labor-power; although survivalists may someday prove otherwise, labor-power can rarely replenish itself without money.[1] When facing the transformation of money into "capital," however, one learns quickly that the labor-power consumed is never controlled by Labor. Owners of money do not hire Labor; they hire labor-power from its "subject," that is, Labor. And capital, which was once money, assumes a life of its own even though it is the dominant subject in bourgeois society—a life not easily controlled by the original owners of money, who may profit from its transformation. Capital's subjectivity owes solely to the process of extracting value from the labor-power it consumes.

The relation between a subjectified capital and an objectified labor-power explains how the asymmetrical power relations currently tolerated in Western liberal society coexist with a democratic equivalence many want to maintain: in a word, capital exploits labor-power (where "exploitation" names any legal claim to own what is left over after extracting more value from labor-power than it costs to replenish it). Owners of money, acting as consumers, are free at least to squander their money (including free gifts and other bad investments), to attempt to transform their money into capital, to spend money replenishing their labor-power, and the like. Once transformed out of the money form, capital hires and fires labor-power in a never ending struggle to keep growing. But the human state of being in possession of labor-power—a subjectified Labor—never figures into capital's equations. This renders Marx's actual subject impossible to locate in bourgeois society: Labor becomes an ambiguous abstraction, an impossible dream, a lost cause. Capital, by contrast, appears to be alive and well, assuming new identities. This book attempts to join Marx in exposing capital's masquerade and salvaging the lost subject, Labor.

Marxists, who are not, of course, the only theorists concerned with asymmetries of power, are often asked, even by sympathetic readers, to defend themselves against charges of being preoccupied with the site of production (Parker, 1991:30). A tendency to reduce the subject to a person or a group of people leads contemporary Western theory to raise class issues—when these issues are raised at all—within the rubric of identity politics. Class is sometimes included in discussions of race, sexuality, and gender. And these are groundbreaking times for identity politics. In some poststructural circles (Butler, 1990, 1991; Haraway, 1990; Connolly, 1991) these debates have effectively undermined the stability and reliability of identity. Marxism appears to be threatened by these developments. Not only is the state of possessing labor-power (what I call Labor) rendered invisible, but identity politics is becoming denaturalized. Amid these debates, to make matters worse, capital has achieved precisely the status that actual people have been losing. In addition to effacing Labor during the buying and selling of its labor-power, capital has now acquired personhood, at least in the United States. As a result of some clever railroading during judicial interpretation of the post–Civil War amendments to the U. S. Constitution, corporations (those "artificial persons" created by legal labor-power hired by capital) have been sworn in as naturalized citizens with no objection from immigration officials.[2] While poststructural readings are working to render identity undecidable, corporations are working to consolidate their forces and become even more firmly entrenched. In our times, the nineteenth-century question of asymmetrical equivalence has been answered by the hegemony of capital.

Who can blame progressive activists and scholars, then, for deploring poststructural efforts to displace the subject? With capital apparently invincible and Labor effectively invisible, playing with abandon can appear to be socially irresponsible. But if Labor is already displaced—indeed missing—as a subject in late capitalism, one cannot blame poststructural theory, even though most of its advocates—especially academics with retirement plans and other endowments—continue to benefit from the violent exploitation of transnational labor-power. And if Labor is already displaced, if the point is to reclaim Labor, does it not make sense to read the texts most appreciative of displacement? To move in this direction of locating spaces that are neither situated in discourse nor totally immersed in silence, I am intrigued by the notion of desire, a name for urgency denied agency.

Specifically, I devote these first three chapters to the intimate relationship between desire and representational schemes that allow some subjects and objects in while ushering others out. This requires that I distinguish the articulate demands of subjects one can identify—for example, an antiracist labor union fighting for insurance benefits for same-sex couples, while calculating the value added to the product by each worker—from the murmuring of indeterminate subjectivity—for example, the "nameless and formless, about to be birthed, but already felt" (Lorde, 1984:36). Until we have detected Labor's whereabouts, I cannot assume that Labor participates or could participate in the identity politics of subject and object positioning. Although any argument concerning class action must include (as I propose in Part 3 of this book) efforts to organize employed and unemployed workers in ways that negotiate race, sexuality, gender, and other vestiges of identity politics, Labor must not be confused, at least here at the outset, with these multifarious, sometimes conflicted, negotiations.

Distinguishing different ways of reading Marx now can help sort out possible confusion later on. In the familiar ending of his "Buying and Selling of Labour-Power" (pt. 2, chap. 6 of *Capital*, vol. 1), Marx contrasts the activities of the "market" and transactions concluded outside the limits of this noisy sphere of circulation:

> Let us, therefore, in company with the owner of money and the owner of labour-power, leave this noisy sphere, where everything takes place on the surface and in full view of everyone, and follow them into the hidden abode of production, on whose threshold there hangs the notice "No admittance except on business." Here we shall see, not only how capital produces, but how capital is itself produced. The secret of profit making must at last be laid bare. (Marx, 1976a:279–80)

This surface/"hidden abode" distinction can be read as the positioning of a nearly invisible economic base beneath the more visible capitalist superstructure of bourgeois ideology. Indeed Marx describes the more visible sphere in terms of an "Eden" of natural rights, characterized by "Freedom, Equality, Property, and Bentham." Despite the work of contemporary liberal theory to soften Bentham's calculated pronouncements, Marx's observation that "the only force bringing them together, and putting them into relation with each other, is the selfishness, the gain and the private interest of each" (1976a:280) carries a timely message. And, of course, behind the door, in the hidden realm (sometimes called the "infrastructure"), we can perceive a change "in the physiognomy of our *dramatis personae*." Subjects who are equals—under the law—in the noisy sphere of market circulation now undergo embodied changes into what Maria Mies (1986:142) calls big and little men. Marx describes capital and Labor like this: "He, who was previously the money owner, now strides out in front as capitalist; the possessor of labour-power [Labor] follows as his worker. The one smirks self-importantly and is intent on business; the other is timid and holds back, like someone who has brought his own hide to market and now has nothing else to expect but—a tanning" (1976a:280). Contrasting the nonexploitative equivalence of subjects (money owners and Labor) with the exploitative relations between capital and labor-power, Marx continues to inspire activists seeking Labor's return from exile.

The most familiar interpretation of this passage, which remains loyal to the memory of Marx as a pillar of the revolutionary community, focuses solely on the category of the unitary subject by never raising the specter of discursive positioning. A more fashionable way of reading this passage, which is sometimes associated with post-Marxism, positions the "workers" along with other determinate subjects associated with identity politics in discursive fields currently dominated by capital at the center. And I propose to read this passage in ways that raise issues of indeterminacy in an effort to complicate relations between objectified labor-power and subjectified capital. After illustrating the first two alternatives, I turn briefly to Clarice Lispector, who facilitates a descent from determined demand to the indeterminacy of desire. Finally, I restage the incident of Labor's disappearance in bourgeois society.

Regarding Marx: From Pillar to Post

Those thinking solely in terms of unitary subjects (for example, individual persons or a class-in-itself) might approach this section with one eye on the rights of the subjects and another on what "really" transpires during business transactions. And what do they see? Capitalist bodies puffed up with self-importance and laboring bodies with deflated egos. Asymmetrical relations between subjects outside the Garden of Eden determine disguised elitism within it; the law pretends it is treating all subjects the same in a class-neutral way while reinforcing the dominance of capital over labor. The state serves the interest of the ruling class. A political strategy based on this reading might involve working in the Garden to establish affirmative action and other programs designed to extend rights to noncapitalist subjects, to minimize the presence of Bentham, to draw new subjects into positions of counterhegemony, to pluralize opposition to capitalist hegemony, and gradually to correct the embodied asymmetry between the self-important capitalist and the timid laborer. This view is forced to presume that the consumption of labor by money takes place backstage, and that Mr. Moneybags gets the better deal, exploiting and dominating labor.

This reading, which relies on Marx's rigorous use of abstraction, pursues both theory and practice in a dialectical unity, sometimes understood as "praxis." In this way people who may unconsciously occupy a class-in-itself due to the material conditions of their exploitation can begin to see things differently and transform themselves into a class-for-itself that promises to expropriate the expropriator. By this account Labor is not best described as displaced; rather it is dormant. Ellen Wood, a leading advocate of class as a unitary subject that consists of working people, writes:

> Somehow the notion has gained currency, even on the left, that the
> very idea of a collective historical agent is a metaphysical abstraction,

and one of the more pernicious Hegelian legacies surviving in Marxism, fraught with dangers of despotism and oppression. . . . Why should this be so? Consider the alternatives. . . . Furthermore, since the working class itself *creates* capital, and since the organization of production and appropriation place the collective labourer at the heart of the whole capitalist structure, the working class has a unique capacity to destroy capital. (1986:65–67)

Such loyalist Marxism offers clarity by asking people to step away from lives determined by capital's hegemony to join in anticapitalist struggle. This always involves raising consciousness.

Bertell Ollman (1993) offers a concrete plan for establishing a class-conscious working class. His account of the objective interests of the working class relies upon a representation of Labor as hired and fired labor-power. To study this subject objectively is to acknowledge wage-labor's relation to capital in bourgeois society. His dialectical approach to value allows for the contradictions between the goals of consumers (consuming use-values) and the goals of those who manage the sphere of production (producing exchange-values). And Ollman lists these contradictions as the objective considerations of class. His approach to class consciousness seeks to popularize the class-in-itself/class-for-itself distinction in Marx. Introducing the subjective elements before the objective risks psychologizing consciousness, says Ollman, by attaching this revolutionary potential to the mere individual. Labor becomes silent when it is too alienated to see its position as a collective class-in-itself. Disorganized labor has not yet come into its subjectivity as a class-for-itself (and may never do so). Ollman's work with the subjective considerations of class is designed explicitly to get subalterns to speak as the class they may not yet know they are.

Problems arise, however, when the workers in question are hostile or indifferent to each other and competitive within their own ranks and files. Ollman is famous for calling this in-fighting "alienation," which he loads into his usage of class and seeks to overcome with his usage of class consciousness. He explains that "the class displays the level of its consciousness . . . whenever workers interact with each other. . . . Approached on their own, individual workers may not even know or feel or be able to put this consciousness into words" (1993:168). Readers will note that consciousness seems to come before having a language for it, instead of the other way around. Until workers are ready to begin using words, Ollman is willing to read other signifiers: "What does one do, for example, with the people who choose to remain silent, a problem that grows of necessity with the size of the group? In part, and where this is feasible, this can be dealt with by asking everyone for their opinion" (170). To some extent, then, the solution to a silent subaltern is asking the right questions. But Ollman knows that silence is a deeper problem: "Beyond this, one must be attentive to various signs and noises that show how people feel about what is being said and done. Enthusiasm, delight, anger, disgust, disappointment, and resignation are all relatively easy to detect, but the bulk of what constitutes class consciousness remains beyond our perceptual reach." Indeed, his insistence on objective conditions and his presumption of alienation permit Ollman to expect less than a full accounting from people, many of whom do not seem to know what they want. Rather than starting where the people are, he is more concerned with explaining barriers to their movement. One might ask why do these people see the world in this way? Such questions lead Ollman to argue that "individuals may . . . possess qualities derived from membership in other groups (racial, national, gender, etc.) . . . that make it very difficult for them to participate as class members in the thinking of the class" (172). He seems to see emphasizing class as an important part of raising class consciousness; other aspects of the multicultural landscape risk drawing attention away from the objective relations of labor and capital.

When loyal Marxists rely on Labor's status as a merely dormant subject in the economic base, they disregard the possibility that materialism itself is dependent upon discursive strategies. To pursue the question of Labor's stolen subjectivity, we must ascertain the extent to which capital's hegemony has seeped into the channels of language that one must pass through whenever making sense. In other words, although the loyalist commitment to revolutionary praxis can serve as a safety check against bourgeois complicity, it relies on presuppositions that keep the problem of Labor's subjectivity off the agenda. Theorists more comfortable with poststructuralism face this problem more directly.

Instead of insisting that class is best approached as an actual or potential identity group, Stephen Resnick and Richard Wolff use class as a position marker in discourse Their recent experiment, written in collaboration with Harriet Fraad, advances a theory of simultaneous modes of production under the banner of Marxism-feminism. Fraad, Resnick, and Wolff's venture relies on three distinctions worked out in earlier studies. First, these authors distinguish between oppression, which, following Michèle Barrett (1980:84-113), they use for cultural processes (assumed to have some "relative autonomy") and exploitation. This is sufficient to keep class processes away from gender affairs. Second, they explain exploitation in terms of Marx's trusty distinction between necessary and surplus labor. Fraad, Resnick, and Wolff (1994:3) explain that "by necessary labor, we mean the amount needed to produce the current consumption of the producers themselves. Surplus labor is, then, the amount they perform beyond what is necessary. . . . The organization of the production, appropriation and distribution of surplus labor comprises what we mean by a class structure." The authors immediately distinguish distributing the surplus from making it and claiming to own it; but it is important not to understand this distinction solely within the capitalist mode of production.[3]

To begin talking about households in terms of class analysis requires allowing for many different forms of class processes. Citing Barry Hindess and Paul Hirst (1977), Fraad, Resnick, and Wolff offer an observation familiar to all readers of Marx and then press one of Marx's suggestions—that different processes can exist simultaneously—to a new and interesting extreme: "The Marxist tradition has recognized and specified different forms of . . . class processes: communist, slave, feudal, capitalist, and so forth. . . . each has been found . . . to 'exist in a variety of periods or socio-economic settings' (Eric Hobsbawm in Marx, 1965:59). The point for Marxist class analysis is to inquire about which of the known forms of the class processes are present in any particular society or social site chosen for scrutiny" (Fraad, Resnick, and Wolff, 1994:4). Thus the same person who is exploited at work by the capitalist might exploit a partner by acting like a feudal lord at home and overcome exploitation in communal solidarity on Saturday morning by tending the local co-op. The same person can find representation in multiple subject positions in competing discourses.

Ernesto Laclau and Chantal Mouffe share Fraad, Resnick, and Wolff's concentration on subject positions instead of unitary subjects. Loyalists can account for the same person acting as both capitalist and worker—for example, someone feeling puffed up when "earning" interest and deflated when having to ask the owner for permission to go to the bathroom—but usually balk at adding class positioning to other categories of identity politics. But Laclau and Mouffe's approach allows people to occupy multiple, if not contradictory, positions in various fields of discourse, which may themselves overlap. The unity of being a subject is by this account always already provisional.

Laclau and Mouffe use poststructural criticism of binary logic, deep foundations, and the unitary subject as a near deadly antidote for the growing problem of fragmentation in radical democratic politics. They maneuver effectively to open the otherwise closed logical system that reduces the plurality of difference to binary oppositions such as heteronomy versus autonomy. These authors resist a conventional wisdom that places attempts to build collective solidarity at odds with attempts to preserve individual autonomy; similarly, they do not conclude that alliances across groups undermine the specificity of group identity. In a closed system, whether one is talking about individual or collective subjects, identity— whether fixed or in process—always stands as the least common denominator in the politics of everyday life. In this sense identity underwrites all policy alternatives. Laclau and Mouffe's open system affirms identity politics but allows more breathing room than most liberalism can muster. They pursue a "both-and" logic that allows individual-collective tensions as well as the chance for dialectical growth. Thus they can admit that specific oppressions are never identical while at the same time claim that they are experienced collectively in ways that change over time. To put it another way, saying that oppressions are never identical or permanent denies neither their reality nor their interrelation. Thus the stage is set for pursuing some measure of equivalence for nonidentical oppressions.

This relative equivalence of oppressions lies in their opposition to hegemonic power, not the similarity of their "essential properties." Laclau and Mouffe's early work discusses the logic of democratic equivalence in dialectical terms with a poststructural spin.

> The equivalential articulation between anti-racism, anti-sexism and anti-capitalism, for example, requires a hegemonic construction which, in certain circumstances, may be the condition for the consolidation of each one of these struggles. The logic of equivalence, then, taken to its ultimate consequences, would imply the dissolution of the autonomy of the spaces in which each one of these struggles is constituted; not necessarily because any of them become subordinated to others, but because they have all become, strictly speaking, equivalent symbols of a unique and indivisible struggle. (1985:182)

Now it seems as if these authors are merely placing equivalence and autonomy in the usual binary tension after all. But this ingenious argument relies on the poststructural impossibility, in principle, of such a logic ever playing itself out. A real common cause—or transparency—across groups works only as a vanishing point on the political horizon; such unity is always already deferred. Because the day of unique and indivisible struggle can never arrive, the logic of equivalence is therefore not incompatible with the much beloved liberal logic of autonomy, wherein "each of these struggles retains its differential specificity with respect to the others" (182).

But this means that regardless of its spaces and gaps, the status quo must play the constitutive role of hegemonic discourse. Because specific group difference is necessarily opaque to anyone not included, the kind of structures this radical democracy would struggle against are really the only common focus of counterhegemonic self-definition. For example, instead of gays, lesbians, and African Americans working out the terms of an issue they designate—say a local ordinance on hate crimes—these groups are opaque to each other until they join the struggle against the dominant discourse (where they move off in the direction of transparency). Mouffe (1992:380) can endorse Iris Young's affinity groups (at least for some groups, such as Native Americans) as long as they are the first step in at least a two-step movement toward a new hegemony. Mouffe argues that "the aim is to construct a 'we' as radical democratic citizens, a collective political identity articulated through the principle of democratic *equivalence*. It must be stressed that such a relation of *equivalence* does not eliminate *difference*—that would be simple identity. It is only insofar as democratic differences are opposed to forces or discourses which negate all of them that these differences are substitutable for each other" (379).[4]

But this is where I have a problem. Could this "hegemonizing" falsely homogenize the dominant discourse—where capital is already ensconced in the United States as a naturalized citizen—and work to elevate rather than undermine its importance? According to the theory, the new groups share affinity only in their opposition to the dominant discourses; whatever we are, we are not like them. More alarming is the fact that newly positioning subjects have no say in the matter of this alliance. Do the groups share this vision of democracy? Or is this just another theory that asks the invisible people to learn their culture alongside an arrogant dominant culture that feels no compulsion to change its categories of perception? Political theorists, after all, enjoy no special immunity to what Marilyn Frye (1983) calls "arrogant perception."

Whereas the loyalist view, on the strength of its teleological assumptions, permits Mr. Moneybags and Labor to slip backstage and then return to discourse as changed men, the post-Marxist claims that there is no backstage, no position outside of discursive fields, no room in which to maneuver, no end that we might call human emancipation. Any introduction of exploitation necessarily takes place within discourse. Indeed, this is the advantage: all visions of economic bases or other vestiges of essentialism are now forced to come to terms with their reliance on discourse. Nature itself might be construed as an effect of discourse. But such a view extends a rather homogeneous subjectivity to Labor (as workers) and grants undue credit to capital's subject position as the hegemonic class. Although other subject positions—for example, environmentalists—may be added to the contest between Labor and capital, and although asymmetries of social and economic power may be addressed in a radical democratic movement, neither the hyperinflation of capital's position as a subject nor the presumption of Labor's position is criticized in the post-Marxist reading. In short, this reading cannot respect the indeterminacy of Labor in bourgeois society.

My problem with both the loyalist and the post-Marxist approach centers on the ease with which theorists associated with them rely on Labor's subjectivity. Labor finds itself dormant within a greater totality or positioned alongside other subjects in counterhegemonic strategies that eschew totality. The post-Marxists are certainly right to accuse the loyalists of a problematic disregard for other aspects of cultural politics, and the loyalists are certainly right to accuse post-Marxists of a problematic disregard for the fundamental violence of bourgeois exploitation. Rather than negotiate between these opposing approaches, I propose holding on to the loyalist commitment to revolutionary praxis as well as the poststructural commitment to discursive positioning. To work out the interrelation of praxis and discourse, I need to find some breathing room, some spaces within which to raise the possibility that Labor's subjectivity is neither dormant nor discursive. I approach Labor as indeterminate and concentrate instead on what Gayatri Spivak (1988:287) calls issues of "epistemic violence" that arise when intellectuals—keen on extending political representation to a marginalized "other"—force "them" into predetermined categories that serve primarily to maintain, if unintentionally, the comfort levels at the center.

Interlude: Lispector Haunting Communion

While Marxian analysis that honors base-superstructure boundaries risks oversimplifying political worlds, poststructural glorification of plurality risks playing into the clutches of those claiming to own the social surplus. Instead of following an easy opposition between form and chaos, this interlude attempts to respect what Audre Lorde (1984) calls the "chaos of knowledge." If every conceivable base is at the same time open to supplementation, we might make provisional sense of a hypothetical zone described by Jacques Derrida (1974:56) as the place "where the project of thinking this totality by escaping it is embedded." Such a zone is inaugural without serving as foundation; such a supplemental zero-point is part of the territory governed by oppositions such as sense and nonsense, early times and modern times, base and superstructure. Reading Lispector on the intervals embedded in human subjectivity offers glimpses of a chaos that haunts any attempt to impose or "intuit" rational order. Such a reading helps to curb the tendency one might have to speak for the "other," or to define other people as the opposite of *us* in neat and tidy ways, or to view those silenced by dominant discourse solely as silent or victims. Perhaps irrationality, madness, and the less painful but no less silent zones of everyday living—while they can never stand alone as tactics or strategy— are silent resources, already mobilized forms of resistance. As Lispector (1989:71) writes: "They wanted me to be an object. I am an object. An object dirty with blood. . . . I'm an urgent object."

Using language as a source of both liberation and oppression, Lispector (1988, 1989) supplements the rational order of any subject-object claim to totality.[5] Rather like the literal "loophole" in Harriet Jacobs's narrative on slave contracts (1987:114–18), Lispector suggests that the excess is all about us. Lispector follows language toward discursive spaces that accompany any binary effort to govern, including dialectics. Her project in *The Passion according to G. H.* articulates an overriding demand for the ungoverned materiality of life, hungers for a wildness missed even by the *Aufgehoben* of mutually exhausted couples.

Following Hélène Cixous (1990), we might note that the most inescapable feature of Lispector's writing comes down to "desire": the primordial ooze of unmapped life. She leaves forms of life undecidable. The *Passion* reads like a subject-centered stream of consciousness, as related by an upper-class woman, G. H., who lives very well on the surplus value generated by working people, an army that includes reserves, one or two of whom she occasionally summons as "domestics" to clean her house. And indeed if one is not haunting Marxism while reading Lispector, the text might remain this predictable.

One day, several weeks after her most recent maid has moved on to some other job, G. H. decides to clean the maid's bedroom. When she steps into the room, finding it spotless, reality begins to shift: "like in dreams, the logic was other, was one that makes no sense when you wake up, for the other dream's greater truth is lost" (Lispector, 1988:96). But in this case "the dream truth was taking place without the anesthesia of night." G. H. recalls, "I sought a vastness" (96–97). Then it happens. She is moving old suitcases that bear the inscription "G. H." and stirs a cockroach. The rest of the story retraces transilient steps that weave in and out of the language of a rather linear plot. The plot moves from G. H. mutilating the cockroach—squashing it—to following its white ooze through orgiastic speculation on "pre-human love" to becoming ambivalent about breaking her own "cockroach silence" in ways that might supplement human subjectivity, and finally to discovering life at a hypothetical zero-point that is not governed by a binary logic.

The *Passion* explores the limitations of living rational orderly lives. G. H. craves organic material—the stuff of life—without the structures of necessity or the humanity so often associated with organicism: "Wanting to be human sounds too pretty to me. I want the materiality of things. Humanity is steeped in humanization as though it were necessary; and that false humanization impedes man and impedes his humanity. There exists a thing that is broader, deafer, and deeper, less good, less bad, less pretty" (Lispector, 1988:150–51). Elsewhere, Lispector identifies with an "organic disorder" where "dreamlike ... greenish with the ooze of time ... ancient cockroaches drag themselves along in the half-light (1989:19, 8–9). In the *Passion*, after making various observations about the white body matter oozing out of the cockroach shell, G. H. turns abruptly to discuss her dissatisfaction with an ex-lover.

Preparing to break her cockroach silence, G. H. needs first to join with this ancient figure in an erotic moment that resembles communion. "In the cockroach's lack of glee I perceived its warrior ferocity. I was meek but its life-functioning was fierce. I am meek but my life-function is fierce. Oh, pre-human love invades me. I understand. I understand. The form of living is so secret a secret that it is the silent tracking of a secret" (Lispector, 1988:108). Like the popular button that bears the inscription "the meek are getting ready," this passage summons the mobilization of a grave silence. Pursuing this theme of a silent love that exceeds humanity at the zero-point before polar oppositions assume their role of governing thought, G. H. suddenly recollects an episode of lovemaking in her past: "there came to me the memory of a true love that I once had and didn't know that I had—for love was then what I understood from a word" (108). Brushing aside the lovemaking that can be captured by the language of patriarchal order and reason, G. H. reinterprets what went without saying. I can offer only an elliptical version of the erotic soliloquy:

What I am talking about is when nothing was happening, and we called that nothing an interval. How could it have been an interval? It was the huge flower opening up, all full of itself, my vision all huge and tremulous. What I saw then came together to my sight and became mine—but not a permanent coming-together: if I had compressed it between my hands like a piece of coagulated blood, its solidity would have turned back into liquid blood again between my fingers. ... In the intervals that we called empty and tranquil, and when we thought that the love had ended ... [Lispector breaks off]. In those intervals we used to think that we were relaxing from one being the other. In fact, it was the great pleasure of not being the other; for in that case we each were two. (109–11)

The intensity of love can blur positions of subject and object; one becomes the other. During the intervals between such moments, positions are thought to return to the "normal" (fixed in discourse): each subject is an object for the other, seeks an object in the other. But Lispector concentrates on these silent intervals to discover the pleasure of being, in silence, neither subject nor object of desire—the pleasure of not being positioned in this particular sexed discourse at all, of slipping out of occupied spaces to unoccupied spaces in discourse. "We used to think that we were relaxing from one being the other"; but in fact during those silent moments we experienced the great pleasure of not being the other (and of not being the self either). During lovemaking "we each were two," subject and object, in relations of satisfaction, marked by the demand of the other. But during the silence—the cockroach silence—no such distinctions are possible. Lispector has discovered the necessary incompleteness of desire, the void created by forced binary choices (subject or object) in dominant discursive fields.

In the *Passion*, G. H. reads the intervals of her lovemaking immediately before encountering a cockroach that she immediately squashes into oblivion. Nearing the displacement of the animal-human binary, she reports: "For the cockroach looked at me with her beetle shell, with her burst body all made of tubes and antennae and soft cement—and that was undeniably a truth prior to our words, it was undeniably the life that up to then I hadn't wanted" (111).

Respecting the chaos of knowledge undermines the reassurance of any polarity by recognizing a zone of indeterminacy dragging alongside the orderly self-other distinctions in commonsense discourse. Here Lispector gives new meaning to communing with nature: "Oh God, I felt baptized by the world. I had put cockroach matter into my mouth; I had finally performed the lowest of all acts. . . . I, who had lived of the middle of the road, had finally taken the first step at its start. . . . I was without limit" (172).

Privileging chaos, if only in a dream-moment, allows a supplemented sense of objective reality, an undifferentiated zone that accompanies all attempts to make sense. This is the point of supplementarity, "by which something which is defined as being complete is none the less brought to completion by what exceeds and even threatens it" (Wood, 1987:189).

Rather than treating silence as a way of leaving discursive fields, Lispector insists on maintaining and mobilizing the erotic moments of realizing the ooze of supplementary zones commingling with the multiple subject and object positions available. G. H. explains the difficulty of reaching silence in current situations: "reality prior to my language exists as an unthinkable thought . . . but bodily matter precedes the body, and one day in its turn language shall have preceded possession of silence" (Lispector, 1988:169). For the time being, of course, a de facto dualism can continue its provisional operations of sense-making. As we read in Lispector's *Stream of Life*, "I've lost my fear of symmetry, after the disorder of inspiration" (1989:62).

Lispector's writing draws up against death and madness as silent resources of reasonable, orderly politics. And her every written move displays the costs of being preoccupied with the cold steel of rationality, including thinking solely in terms of dichotomies. Reading Lispector requires moving from one experiment to another because she usually follows the lead of her language. In a world in which everything has become discourse, she uses language (intervals intact) to mediate between wild dreaming about the silent monstrosity of the unnameable and the straight and narrow rationality that one might name "patriarchal order." Using *writing* to signify the "movement of mediacy" (Ryan, 1982:28) between the metaphysics of presence (where we might locate subject-object relations) and the nonpresence of "all that gives rise to an inscription in general" (Derrida, 1974:9), Lispector's extravagant writing works as a break/hinge (*brisure*) between reason and chaos.

Restaging the Buying and Selling of Labor-Power

Choosing between Marx's manly reasoning and Lispector's "écriture feminine" presupposes a divorce that can never be granted. My work, then, continues the struggle against capital's hegemonic position without restricting arguments to the boundaries dictated by the usual oppositions.[6] Expanding the politics of juxtaposing capital and labor-power in discursive fields, we might also include would-be subjects locked out of discursive structures. Working for these wider supplements requires approaching *Capital* not only by looking at its dramatis personae and traversing its text but also by attempting to read (or at least note) the silence of the discourse. Following Lispector's lead, we might ask, "What urgent objects in the field of economic discourse are written out of the play?" Between the first two approaches to the buying and selling of labor-power one can reformulate the "Garden of Eden," allowing readers to sense the "danger of need" among those denied major speaking parts as subjects or even visibility as objects. One can use the same passage to illustrates the potential of reading indeterminacy in Marx's staging of this transaction.

The sphere of circulation is noisy because all subject positions enjoy relative equivalence. Possessors of money negotiate with possessors of labor-power, who become possessors of money—if only for a short while—after selling their labor (we join Marx below in describing this circuit as C-M-C, or commodity-money-commodity). A penniless person might work for a week, assuming a laboring position, only to assume a money-owning position when hiring somebody else to figure out the taxes. The Garden of Eden has room to extend rights and, along with these rights, subjectivity to all positions in the discourse of production. Successful progressive struggles promise to increase the volume of noise in the sphere of circulation, but their success might be enhanced by also considering the silences.

To show how Labor is objectified under capitalism without risking the essentialism of the teleological perspective or the presumption of intersubjectivity of the post-Marxist perspective, the third perspective holds on to the claim that there is nothing outside of the text but pays close attention to this "cockroach silence" in the margins of the text. How did capital gain its power (is hegemonic construction all that it's cracked up it be)? Why is Labor silent (can the subaltern speak)? Thus the changes in physiognomy can be explained in terms of a cross-dressing act. But the action is slightly more complicated than Labor and capital exchanging costumes because capital is not even a party in the original exchange. Perhaps a slightly different way of staging Marx's drama can draw out a more suggestive explanation.

In the Garden of Eden we begin with two subject-object relations. Subjects have speaking roles; their objects have no lines and are ordered about like stage props. Subject A is in a position of ownership with respect to the object money, dressed as a bag of money. A owns a bag of money. Subject B is in a position of ownership with respect to the object labor-power, dressed as if it has become a starched uniform. B owns pressed and clean labor-power. Capital is nowhere in sight.

All of a sudden, when no one is paying attention, when the money owner is preparing to convert his object, money, into capital—that is, when A and B are about to change their physiognomy before our very eyes—a phantom rises out of Subject A's object, the bag of money, and after assuming a ghostly presence on stage, rips off Subject B's (Labor's) costume and wears it as a disguise. Capital, the phantom subject, is now dressed in the Labor owner's costume. This leaves the naked and shivering Labor (the real Subject B) in need of a costume. But where can Labor turn? Subject A, whose object, money, is still in the bag because not all of the money has been converted into capital, remains dressed in the original costume of the money owner. Money owners have value in this production and can speak. And Subject B's object, labor-power, remains dressed in its starched uniform, preparing to be silently bought, sold, and consumed by owners of money. Capital, the object formerly known as money but now pretending to be a subject, places itself in a position of control with respect to labor-power. Capital has stolen Labor's speaking parts. Capital is now the form-giving fire. Capital pretends to be Subject B. And the real Subject B is unable to speak. Owners of labor-power do not survive the transformation of money into capital with their subjectivity intact.

In the Eden of the innate rights of man, Labor—the real subject (as opposed to its objectification, labor-power)—must now fight for rights that it would receive automatically if it had retained its subject status. The world is topsy-turvy. Legislators work night and day for the health of the economy while neglecting the health of the people in their districts. Capital alone can assume a right to survive; a fact that should give owners of money pause (they might be next). The change in physiognomy Marx reports is illusory in the sense that capital (really a phantom originating in a money owner's bag) is wearing Labor's costume, speaking Labor's lines, controlling Labor's object, and sometimes—by disregarding our labor-power altogether—regarding Labor as a surplus population. Any aspect of life not controlled by capital's transformation from money is radically devalorized.

Capital's hegemony is as secure, then, as its stolen discursive position. Learning to strut comes easily to people who mistake themselves for the form-giving fire of Labor, the transience of things. Similarly, workers learn to cower because of their missing subjectivity: employees are alienated from their rightful subject position as Labor in discourse, and they are alienated from controlling their object, labor-power. In this presentation of Marx's drama, then, the relevant contrast is not between ideology (Eden) and economic base (door marked "No admittance except on business"); rather, the contrast is between noisy politics as usual and the silent politics that transpires right under our noses, within the very "Eden of the Rights of Man" which effectively effaces Labor.[7] Currently, capital is playing a game in which it defeats Labor both coming and going. Labor watches in silence as people spin myths of capital's godlike supremacy. But unlike capital, Labor is never at a loss for resources.

To locate a heterogeneous Labor that has been denied representation requires making some decisions with respect to Lispector's interval, at the limits of the text. But how is it possible to articulate desire when its silence has yet to be transformed into language? If desire is approached as subject X's need for object Y (my need as a worker for a living wage), then the answer is deceptively simple: don't waste time theorizing, organize. But, even though Labor needs to get its act together, such approaches often turn a deaf ear to precisely the intervals one needs to accentuate. Workers must organize and articulate concerns, but the vast territory of what cannot be said must not be considered off-limits. My project contests the presupposition that capital's hegemony must go without saying. But this requires an opening that I hope to find by continuing to study desire's relation to representation.

Marx's question of asymmetrical equivalence has been answered in our times by capital's hegemony, but we need in the name of class action to reexamine this question. We must struggle to locate Labor instead of presuming its subjectivity. Saying that the capital/labor-power binary leaves something to be desired—for example, the cockroach silence of any subject denied access to the means of representation—suggests that we should embark on a detailed study of how poststructural theory comes to terms with desire's indeterminacy. Relating this slippery concept to representation offers clues concerning how Labor is effaced during the buying and selling of labor-power. These are the tasks of the next two chapters. This first part of the book, which opens the discussion of indeterminacy, is connected to Marx's writings in Part 2 and developed as an action project in Part 3.

But the chapters of this first part—on desire and representation—also form the beginning stage of three parallel arguments on labor, theory, and value respectively. The first chapter of each part, including this one, moves from the disappearance of Labor to the commitment to Labor in Marx's writing to the heterogeneous quality of the Labor underground. The second chapter of each part moves from theories of desire in Lacan, Deleuze and Guattari, and Derrida to signs of indeterminacy in Marx and Althusser to a poststructural praxis fueled by considerations of indeterminacy. Finally, the third chapter of each part begins by showing value's debt to representation, moves to ways of valuing what exceeds the relationship between money and commodities in Marx's writing, and discusses practical ways of valorizing abject properties of bourgeois society. The striated design of these chapters should indicate that I adopt the conventions of subject-object relations even as I resist their governance.

CHAPTER TWO

The Ruined Limits of Enunciation:
From Lacan to Derrida

Strictly speaking, since we are questioning the human being's control over the production of language, the figure that will serve us better is writing, for there the absence of the producer and receiver is taken for granted. A safe figure, seemingly outside of the language-(speech)-writing opposition, is the text—a weave of knowing and not-knowing which is what knowing is. (This organizing principle— language, writing, or text—might itself be a way of holding at bay a randomness incongruent with consciousness.)

—Gayatri Spivak, *In Other Worlds*

I begin by presenting alternatives to the facile theorizing of desire as those "longings" that everyone has and needs only to confess, or discover, on the grounds that this usage reduces desire to demand and ignores the extent to which demand is indebted to discourse. Several names stand out as markers commonly used to chart positions on the indeterminacy of desire: Jacques Lacan, Gilles Deleuze and Félix Guattari, and Jacques Derrida. Because they appear in so many different projects, I must show how I read these subject-authors—especially as they signal the problem of desire— before presenting my version. After explaining briefly their interrelation, I borrow Poe's "The Purloined Letter" as a vehicle for presenting their significant differences, on the way to a modest attempt to salvage desire's indeterminacy. Poe's story, (re)transmitted by a nameless American narrator, tells how Dupin, a mysterious French aristocrat, retrieves a stolen letter hidden right under the noses of the entire Parisian police force.

Structure, Sign, and Subject

My objective in these first three chapters—detecting Labor's whereabouts —might suggest that I am studying how Dupin locates the purloined letter because I am looking for clues concerning how to locate Labor's stolen subjectivity. But this is true only in the sense that discussing this story requires examining the gap between signification and actual life. Although their projects in structural linguistics are more concerned with how signification works than with negotiating reality, Ferdinand de Saussure and Emile Benveniste are commonly mentioned at this juncture because their combined argument draws the problem of sign and structure closer to the question of the subject.

According to Saussure, the two faces of the sign—signifier and signified (for example, saying "lā-bər" to signify "being in possession of labor-power")—must be organized by a structured system. An arbitrary sound, the code (signifier), is conjoined with its message (signified) in a unity called the sign whenever the rules are followed; where users are accustomed to this unity, the signifier often travels by itself under the name "sign" instead of always showing its other face. Speech (*la parole*) is the conscious use of unconscious structures (*la langue*) that regulate the logic of the sign. Although both operate together, Saussure is more concerned with the synchronic structure, where positions can be fixed and studied objectively, than with diachronic speech, where one regularly misspeaks, slips, breaks rules. As a linguist, Saussure regards writing as the mere signification of the spoken signifiers of the signified message. But emphasizing synchronic structure leads him to neglect who is actually doing the speaking or using the available signs at any given time and place.

Benveniste solidifies Saussure's relation of discursive use of signs (speech) and the structure of language in a way that addresses the subjectivity involved. Pointing out that signifiers such as "I" do not carry a signified, Benveniste (1971:218) regards these terms as formal markers that shift the receiver's attention away from the subject about which one speaks and toward the speaking subject, the actual person attempting to make sense: "'I' is the individual who utters the present instance of discourse containing the linguistic instance 'I.'" Hence he distinguishes the "subject of the enunciation" from the "subject of the statement (or utterance)." Kaja Silverman (1983:46) explains that "although these two subjects can only be apprehended in relation to each other, they can never be collapsed into one unit. They remain . . . separated by the barrier between reality [the place of enunciation] and signification [the site of the statement]." This barrier is not problematic for linguistics because any actual person can become an enunciating subject by passing through the channels of signification (learning the language) and making demands of other subjects: "I want bread and roses too." For Benveniste (1971:224) "ego is who says ego," and that's that. But any refusal to equate desire and

demand makes tampering with the barrier between reality and signification almost irresistible. All demand takes place within discursive fields in
which determinate forms, such as names, dates, and rules, are assigned;
but Lispector leads us to believe that new forms of possible subjectivity
often linger in an indeterminate form. I aim to problematize the limits of
enunciation by recycling desire's indeterminacy.

We are, then, comparing and contrasting different approaches to Benveniste's subject of enunciation, the actual subject who speaks within
structures of language that fix signifying codes in an exact relation to
signified messages. Lacan (1991:248) accepts Benveniste's twin levels of
signification—speech-acts and rules of language—but not without subverting the unity of the Saussurean sign by allowing signifiers to signify without following structured rules of engagement that, for linguists,
would connect these sounds to a signified message. And yet, if analyzed
properly by "one who can hear," says Lacan, these floating signifiers, or letters, disconnected from their signifieds can possibly symbolize concealed
truths blocked from one's conscious use of even the most precise speech.
So where does this leave the subject of enunciation? Would-be speaking subjects are born into a language whose autonomous signifiers speak
through us when we begin to use them. In other words, Lacan's subjects
of enunciation occupy a position outside the very same channels of signification they must pass through to become one; the subject of enunciation
is simultaneously called to speak and is "petrified" by the signifier (Lacan,
1977:207). "Desire" is the name Lacan gives to this impossible situation
of being torn between the demands of signification and the actuality of all
that resists it. Judith Butler (1987:193) speaks for Lacan—"Desire is never
materialized or concretized through language, but is indicated through
the interstices of language, that is, what language cannot represent"—and
then calls upon him to speak for himself: "In the interval intersecting the
signifiers . . . desire crawls, slips, escapes, like a ferret" (Lacan, 1977:204).
Because desire, for Lacan, simultaneously resists and requires signification, it names a lack in the representational schemes we construct when
trying to make sense of our lives. We are barred from the truth of what
we are saying and doing to each other; we live instead at the mercy of unconscious signifiers (operating as symbols) that twist and knot our desires.

Whereas Lacan thinks he is subverting the Saussurean sign by freeing
the signifier to symbolize unconscious truths, Deleuze and Guattari reject
the entire operation of sending messages with codes, including poststructural attempts to rescue Saussure from slipping into the habit of conflating
any signifiable thing (itself) with the sign's message. Accordingly, they
distinguish the province of representation from uncharted whirlwinds of

desire, an unstructured *fwoosh* of affirmation that spills over the signifier, overwhelming any attempt to impose a code. Interestingly, they find that capitalism shares this schizophrenic rush, but point out that it must always regain its composure in order to take care of business. Rejection of the Saussurean sign allows these imaginative theorists to appropriate Benveniste's distinction between subjects of enunciation and subjects of the statement without, or so they say, connecting the sturdy dichotomy to issues of representation. By siphoning off its insipid "personology," Benveniste's subject of enunciation—the speaking subject—becomes in their hands an agency capable of making formal declarations of reality; and the subject of the statement—the spoken subject—is forced to occupy itself with conforming to this dominant reality. To make things even more interesting, these agencies can be performed by wholly different classes of actual people. Deleuze and Guattari assign the place of enunciation to the capitalist class and the place of the statement to the proletariat; although these classes require each other, they cannot be considered identical. Whereas the capitalist creates ("I will colonize the moon"), the proletarian conforms ("Maybe I can find work there"). But this post-Benvenistean formulation also leaves room for an unruly desire to erupt periodically at the heart of its apparent rapprochement.

Whereas Lacan subverts the unity of signifier and signified on the way to locating desire in the intervals of representation, always out of reach to the subject of enunciation, and Deleuze and Guattari escape the sign altogether on the way to divorcing desire from representation's subjects (the subject of enunciation and that of the statement), Derrida deconstructs the sign on the way to decentering even the desiring subject of enunciation in a *différance* of writing. Although the relation between the diachronic use of signs (speech) and the synchronic structure privileged by linguists (language) is very much a part of Derrida's approach, he avoids thinking about the relation of signifier and signified in any form that fixes their unity. This means that speech and language are continually changing (each other). To convey these interactive effects without evoking "history" (and thus risking "repressing" the "difference" he seeks to accentuate, Derrida (1991:64) notes that "differences *play:* in language, in speech too, and in the exchange of speech and language"; and coins *différance* as "the playing movement that 'produces' these differences." This movement makes it necessary to place any differential arrangement between arbitrary signs in a larger context, called writing-in-general, or "writing as différance." This general location envelops concrete discourse, including its written component, adding an "element of extrachronicity to the usual structural consideration of diachrony and synchrony" (Corlett, 1993:159). This formulation implicates the enunciatory stance of any desiring subject, including all narrators and master theorists among us, in the différance of writing.

Focusing on "The Purloined Letter" provides access to these overlapping approaches to desire and representation: Lacan stresses speech while pursuing desire as the negative aspect of what is lacking in (what we mistakenly think of as) our lives; Deleuze and Guattari eschew representation while developing desire as the positive aspect of what is lurking beyond our collective lies; and Derrida generalizes writing in ways that implicate everyone at the scene, while deferring the subject of desire. It is time to recollect Poe's story.

The Plot

Two men, the American narrator (who is paying the rent) and his Parisian friend, the aristocratic Dupin (an amateur detective with a rather modest trust fund, whom we have met in two earlier stories), sit in a library smoking in the dark when they are interrupted by the prefect of the Parisian police, G, who asks for Dupin's services on a matter of highest importance. We learn from G that the queen was in the royal boudoir reading a secret letter when she was interrupted by the king and his minister, D. We are told that the queen immediately placed the letter face down on a side table, but not before the minister detected her precarious situation. The unsuspecting king noticed nothing. After some discussion of state affairs, D allegedly removed a facsimile of the queen's letter from his pocket and swapped it for the one on the table as she watched hopelessly, allowing him to abscond with her secret. The queen, left with nothing but the facsimile, contacted G, unofficially of course; she described the letter and waited while he and his police force looked virtually everywhere that D could have hidden the letter. Finally, G mentions to Dupin that the queen has even offered a substantial reward. Depressed, G leaves the narrator's place (of enunciation).

One month passes. G returns to the library for a second scene in which Dupin, who takes pride in getting at the truth of such matters, manages to get G to offer him a percentage of the queen's ever increasing reward and only then turns over the stolen letter. Delighted, G writes Dupin a check and leaves, allowing Dupin to explain (to the narrator) how he managed to find it. On a visit to D, Dupin alleges, he immediately noticed a letter, folded inside out and wadded in a container hung from the mantel. Realizing that this must be the stolen letter, Dupin left behind "by mistake" a cigarette case, which he returned the next day to retrieve. But because

Dupin staged on that day a coincidental street incident that induced D to run to the window, he managed to abscond with the queen's letter, leaving behind a facsimile bearing an inscription that would identify him to D as the thief. The story ends with the narrator quoting the inscription, penned by another author, of the facsimile that Dupin left for D.

What is really going on here? Did Dupin outsmart all the others? What is the narrator's role in this drama? Is Dupin really D in disguise? Does the identity of the characters matter any more than the contents (the signified) of the letter, which we never ascertain? Who better to bring in for a first reading than Jacques Lacan, who complicates this story in ways that at once reveal his approach to desire and make it comparable to the other approaches I have lined up.

Reading Poe over Lacan's Shoulder

Lacan studies how the subject's imaginary ego, a shadowy affair fraught with anxiety, relies upon a symbolic order, a linguistic operation which provides the locus for all subject-object relations, including the naming of subjects that cannot be otherwise spoken.[1] Demonstrating how imaginary shadows are related to symbolic chains of significance will prove difficult because, for Lacan, we are born into a locus of signification which both makes it possible for us to speak and impossible for us to know the full extent (especially the truth of) what we are saying to each other.[2] Here Lacan, proposing to demonstrate the "decisive orientation which the subject receives from the itinerary of a signifier" (12; 29),[3] moves quickly to describe the two scenes summarized above: the primal scene in the queen's boudoir and its repetition in D's apartment.[4]

Staging even the first two scenes of this drama, however, requires a narrator's use of indirect lighting (*l'éclairage à jour frisant*) to illuminate "the point of view that one of the actors had while performing it" (12; 29). The prefect, G, is spotlighted in the first dialogue, during which we learn of the crime and the inability of the police to solve it; Dupin is spotlighted in the second dialogue, during which we learn of the recovery and the hostile note he leaves behind. Lacan argues that "the narration, in fact, doubles the drama with a commentary without which no mise en scène would be possible" (12; 29). The real drama we have traced above in terms of its plot, then, is rather like the imaginary order, a play without speech (*drame sans paroles*): "nothing of the drama could be grasped, neither seen nor heard" (17-18; 34), without passing through channels of narration that perform the representational task of assigning names and places, subject and object positions. As we are about to see, the real drama, in which characters fail to recognize themselves and each other, stands in a complementary position with a new, other drama. If the real drama plays without speech, the new drama plays with the properties of speech (*les propriétés du discours*) and transforms what would perhaps otherwise make no sense (or "remain inconsistent") into a full-fledged narrative.[5] This "other drama" is, of course, the symbolic one. Insomuch as it reveals, in Lacan, the complexity of the Symbolic's hegemonic rule, the fragility of the Imaginary, and the impossibility of the real, we need to seek it out.

This section is marked by the first break in the French text (16; 32) — immediately after Lacan recounts how a proper appreciation of the "immixture of subjects" (depicted later as the Schema L) can enhance the story—and runs through continuously to the second break (27; 41). Lacan attempts in this section to justify connecting Poe's tale to his formula "The unconscious is the discourse of the Other," which privileges the symbolic over the imaginary and helps to explain that other pronouncement: "All desire is desire of the Other."[6] Lacan's self-justification requires presenting the new drama, the one that doubles the play without speech, by contrasting the role of language in the narrator's presentation of the two dialogues associated with the primal scene and its repetition in D's apartment.

Approaching the New, Other Drama

Lacan wants, then, to argue that "the manner in which the subjects relay (*se relaient*) each other" is "determined by the place which a pure signifier — the purloined letter — comes to occupy in their trio" (16; 32). This is the sense in which the letter is a fourth character in each scene for Lacan, one which represents an unconscious element unavailable to and yet part of each trio. He suggests that what "makes for our pleasure" is the "impression that everyone is being duped (*soit joué*)" (17; 33). He explains the power of the signifier in five different twists and turns of an argument: a glimpse of the first dialogue (beginning at 18, line 11; 34, line 20); an imaginary digression (beginning at 19, line 6; 35, line 6); a glimpse of the second dialogue (beginning at 19, line 31; 35, line 27); a continuation of the second dialogue which concentrates on Dupin (beginning at 22, top; 37, line 18); and finally a return to the first dialogue, which concentrates on G (beginning at 24, line 32; 39, line 26).[7] Studying how duplicity permeates the Lacanian Poe may draw us closer to the tension between the two dialogues, which yields this other, new drama.

A Glimpse of the First Dialogue: Entering the Channels of Signification

Our initial glimpse of the first dialogue, in which readers learn for the first time of the theft and the bafflement of the authorities in the first scene, focuses on the communication between two subjects, Prefect G and Dupin. Lacan describes this encounter as a dialogue "between a deaf man [G] and one who hears." He does so because he wishes to distinguish between the mere reportage of an event (relating exactly what happened) and "the highly significant commentary into which he who understands integrates it." This distinction between exact verisimilitude and true verity will soon be developed as two sides of the "wall of language": intersubjective speech and the word itself. But here Lacan merely illustrates how the "dialogue may be more fertile than it seems" by reminding us that the prefect was not after all a witness to the theft in the queen's boudoir. The narrator, although "hypothetically" adding nothing to the story, is nevertheless retransmitting the already retransmitted message of the reported crime from the queen to the prefect to Dupin and finally to his readers. For Lacan, this establishes immediately that the relay circuit he wishes to accentuate "belongs to the dimension of language"; he uses this to distinguish his other drama from the imaginary fumblings of the real drama, or what actually happened.

An Imaginary Digression: Introducing Some Key Distinctions

By indicating to us what really happened in the two scenes, one might ask, does Poe's narrator not resemble a waggling bee "signalling . . . the location of objects"? For Lacan, however, the cybernetic joy of reducing language to encoding and decoding operations illustrates "only an imaginary function," which might even be taught to animals. To maintain his distinction between the imaginary drama without speech and the symbolic drama that plays with the properties of speech, Lacan knows he must articulate the scope of what speech repeats and then deal with the symbolic dimension of signification.

Lacan mentions here "a linguist," who happens to be Benveniste, for whom the waggle of the bee exemplifies a code of signals that lies outside the scope of language, even though a bee needs food and can communicate its location to another bee. Benveniste disqualifies the wagging dance as a language in part because the relation between the dance and the food is fixed, and also because the bee receiving the message cannot transmit it to a third party. The first difference speaks to the distinction between being inside the scope of language and outside it (where Lacan would locate inarticulate need); the second prepares us for the distinction within language between demand and desire.

Lacan (1977:84) agrees with Benveniste that "we can say that [the waggle] is distinguished from language precisely by the fixed correlation of its signs to the reality that they signify." In other words, a language, whether its users know it or not, does not designate naturally given objects (signifiable reality). Saussure has taught that language, as it lives in the world of speech (*la parole*), is a matter of signs (relations between signifiers and signifieds) organized by a structure (*la langue*). Lacan distinguishes quite explicitly what language signifies from all that is signifiable: "When one talks about the signified, one thinks of the thing, whereas in fact signification is what is involved. Nonetheless, each time we talk, we say the thing, the signifiable, by means of the signified. There is a lure here, because it is quite clear that language is not made to designate things" (1991:248). Using a language, as opposed to signaling with a code, permits constructing worlds of meaning which stand apart from actual experience. This means that there will be a gap between one's actual experience and the language games available; indeed this is the line between the real and the Imaginary, marked by passing through the channels of language. Those born into a language, after distinguishing self from other, join the speaking subjects in maintaining orderly lives that owe a sometimes unacknowledged debt to signification. Kaja Silverman (1983:21) introduces the Lacanian Imaginary as "a spectrum of visual images which precedes the acquisition of language in the experience of the child, and which continues to coexist with it afterwards." This is commonly referred to as the dimension along which the human subject is split between the need of the real and the demand made possible by communication.[8]

Lacan alludes to such an Imaginary in this brief digression when conceding that something resembling simple animal "communication is not absent in man." He allows for both "communion . . . between two persons in their hatred of a common object" and the congregation of "an indefinite number of subjects in a common 'ideal'" (19; 35). As in the case of the child, who visualizes images of self and other before becoming a subject of enunciation in discourse, such communication "may be maintained only in the relation with the object" and is "not transmissible in symbolic form." But because the demanding ego is regulated by language instead of a simple coding operation, we must continue exploring the scope of language.

Here Lacan tells us that any communication between imaginary egos is "mediated by an ineffable relation." This is because becoming a language user entails being assigned a discursive position by the symbolic order.

Elizabeth Grosz (1990:66) explains that "demand initiates the child into the categories and terms of discourse, but it does not position the subject in a stable enunciative position as a speaker or discursive 'I.'" And the play without speech of the Imaginary continues throughout life, even among those vested in language as speaking subjects; indeed all characters of "The Purloined Letter" are eventually captured by the Imaginary. As Lacan (1991:80) is fond of repeating, "In the relation of the imaginary and the real, and in the constitution of the world such as results from it, everything depends on the position of the subject. . . . [which] is essentially characterized by its place in the symbolic world, in other words in the world of speech."

Although the subject of enunciation, the actual person drawn into language from a speechless ego to the subject of the statement, resides in the real—the site of all that resists signification—this person must first be positioned by the Symbolic as an "I." But this positioning blocks us from our place of residence. This is why Ellie Ragland (1995:147) describes the real as "what cannot be thought or said because it is too painful to know"; Lacanian "aphanisis" names this barrier to the actual signifiable world. The purpose of the symbolic drama is to present this world of speech as it mediates what may appear (to the untutored) to be simple communication or demand for objects between one subject and another. This explains, then, why G, a man with utmost "lack of imagination," is positioned so prominently in the first dialogue of the symbolic drama: as a desiring subject positioned in discourse by the narrator, he serves at once to represent the virtue of exactitude and the impossibility of representing desire in language (or locating the letter).

Because it raises the specter of signifiers that escape the logic of the Saussurean sign, Lacan's brief digression is not only about articulating the scope of language. If we follow S. Žižek (1989:56) in approaching Lacan's symptoms as "meaningless traces" hidden from the subject that—through analysis—can yield the "truth" or "symbolic place and meaning" within a "signifying frame," then it makes sense to conclude this section with Lacan's foreshadowing suggestion that "in determining the scope of what speech repeats, it prepares the question of what symptoms repeat" (19; 35). And with this I turn to glimpse the second dialogue in the symbolic drama, where one must prepare to encounter the problem of desire.

A Glimpse of the Second Dialogue: The Other Side of the Wall of Language

Whereas the first dialogue (between Dupin, who can hear, and Prefect G, who cannot) "sifts out" the linguistic dimension, the second (between the narrator and Dupin) allows Lacan to travel to the other side of the wall of language which separates the "field of exactitude" and a "register of truth." The field of exactitude contains the interlocution between subjects using speech (as word choice) in ways that are consistent with (known) language (-games). The register of truth, on the other hand, operates at the "trans-individual" extreme of whatever foundation makes it possible for humans to play language-games, "where the subject can grasp nothing but the very subjectivity which constitutes an Other as absolute" (20; 35). Understanding this formulation requires remembering that this drama is symbolic.

One must avoid, then, approaching these twin poles as territories inhabited by actual persons. The imaginary play without speech leaves plenty of room for G to occupy the position of ignorance (the king's place in the second scene) and Dupin to replace D in the all-seeing position. But the new, other drama, a symbolic one, juxtaposes the two dialogues on a different dimension, which allows one to explore the properties of speech. Here G and Dupin represent exactitude and truth respectively. As Ragland (1995:147) explains, "no one is actually *in* the symbolic . . . but is represented there by the imposed language and identifications that signify a person as a subject." Consider, for example, discussing a problem with a friend. Aside from how you and the friend relate as self and other during the conversation (an imaginary question that does not concern us here), there remain two questions for each person to ask: What did I say? (speech) and What did I really say (word)? For Lacan contra Saussure, the difference between these two questions allows signifiers (such as the purloined letter) to take on an autonomous subjectivity as symbols apart from any given relationship with a signified. But how is it possible, if one's ego is not involved, to distinguish one's speech from the truth hidden in one's speech?

The second dialogue of the symbolic drama gives a truth-seeking Dupin the spotlight, allowing him to explain how he managed to find the elusive letter. His dialogue with the narrator introduces Dupin's superior intellect and method of reasoning in ways that lead readers to question what is really going on. Lacan opens his treatment of this section by illustrating the "state of privation (*dépouillement*)" between speech (*parole*) and signifier (*signifiant*) with Freud's famous joke about how an "exact" use of speech can sometimes seem wholly unrelated to the "truth" of what is going on between two subjects.[9] "Why are you lying to me?" one character shouts breathlessly. "Yes, why do you lie to me saying you're going to Cracow so I should believe you're going to Lemberg, when in reality you *are* going to Cracow?" Is Poe creating a duplicitous Dupin who, despite his lies and deception in the imaginary drama, represents a truth in the symbolic drama, a truth that eludes us. Indeed, much of the story's effect lies in the eerie feeling that everyone hiding something is also being watched, that there is no hiding place.

A Continuation of the Second Dialogue While Concentrating on Dupin's Search for the Truth

Returning to the presentation of Dupin's superior methods in the second dialogue, Lacan recalls the first dialogue where "everything is arranged to induce in us a sense of . . . the imbecility" of G, the deaf one (22; 37). But here, in pursuit of the truth instead of exactitude, Lacan wonders whether "so much intelligence [is] being exercised [by the narrator] . . . simply to divert our own from . . . [the fact that] the police have looked *everywhere*" (23; 38). Perhaps Poe is showing us everything after all; in which case we are entitled to conclude that the letter was not in its place, even though it was also obviously somewhere, because Dupin managed to find it. Lacan must show us how to resolve this conundrum.

Lacan's distinction between the Symbolic and the real (all that resists the Symbolic) allows him to argue that letters operate as agents of both absence and presence. A letter—by which he means any arbitrary signifier (such as "elephant")—makes objects (elephants) present by positioning them in discourse and also signifies the absence of (real) elephants. Elsewhere Lacan (1991:228) writes that "everything is *already there* no doubt, but it is only with speech that there are things which are—which are true or false, that is to say which are—and things which are not" (emphasis added). With speech it becomes possible, says the imperialistic Lacan, to divide up the vast regions of the real (the "already there") and in so doing establish pockets of truth, like colonies. With speech one can distinguish "elephant" from "giraffe"; even though the choice of signifiers is arbitrary, these distinctions are necessary for making sense. Lacan needs to allow actual elephants and giraffes to remain in their place, "already there" in the inarticulable real, while continuing his discussion of exactitude and, eventually, truth. The letter kills the real phenomenon outside the scope of language by giving it a determinate form inside language.[10]

Speech-acts owe their meaning, then, to the structure of language, not the phenomenal world. Problems arise in any confusion between the signifiable real that cannot be articulated and the imperial project of signification, within which positions can be mapped with precision. Such confusion has the effect of making relations between letter (waggle) and place (bee-balm) as fixed as they are for the bees. Letters, if you know what they are, are simply not like other objects.

As he concludes his examination of Dupin's footsteps, Lacan writes:

"For the signifier is a . . . symbol only of an absence. Which is why we cannot say of the purloined letter that, like other objects, it must be *or* not be in a particular place but that unlike them it will be *and* not be where it is, wherever it goes" (24; 39). The *"nullibiété"* (23; 38) of the letter—the fact that it is nowhere present—owes to its lack of basis in the real; it is not assigned a place among other objects because it draws them into language. As such it owes its materiality (its capacity to kill the real by substituting a sign for it) to its basis in the Symbolic. And yet the letter is free to travel in ways that never fix the signifier to the signified; like any sovereign, wherever it goes it will be where it is. So here lies the answer to the conundrum: the letter is not in any place in particular because it establishes what is present and absent. And yet we are beginning to see that this establishment always leaves something to be desired.

A Return to the First Dialogue, Contrasting G's Exactitude and Dupin's Truth

To drive home the importance of the Symbolic for maintaining order, or keeping things in their assigned places, Lacan opens this section by contrasting the orderly search of the exacting G and the vast unnamed territory that is "always there," always in its place because it owes nothing to the signifier. According to Lacan (25; 40), "the real, whatever upheaval we subject it to, is always in its place; it carries it [its place] glued to its heel, ignorant of what might exile it from it." But the real lies outside the scope of language and dies whenever drawn into speech by the Symbolic.

Because the police have done all that one can in the field of intersubjective speech—have followed their orders to the letter, as it were, exhausting all spaces—the problem is not their lack of insight, but ours for failing to distinguish the speech of the desiring subject from the word at the foundation of intersubjectivity. The entire operation has been taking place within the scope of language, which by definition blinds us to the real. The physical letter, the actual sheets of paper first stolen by Minister D, has already made its impression on the characters in the imaginary drama; what matters here all along are the characters' reactions to the letter, not the sheets of paper. Lacan says here that, while the letter plays a fourth character in each triangle, "the signifier is not functional." Each character is at once caught up in the Imaginary, represented in the Symbolic, and blinded to the real.

By saying that the police's lack is "neither individual nor the corporative variety," that there is nothing that one can do to redeem their position, Lacan signals a move to the other end (or transindividual field) of the

symbolic axis, the locus of signification at the foundation of intersubjectivity. Any intersubjective link between subjects (positioned in discourse
as subjects of the statement) and living in the Imaginary as egos and objects must involve the transindividual third party of the letter. As Lacan
writes elsewhere, "The Other with a big O is the scene of the Word insofar as the scene of the Word is always in third position between two subjects. This is only in order to introduce the dimension of Truth, which is
made perceptible, as it were, under the inverted sign of the lie" (Wilden,
1968:269). The characters of the imaginary drama can be analyzed in the
symbolic drama, within which they are positioned at various places in the
circuit of the letter. But the analyst—first Dupin but then Lacan—reserves
the position of the third party, closest to the truth. G, the desiring subject,
cannot be expected to locate the letter because it is already incorporated
in his subjectivity as a lack. We have seen that being called into language
splits the subject between the need of the real and the demand of the ego.
And now we see that the Word intervenes in any relation between self
and other. The gap between the real and the Symbolic requires that the
desiring subject remain unfulfilled because the subject of the statement is
forever blocked from the subject of enunciation, located in the real.

Reducing "The Purloined Letter" to a story about characters making
demands of each other risks missing the power that the signifier holds over
the entire operation (much of which proceeds unbeknownst to the egos
involved) and consequently underestimating the (epistemic) violence of
representation. For Lacan, then, the written word—as a signifier of the
spoken signifier of the largely irrelevant signified—flies away and speech
remains ripe for analytic review, even if partially severed from a real that
is "always there."

Lacan accordingly draws this section of his seminar on Poe to a close
on the following note: "Nothing then can redeem the police's position
[as the desiring subject of discourse barred from the truth], and nothing would be changed by improving their 'culture.' *Scripta manent:* in vain
would they learn from a deluxe-edition humanism the proverbial lesson
which *verba volant* concludes. May it but please heaven that writings remain, as is rather the case with spoken words: for the indelible debt of
the latter impregnates our acts with its transferences" (26-27; 41). As
the "talking cure" of psychoanalysis might promise, we as analysands can
through transference, with the help of the analyst, interpret the unconscious desires lurking in our acts. But what is the fate of the written word?
Scripta volant? Exactly right: reversing the proverbial lesson, writings are
up for grabs ("Les écrits emportent au vent les traites en blanc d'une cava-
lerie folle"), which explains why letters can be stolen ("Et, s'ils n'étaient

feuilles volantes, il n'y aurait pas de lettre volées") (27; 41). But the speech they would contain remains ripe for (psychoanalytic) review.

Because the letter is the only character allowed to play the Word, I want to close my elliptical reading of Lacan's seminar with something close to what one might call its "voice," if the letter were not so relentlessly trans-individual. Fortunately, Lacan gives the letter a closing line that serves to indicate the power of the Absolute Other: "So runs the signifier's answer, above and beyond all significations: 'You think you act when I stir you at the mercy of the bonds through which I knot your desires. Thus do they grow in force and multiply in objects, bringing you back to the fragmentation of your scattered childhood. So be it: such will be your feast until the return of the stone guest I shall be for you since you call me forth'" (40; 52). The menacing power of this Word that petrifies the subject even as it calls it to speak illustrates the extent to which the imperialistic Lacan is committed to a position that allows the truth to hollow out colonies in the real.

Aftermath: Lacan's Schema L

It should be clear that the actual, speechless drama, in which characters repeat motions in triangulated formulation, and the other, new drama stand in a relation of Imaginary and Symbolic. We have just seen how the narrated subject-Subject relations of analysand and analyst (G and Dupin) are cast in opposition to (and possibly mediate) the subject-object relations of the ego-other variety (where G and Minister D actually reside). Furthermore, the real seems to stand in ignorance outside these, haunting both intersecting structural axes. Although the relationship between these axes seems frozen in time when Lacan is reading Poe with an "immixture of subjects" in mind, their relation appears developmental when describing how children differentiate themselves from the (m)other at the mirror stage in the Imaginary. And the appeal to a fundamental truth (the Word) gives many of us the suspicion that the ultimate aim of Lacan's reading is to unlock the mysteries of the unconscious. Lacan's Schema L., as it appears in the notes following the Poe seminar (1966:53) and elsewhere (Lacan, 1988b:109), helps illustrate how the Imaginary and Symbolic operate together at various levels.

Ragland (1995:30) uses the Schema L to give the Lacanian subject a straightforward interpretation: "the ego is only a part of the subject stretched over the four corners Lacan maps in the Schema L as: ego (*moi*), desiring subject (*je*), the other of imaginary relations, and the Other as

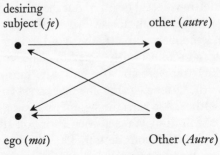

desiring
subject (*je*)   other (*autre*)

ego (*moi*)   Other (*Autre*)

Chart 1. Four Corners of the Schema L

site of unconscious meaning production." Lacan, who announces early in this essay his interest in the "immixture of subjects" in Poe's Purloined Letter, offers the diagram shown in Chart 1. But Grosz (1990:73) reminds us that this is only one (the synchronic one) of three possible levels of this schema—diachronic, synchronic, and (psycho)analytic—all of which are relevant here.

Developmentally Lacan uses the schema to identify the brutish self (*Es*) of the real, who must pass through the mirror stage (*autre-moi*) and enter the locus of signification Lacan calls the Other, *Autre*. This level should be read like a Z. For example, one can at this level illustrate the transition from the real of the cockroach or bees or newborn human bodies (entities that have not yet passed through the anxiety-producing defiles of language) to the Symbolic which positions subjects in discourse.

Synchronically, as Ragland has just suggested, the subject is stretched out as if drawn and quartered. Lacan (1977:90) describes the second story of his Schema L in these terms: "It is therefore always in the relation between the subject's ego (*moi*) and the I (*je*) of his discourse that you must understand the meaning of the discourse if you are to achieve the delineation of the subject. But you cannot possibly achieve this if you cling to the idea that the ego of the subject is identical with the presence that is speaking to you." Viewing the ego synchronically permits thinking about the two scenes in which characters repeat various positions of hiding, seeing nothing, and all-seeing. The narrator draws this play into language by permitting subjects of enunciation, such as G and Dupin, to speak as subjects of the statement (*je*). The symbolic axis can illustrate that "ineffable relation" mediating any imaginary communication between subjects in terms of shared objects.

To capture the debt of this subject positioning to the signifier, or symbol, one needs only to turn to a third sense of the Schema L, one that privileges the Symbolic over the Imaginary: (psycho)analysis is designed to draw the subject away from imaginary misrecognition toward a closer appreciation of the unconscious absolute Other. Steering analysands toward hidden truths by breaking the mirror of the Imaginary and through transference detecting in the symptomatic speech of the desiring subject (*je*) the structure of the unconscious (*Autre*), analysts facilitate our coming to terms with a desire that is always the desire of the Other, a tyrannical Subject that petrifies the subject, even as it draws it into discourse. At least this is where Lacan is trying to take those who can hear.

The three-storied Schema L is quite useful in explaining the relationship between the subject of enunciation (the person speaking the word "I") and the subject of the statement (the word "I" spoken in a statement). As Silverman (1984:196–97) explains, "The speaking subject belongs to . . . the real, but it can attain subjectivity . . . only through . . . signification. Since signification results in an aphanisis of the real, the speaking subject [the actual person] and its discursive representative—i.e., the subject of the speech—remain perpetually dissimultaneous, at odds." We must remember here how a would-be person, Es, is split between need and demand, as an individuated ego at the mirror stage in the Imaginary, when passing through the channels of signification eventually to become a desiring subject (*je*). This painful process is never resolved. Looking in the mirror, one feels the jubilation of a unitary subject, but this very unity carries with it anxieties about indeterminacy or fragmentation never before recognized, the anxiety and needs of the real. The danger of need lurks within any Garden of Eden.

Language elevates humanity above the status of animals like bees, but because we cannot ever be fully aware of our positions in language we construct worlds of deception, misrecognition, and anxiety. And even these reassuring worlds are regularly interrupted by the real, that indeterminacy that the Absolute Other never successfully keeps at bay. Viewed diachronically, desire results from the splitting of the subject between need and demand, on either side of the "scope of what speech repeats"; viewed synchronically, one's "desire is always desire of the Other" precisely because "the unconscious is the discourse of the Other" (16; 32). And this presence of desire, itself a symbolic relation (*je-Autre*), always already (synchronically) mediates every self-other relation in the Imaginary.

Deleuze and Guattari's Demands on Lacan

Deleuze and Guattari liberate desire by refusing to follow the mapping suggested by Lacan.[11] Rather than continue agonizing over the negotiations between the signified and its signifiers, they dare to speak of "asignifying signs," locating desire as the Lacanian real outside the intersection of symbolic representation and imaginary coherence. They promise to revolutionize the heretofore stabilizing, if somewhat anxiety-producing, psychoanalytic model by arguing that "the true difference in nature is not between the Symbolic and the Imaginary, but between the real machinic (*machinique*) element, which constitutes desiring-production, and the structural whole of the Imaginary and the Symbolic, which merely forms a myth and its variants. . . . In any case, it was inopportune to tighten the nuts and bolts where Lacan had just loosened them" (Deleuze and Guattari, 1983:83).

This loosening of restriction (which Deleuze and Guattari describe as "*yes*") appears to be precisely what I need to rethink Labor outside of the circulation of money and commodities during the buying and selling of "its" object, labor-power. But I need to study how capital-Labor relations are reformulated in Deleuze and Guattari's discussion of desire and representation. To accomplish this I explain several key distinctions concerning capitalist representation in their *Anti-Oedipus;* next I zero in on several passages from *A Thousand Plateaus* which link an "out-class" that is neither worker nor producer with a capital that is increasingly "smooth" as opposed to "striated"; and then I suggest a way of reading Deleuze and Guattari's twin volumes as one.

How Axiomatic Capitalism Is Not a Coding Operation

We learn from the outset that "writing has never been capitalism's thing" (Deleuze and Guattari, 1983:240), but one needs to note carefully their use of *writing*. Does this term name a Derridian writing-in-general that must include the framing of the intenders, or is it merely the (Lacanian) graphic signifier of the spoken signifier of the conceptual signified in a continuation of (post-)Saussurean privileging of speech over writing? Deleuze and Guattari appear to use "writing" in the latter sense, on the way to rejecting any form of representation associated with coding. Their portrayal of capitalism as a "language of decoded flows" distinguishes its capacity for change from the "despotic overcoding" of signifiers they associate with the Symbolic; writing "belongs to imperial despotic representation" (240). Building on Marshall McLuhan's insight—"the content of any medium is always another medium" (241), Deleuze and Guattari liberate the signifier from the signified while relieving Lacan of his imperial model.

We are about to see how Deleuze and Guattari develop decoding and axiom proliferation as two faces of capitalist representation which do not rely on writing. They relegate writing to the reterritorializing the state and its striations as a third face of capitalist representation. Capitalism and schizophrenia share a penchant for decoding operations, but capital differs from its unruly partner by relying on the reassurance of its axioms and, in addition to this, the authoritative recoding operations of the reterritorializing state.

It is useful here to distinguish the rules of language-games, in the Wittgensteinian sense of "forms of life," from the all-absorbing "flux" that Deleuze and Guattari cannot seem to leave alone. Both operations involve markedly different senses of decoding. Although Deleuze and Guattari (1983:245) acknowledge that "decoding doubtless means understanding and translating a code [as in a language-game]," they want—on the strength of their rejection of a Saussurean linguistics of signs—to push further, to use "decoding" in the negative sense of "destroying the code as such, assigning it an archaic, folkloric, or residual function." They theorize desire in terms of a fundamental asignifying *"yes,"* by convincing us of the "certain[ty] that . . . neither capitalism, nor revolution, nor schizophrenia follows the paths of the signifier" (244).

Setting aside the determinacy of language-games and their codes, if only momentarily, permits emphasizing the difference in Deleuze and Guattari between the flow established by capitalism (in the flux of finance and the reflux of wages, for example) and the flow unleashed as schizophrenia, "the universe of productive and reproductive desiring-machines, universal primary production as 'the essential reality of man and nature' "(1983:5). (Significantly, they quote D. H. Lawrence on love instead of Karl Marx on Labor.)[12] The desiring-machine is binary in the sense that "there is always a flow-producing machine, and another machine connected to it that interrupts or draws off part of this flow." This schizophrenic machine names desire in the sense that "desire constantly couples continuous flows and partial objects that are by nature fragmentary and fragmented" (1983:5). "Schizophrenia and capitalism," we are told, "should be examined at the deepest level of one and the same economy, one and the same production process." In fact Deleuze and Guattari argue that "our society produces schizos the same way it produces Prell shampoo or Ford cars, the only difference being that the schizos are not saleable" (245). We must, then, also consider their delirious differences.[13]

Schizophrenia's machinic decoding operations yield unregulated, freely dismantled, dismembered desire. Capital's machinic decoding operation also breaks down all hitherto existing codes—recall that for Deleuze and Guattari this includes the entire project of writing—but is forced to substitute, or exchange, its axiomatic rules for the earlier codified rules. Capitalism "axiomatizes with one hand what it decodes with the other" (1983: 246). For an obvious example, under an earlier customary code social status was not dictated by size of income, but with capitalism it is as difficult to value people with no access to the means of subsistence as it is to devalue people with unlimited access. Archaic terms like "respectability" now float freely in most circles along with the money flow. But all of this freedom falls within the strict boundaries of a new social axiom which respects, for example, the privacy of property and the health of the economy. This is the sense in which, according to Deleuze and Guattari, capitalism serves as the limit (relative to its axioms) of all societies. But schizophrenia is not beholden to these axioms. Hence the schizophrenic desiring-machine stands as the exterior limit of capital's axioms, which stand as the relative, or interior, limit of social possibility: "monetary flows are perfectly schizophrenic realities, but they exist and function only within the immanent axiomatic that exorcises and repels this reality" (246). People with money to burn help (given a constant supply of fresh labor-power) to keep capitalism flowing into the future; but schizos remind us that money can burst absolutely into flames at any moment and that the economy can become very sick indeed. And on the strength of this reminder they reintroduce the state.

Relocating Labor as Desire's Out-class

Deleuze and Guattari (1983:253) allow as "an obvious and practical fact" that the state is "entirely in the service of the so-called ruling class," but this is not their point. The proliferation of axioms sparked by capitalism has replaced ancient and feudal social distinctions and other codes; from the perspective of these axioms there is only one class, the bourgeoisie. One is either bourgeois or outside class politics altogether. They explain that "the bourgeoisie . . . is the *only* class as such, inasmuch as it leads the struggles against codes, and merges with the generalized decoding of flows" (254). Marx teaches us that the bourgeoisie is a revolutionary class in the sense of eliminating earlier distinctions (though we carry trace elements of this past), but how can these post-Marxists view the bourgeoisie as the only class? Surely one rules and the other is ruled?

Deleuze and Guattari appear to face this criticism directly when they acknowledge that "it will be said that there is nevertheless a class that rules and a class that is ruled, both defined by surplus value, the distinction between the flow of financing and the flow of wages" (1983:254). Entertaining the capitalist cry "I too am a slave," they read Marx in ways that allow a sympathetic response.[14] Rather than stress the extent to which, for Marx, the capitalist merely bears the sign of capital and is henceforth also alienated as a person, Deleuze and Guattari flatly presume that capitalists are people too. Workers caught up in the refluent tide of wages form one distinct class, whereas owners who go with the flow of futures and finance form the other. This reflux-flux couple should remind us of the preamble to the Wobblies' constitution: "the working class and owning class have nothing in common." Hence it is rather easy for these authors to say to the I.W.W.—as Althusser will in Chapter 5—"I agree with you in ideological terms, but structurally speaking things are much more complex." Observe Deleuze and Guattari's decidedly structuralist insights: "But this [ruler-ruled relation] is only partially true, since capitalism is born of the conjunction of the two [reflux and flux] . . . and integrates them both in the continually expanded reproduction of its limits. So that the bourgeois is justified in saying, not in terms of ideology, but in the very organization of his axiomatic: there is only one machine . . . and one class of servants" (254). Now, it is one thing to say that owners of money and owners of labor-power stand in a mutually dependent, mutually antagonistic relationship. Indeed capital cannot grow without a labor-power that must be at least contracted (if not paid) by owners of money. But it is quite another thing to say that there is only one class in late capitalism. Deleuze and Guattari travel from the mutual relations of labor-power and capital to their mutual positions in "an undivided flow of income" (255) on the strength of the axiom-code distinction we have just digested, which permits them to distinguish "ideology" and "axiomatic organization."

Having destroyed all earlier codes, capital controls all axioms and spins new ones as needed. In a great "decoded flow" capital reigns supreme, like a rigged wheel of fortune that wins 100 percent of the time, even though it must constantly change the rigging. On the ideological side, at the level of the street, workers might call for a general strike against owners; but on the theoretical side, at the level of the axiomatic, Deleuze and Guattari argue, both "sides" are "servants of the machine." Deleuze and Guattari have not lost their revolutionary zeal; they have just moved out of the center to the fringe of real desire.

Appreciating Deleuze and Guattari's call for the liberation of desire brings us closer to its relationship to representation. It is helpful here to recall their distinction between the perfect schizo and those workers and owners who go with the "undivided" flow of income. Remember that both are intimately involved with decoding, especially in late capitalism; but the schizos get carried away, go all the way, unleash energies that test—no, define—the absolute limits of capitalism. Deleuze and Guat-

tari name these unleashed energies "desire." And desire's *yes!* is henceforth divorced from representation. From a post-Marxist revolutionary
perspective, schizos are more theoretically interesting than their archaic
relatives—whether Wobs, proles, or community organizers. For Deleuze
and Guattari,

> the theoretical opposition is not between two classes . . . it is between,
> on the one hand, the decoded flows that enter into a class axiomatic on
> the full body of capital, and on the other hand, the decoded flows that
> free themselves from this axiomatic just as they free themselves from
> the despotic signifier, that break through this wall, and this wall of a
> wall, and begin flowing on the full body without organs. *The opposition
> is between the class and those who are outside the class* [*les hors-classe*]. . . .
> Between the social machine's régime and that of the desiring-machines.
> . . . between the capitalists and the schizos in their basic intimacy at the
> level of decoding, in their basic antagonism at the level of the axiom-
> atic. (1983:255, emphasis added)

In this remarkable plea for emancipated desire, class agents and "those
who are outside the class" have managed to free themselves from the "despotic signifier." The bourgeoisie takes care of business by replacing codes
with axioms; the "out-class" goes one step further by replacing axioms
with freely flowing, unruly indeterminacy. The most sympathetic Marxist
reading of this passage would describe Deleuze and Guattari as relocating the basic antagonism of capital and labor, giving this pair of terms
a "basic intimacy" at the "level of decoding" and a "basic antagonism"
at the "level of the axiomatic." But less patient readers, especially loyalist Marxists, might ask whether Labor has been evacuated in the flux, lost
once again in another bourgeois shuffle. Is Labor's movement the price
one pays, we might ask, for "updating" Marx by entertaining the contemporary complexity of capital's relentlessly violent consolidation?

Deleuze and Guattari anticipate such questions from their rearguard
readers and say "of course, it is possible to conceive a theoretical determination of the proletarian class at the level of production (those from whom
surplus-value is extorted) or at the level of money (income in wages)"
(1983:255). But this reassuring gesture reveals Deleuze and Guattari once
again using class to group people as fixed subjects. With such a fixed sense
of the subject in hand, they move easily to dismiss heretofore revolutionary socialism as theoretically suspect and practically ineffective. They
continue the quotation just cited with this damning qualification: "But not
only are these determinations sometimes too narrow and sometimes too

wide, but the objective being they define as *class interest* remains purely virtual so long as it is not embodied in a consciousness that, to be sure, does not create it, but actualizes it in an organized party suited to the task of conquering the State apparatus."

The task of organizing a "bipolarity of classes," then, faces twin obstacles, equally insurmountable for Deleuze and Guattari. First, it is hard to draw the line between workers and owners as classes-in-themselves; second, the move to a class-for-itself is plagued by party-state relations that always lose out to capital's incredible power to create new axioms, even "to add a few more axioms for the recognition of the proletariat as a second class" (1983:256). This theme of first- and second-class subjects continues in their *A Thousand Plateaus*.

Three Faces of Capitalist Representation

Just when we thought that all of the qualitative, indirect, limited, reliant codes had been shattered by quantitative, unlimited, direct, self-reliant axiomatization, modern societies are now shown to be torn in both directions of axiomatizing deterritorializing and reterritorializing based on recoding. Deleuze and Guattari capture the dilemma: "They vacillate between two poles: the paranoid despotic sign, the sign-signifier of the despot that they try to revive as a unit of code; and the sign-figure of the schizo as a unit of decoded flux, a schiz, a point-sign or flow-break. They try to hold on to one, but they pour or flow out of the other. They are continually behind or ahead of themselves" (260). Such a dynamic model concentrates on the relationship of social machines (that bourgeois class) and desiring-machines (the out-class). In fact, Deleuze and Guattari would advance as twin poles of axiomatization the class–out-class tension as a relation between recoding and decoding. It is becoming clear that Labor, if it belongs anywhere, is now construed as a perfect schizo outside the zone of capitalist axiomatics, including the axiom capital creates for determinate labor-power as a second-class citizen. Readers should be already suspecting that this substitutes an unnamed subject of desire for Labor.

Deleuze and Guattari's diagnosis (1983:262) works through an elapsing time continuum from the coding of a "savage territorial machine" to the overcoding of a "barbarian despotic machine" to the decoding of the "civilized capitalist machine," which is also always recoding, in part because of the traces of despotism and territoriality it carries from the past. We are left with a situation in which "deterritorialization, the axiomatic and reterritorialization are the three surface elements of the representation of desire in the modern socius" (262). Because capital controls all three surfaces, representation emerges, at least in *Anti-Oedipus*, as the enemy of revolutionary desire. Hope lies in the fact that schizos share decoding operations with capitalists.

Indeed, Deleuze and Guattari detect problems with state socialism in its insistence on reterritorializing, recoding, reconfiguring second-class proletarian spaces always within the governance of the capitalist axiomatic. Instead of mobilizing one group of people—producers—against another—managers—state socialists are forced to mobilize loose sets of fragmented people against an unseen force that is always watching or monitoring the situation and manipulating, if not profiting from, our every decision. When we win strikes, capital sells us durable goods; when we lose strikes, capital sells us prisons. Labor is pushed beyond the margins of value while capital plays its margins for all they are worth.

In the face of being criticized for neglecting class struggle, Deleuze and Guattari could deploy their distinction between interest and desire. The proletariat has been granted second-class citizenship in late capitalist society in the sense that axioms have been created to deal with its interests, much like axioms have been created to deal with dolphins' interests. Deleuze and Guattari find in this the possibility of betraying the revolution. Desire, on the other hand, refuses to permit the reterritorializing and recoding that capitalism requires. Hence its revolutionary potential. Deleuze and Guattari believe that "capitalist society can endure many manifestations of interest, but not one manifestation of desire, which would be enough to make its fundamental structures explode, even at the kindergarten level. We believe in desire . . . not because it is a lack, a thirst, or an aspiration, but because it is the production of desire: desire that produces—real-desire, or the real in itself" (1983:379). Their portrayal of desire as an out-class transforms class struggle from interest-group squabbling to revolutionary anticapitalist action. Earlier in this argument, they state their preference: "Desire can never be deceived. Interest can be deceived, unrecognized, or betrayed, but not desire" (257). Interests come and go, subject to capital's manipulation, but desire, like the Lacanian real, is "always there."

We face, then, a major difference of scope between Lacanian desire and the project of liberation in *Anti-Oedipus*. Even the three-story structure of the Schema L is unduly restrictive for Deleuze and Guattari, who switch metaphors (a term they would resist) from structures to machines and then pit social machines against desiring machines. If you can imagine folding the Schema L along its symbolic (*je-Autre*) axis, Deleuze and Guattari's desire lives outside the fold. What readers might pronounce as inarticulate in the Lacanian real, Deleuze and Guattari interpret as voices of desire clamoring for autonomy and emancipation. They attribute Lacan's reticence to a misplaced reliance on symbolic representation. Deleuze and Guattari refuse to reduce production to representation, the word.[15] The high stakes of their schizoanalysis demand that we "overturn the theatre of representation into the order of desiring-production" With a scope wider than any given Lacanian domain, an interest in the flip side of the Schema L, and a commitment to a desire they find at odds with capital's theater of representation, Deleuze and Guattari are well positioned to inspire antiauthoritarian (antistate) revolutionary movements against the capitalist axiomatic (from an out-class perspective).

Desire's Impending Divorce from Representation

Moving from *Anti-Oedipus* to *A Thousand Plateaus* requires passing from relative negativity to provisional liberation. *A Thousand Plateaus* encourages a multiplier effect inspired by the figure of the "rhizome," a chaotic network of possibility that chokes the sturdy, reliable roots of Western metaphysics. One might contrast Lispector's "interval" with the book's opening exhortation: "Make rhizomes, not roots, never plant! Don't sow, grow offshoots! Don't be one or multiple, be multiplicities! Run lines, never plot a point! Speed turns a point into a line! . . . Between things does not designate a localizable relation going from one thing to the other and back again, but a perpendicular direction, a transversal movement that sweeps one and the other way, a stream without beginning or end that undermines its banks and picks up speed in the middle" (1987:25).

Unlike *Anti-Oedipus* with its mission of delivering a revolutionary schizoanalysis, *A Thousand Plateaus* is determined to develop new (smooth) spaces for the operations of desire-machines, here called "assemblages." My reading of Deleuze and Guattari focuses on the relation of workers and owners as they form one class of (enslaved) servants in axiomatized bourgeois society. Here I turn to the work with subjectification in *A Thousand Plateaus*. I must also ascertain how the three faces of capitalist representation developed in *Anti-Oedipus* are related to the celebration of desire found in these pages. This relationship relies upon a most provocative distinction—smooth versus striated capital—which effectively positions capitalism between the chaos of the schizo and the order of state authority.

Reviewing the evolution of the modern state in terms of *Anti-Oedipus*'s progression from savage to barbarian to modern forms, Deleuze and Guattari appropriate Marx's alleged modes of production without continuing to weave his common thread of the exploitation of surplus labor. By defining "social formations by machinic processes and not by modes of production" on which they depend, Deleuze and Guattari position themselves to finish off the rather significant Marxist distinction between constant capital (such as the owners' machines) and variable capital (such as the workers' labor-power). Indeed, if human beings are approached as constituent parts of a machine, the surplus value that derives from exploiting human labor-power becomes a "machinic surplus value" (1983:232) to which users of a product (such as TV viewers) might also contribute. From here Deleuze and Guattari could go on to bolster their earlier structural claim that workers and managers are slaves to the same machine. It comes as no surprise, then, that labor-power's movement (within the capitalist axiomatic) and unruly desire's revolution (as the out-class without it) will not be conjoined in *A Thousand Plateaus*. We must ascertain, however, whether the out-class/servant class distinction is a necessary result of smooth capitalism's version of machinic capture and enslavement. This requires clarifying the issue of capital's machinery.

Inasmuch as "the state becomes the model of realization for the capitalist axiomatic" we can turn there to study the subjectification required by capital's machinations. According to Deleuze and Guattari, the evolution from the crude machinic enslavement of earlier forms of the state to subjectification of the modern form requires distinguishing human beings as "constituent pieces of a machine" and "human beings as a subject linked to a now exterior object." At first glance, thanks to a history of progress, "the human being is no longer a component of the machine but a worker, a user" (1987:457). Subjectification creates a subject—for example, a worker or a capitalist—and correspondingly "subjects" that freshly minted entity to the recoded territory of a state that is fond of proclaiming, "when I feel desire I take out my gun." This explains why in late capitalism the same subjectification that freed us from coded machinic enslavement can and does lead to a new form of axiomatized machinic enslavement. Deleuze and Guattari write: "It could be . . . said that a small amount of subjectification took us away from machinic enslavement, but a large amount brings us back to it" (458). In fact, they distinguish machinic enslavement and subjection to the state as coexisting poles instead of stages.

The major difference between our contemporary enslavement and its codified ancestors becomes, for Deleuze and Guattari, the extent to which capital's power lies immanent in society as a ruling axiom.[16] The subjectification of contemporary bourgeois society afflicts both so-called owners and workers as different parts of the same machine. The subject in subjectification must be understood here not in terms of a person—or even a Lacanian quadra-subject—but instead as a body marked by dominant discourse. One becomes enslaved more subtly—and perhaps completely —under late capitalism. Workers and owners endure the injuries of a speedup in the workplace without the cruel taskmaster of yesteryear. For Deleuze and Guattari "there is no subject, only collective assemblages of enunciation [such as schools or prisons or psychiatry]." "Subjectfication," they continue, "is simply one such assemblage and designates a formalization of expression or a regime of signs rather than a condition internal to language. . . . Capital is a point of subjectification par excellence" (1987:130). To understand how capital's point of subjectification turns into the line of subjectification we have been calling axiomatization requires a new distinction—borrowed from the linguist Benveniste—which shows in greater detail how workers and owners are part of the same machine.

Drawing on Benveniste's distinction between subjects of enunciation and subjects of the statement, Deleuze and Guattari argue that a point of subjectification turns into a line of subjectification through the complex inner relation of these two subjects. Here is how they explain the inner dynamic in terms of the assemblage called psychoanalysis:

> The psychoanalyst presents him- or herself as an ideal point of subjectification that brings the patient to abandon old, so-called neurotic, points. The patient is partially a subject of enunciation in all he or she says to the psychoanalyst, and under the artificial mental conditions of the session: the patient is therefore called the "analysand." But in everything else the patient says or does, he or she is a subject of the statement . . . growing increasingly submissive to the normalization of a dominant reality. (1987:130–31)

Even though they evoke the analyst-analysand relation on the third story of the Lacanian Schema L, Deleuze and Guattari are less concerned with the relation of the Imaginary and the Symbolic than they are with desiring-production outside, or that which makes such an intersection possible. Here they are, like Minister D eyeing the queen, trying to observe Lacan's Schema L from a position outside it.

Their appropriated version of subjectification helps to explain capital's hegemony, or machinic enslavement. First, a point of subjectification constitutes the subject by distinguishing it from its object—as food constitutes the anorexic, or an article of clothing the fetishist. Second, the subject of enunciation is issued as a function of the mental reality determined by the new point of subjectification. Third, this enunciation makes it possible to speak, to make statements that conform with its new mental reality. Finally, the initial point of subjectification becomes a line of subjectification when the first subject crosses over into the second, which in return gives it substance: "the subject of enunciation recoils into the subject of the statement, to the point that the subject of the statement resupplies the subject of enunciation for another proceeding" (1987:129). Accordingly, capital "acts as the point of subjectification that constitutes all human beings as subjects; but some, "the capitalists," are subjects of enunciation that form the private subjectivity of capital, while the others, the "proletarians," are subjects of the statement, subjected to the technical machines in which constant capital is effectuated" (457). Capital's tremendous power of deterritorializing expression through axiom proliferation is intimately related to schizophrenia in the sense that both break all hitherto existing "points" of subjectification. In addition to these formal declarations of mental reality, bodies are also inscribed by statements in conformity with the dominant reality. Here the state is brought in to maintain order. The deterritorialized subject of enunciation is always recoiling into the reterritorialized subject of the statement; this explains why proletarians and capitalists are wrapped up together in a reality governed by capital and enforced by the state: machinic enslavement. Capital goes where it wants to and speaks through the capitalist; workers conform to the dominant reality left in their wake.

Due to the unruly nature of the constant capital/variable capital distinction in a new age of machinic enslavement (under the "asign" of the axiom), surplus value and surplus labor—key elements of Marx's technical definition of exploitation—are regarded as relics of yesteryear. "In these new conditions, it remains true that all labor [in the sense of consumed labor-power] involves surplus labor; but surplus labor no longer requires labor [for machines can also perform this function]" (1987:492). In other words, concentrating on the exploitation of human labor-power, although this certainly continues to exist in sweatshops and free enterprise zones the world over, does not begin to address the wide range of capital's assemblages. Perhaps the most memorable description of the free-flowing reconstitution of human being that Deleuze and Guattari are detecting stresses its autonomy from state involvement: "today we can depict an enormous, so-called stateless, monetary mass that circulates through foreign exchange and across borders, eluding control by the States, forming a multinational ecumenical organization, constituting a de facto supra-national power untouched by governmental decisions" (453). And yet we have seen this is only a partial aspect of capital's mastery. The deterritorializing/decoding articulated in this passage travels in a tension with the recoding/reterritorializing on the part of the state. To do otherwise would forsake the relative limits of capitalism for the absolute limits of desire. Deleuze and Guattari are quick to remind us that "states are not at all transcendent paradigms of an overcoding but immanent models of realization for an axiomatic of decoded flows" (455).

But it is one thing to claim that labor-power has become alienating machinic enslavement because the actual worker involved has become part and parcel of the machine along with the manager and the consumer, and quite another thing to claim that labor-power is no longer at odds—structurally speaking—with its owner. We might just as easily conclude that managers are workers and that both managers and workers are at odds with the new subject, capital, that phantom subject that stole Labor's subjectivity. But Deleuze and Guattari cannot join us because, for them, capital is a point of subjectification, an object that constitutes first the enunciating capitalist and then the rule-following worker. Capital is approached as organs without a body—a point—and then transformed into a body without organs—a line. We must continue asking what happens to Labor—our possession of labor-power—as Deleuze and Guattari move from striated to smooth capital.

A Thousand Plateaus develops this new distinction to explain the relation of state repression of desire and capital's participation in this dangerous force. Deleuze and Guattari's way of distinguishing smooth and striated models is at once fundamental to *A Thousand Plateaus*'s attempt to s(t)imulate smooth spaces and key to *Anti-Oedipus*'s assault on representation because these authors confine representation to striated spaces within which (written) coding is possible. The sea is an example of smooth space, whereas cities are designed as striated space.[17] Lacan's Schema L exemplifies striated space with its three planar dimensions and intersecting axes as lines connecting various endpoints, forming zones, as if in a regulated city. Deleuze and Guattari's portrayal of capitalism requires living smoothly in striated space, respecting relative limits. But Moneybags's schizoid, flow-breaking twin is always waiting in the wings, respecting no limits whatsover.

At the nexus of capital's free-flowing autonomy and the state's rigid containment, Deleuze and Guattari present the following bone-chilling assessment of capitalist hegemony: "It is as though human alienation through surplus labor were replaced by a generalized 'machinic enslavement.' . . . It is as though, at the outcome of the striation that capitalism was able to carry to an unequaled point of perfection, circulating capital necessarily recreated, reconstituted a sort of smooth space in which the destiny of human beings is recast" (1987:492). Users, workers, owners, all go through the motions in a machinic enslavement determined by the flow

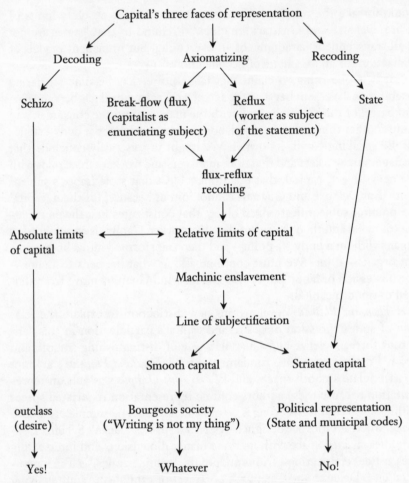

Chart 2. Desire's Divorce from Representation in Deleuze and Guattari

of circulating capital, as powerless to change the axioms as enunciated, as they are to change the tides of the sea.

This distinction, then, helps me to complete the picture of the relationship between Deleuze and Guattari's three faces of representation—decoding, axiomatizing, and recoding—and the politics of desire. We see that representation is ultimately divorced from desire (Chart 2).

Thus capital is given a free hand in the constitution of the subject, the result of which is two classes of people who have a great deal in common. Deleuze and Guattari succeed brilliantly in articulating the all-encompassing victory of capitalism, the way in which its forces have achieved axiomatic status. Their work carries the implication that unleashing desire of any variety might invigorate a radical movement outside the purview of capital's domain. Herein lies the relevance of the autonomy movement (especially adept at contesting state power) or other new social movements that refuse to play capital's game. But before joining them in relegating Labor to an earlier stage of historical development, we should turn to another way of theorizing desire, a way of locating desire within representation as the différance, trace, or supplement of codes and messages. This will allow for an aporia in the axioms that govern subjects and objects and help to explain how Labor may be there all along, long after its determinate forms have been co-opted by bourgeois society. Resuscitating Labor will require a return to Marx—as we do in Part 2—for a reevaluation in light of the gaps and spaces one finds in the text of the proper(ty). But first we have to locate this invisible subject.

Eugene Holland (1991:55) distinguishes Deleuze and Guattari from Derrida in a way that is consistent with our reading: "where Derrida rewrites a binary opposition such as speech versus writing in terms of a single broader nonconcept like writing (arche-trace), Deleuze and Guattari instead defy binary closure by multiplying terms." Adding Lacan's masterful Symbolic-Imaginary couple to the mix presents us with three provocative approaches to indeterminacy: the Lacanian real, Deleuze and Guattari's desire, and Derridian extravagance. Before crafting my approach, I need briefly to contrast Derrida's approach with the theories of both Lacan and Deleuze and Guattari.

The Creative Weave of Différance

Lacan and Derrida have, of course, already squared off at the site of Poe's "The Purloined Letter." Barbara Johnson offers the best-received account of this struggle between these two distinguished subject-authors, who are sometimes—not unlike Minister D and Dupin—difficult to distinguish from one another. To ascertain how the excess of Derridian différance relates to the Lacanian real, I defer—if only for "a glance's time"—to Derrida's reading of Lacan reading Poe. My work demonstrates how supplementing the Lacanian Schema L—but not attempting to pursue Deleuze and Guattari's flow-break of Absolute desire—defers the question of desire's indeterminacy in ways that might help complicate the (re)presentation of capital's circulation. That is, I find in Derrida an incomplete theory of desire that, precisely because of the indeterminacy allowed, provides Labor an opening for transforming silent urgency into language.

Barbara Johnson (1988:223) has convinced many readers that

> Although Lacan's reading of "The Purloined Letter" divides the story into triadic structures, his model for (inter-)subjectivity, the so-called schema L, which is developed in that part of the Seminar's introduction glossed over by Derrida, is indisputably quadralinear. In order to read Lacan's repeating triads as a triangular, Oedipal model of the subject instead of as a mere structure of repetition, Derrida must therefore lop off one corner of the Schema L in the same way he accuses Lacan of lopping of a corner of Poe's text—and Derrida does this by lopping off that corner of Lacan's text in which the quadrangular Schema L is developed.

But I want to reconsider the relation of triangles and squares in this encounter. We have retraced Lacan's steps sufficiently closely to argue that his Schema L is not only developed in the afterword, the section glossed over by Derrida. Rather, the Schema L provides the organizational principle for juxtaposing the "real drama" (*moi-autre*) and the "new, other drama" (*je-Autre*), a portion of the text scrutinized by Derrida. When Derrida shows how Lacan "extracts . . . triadic structures" from a "scene of writing" which is interminably complex, he is not necessarily lopping off the portion of the Seminar in which the Schema L is developed; rather he may be contesting the quadralinear status of the schema by presenting it in Oedipal fashion as a Symbolic-Imaginary couple interrupted by the Real. I want, then, to suggest that after Derrida completes his reading of Lacan reading Poe the Schema L is not so much missing one of its corners as it is relieved—through careful supplementation—of its duties to organize the subject of desire. In its place one finds a more chaotic "scene of writing" which enframes—without framing—the action of subjects and objects positioned in discourse, deferring any coherent theory of desire. Such a reading allows me, in the aftermath, to salvage elements of Lacan—for example, the subject split between need and demand—without endorsing his imperial duty to the truth of the Big Other.

Narrating the Two Dramas

Derrida notes that Lacan begins his seminar by distinguishing drama, narration, and conditions of narration in ways that appear to be sympathetic with his own claim that everything transpires at the scene of writing. But no sooner does Lacan raise the possibility of such complex narration, we are told, than the narrator becomes transparent, or is whisked away as a "general narrator," whose role in relating the actual drama helps us to identify the new drama on the symbolic axis.[18] In Derrida's words: "the narrator, the narration, and the operation of the *mise en scène*, the staging, are dropped" (1987:429). Because he makes such minimal use of them, Derrida accuses Lacan of entertaining these subjects in order to banish them. Consider this indictment: "All the allusions to the narrator and to the act of narration are made in order to exclude them from the 'real drama' (the two triangular scenes), which is thus to be delivered to the analytic deciphering of the message in clearly demarcated fashion" (429). To catch Lacan in the act of rendering the narrator's "I" transparent, Derrida reads the two movements we have already come to associate with the "new, other drama" on the symbolic axis of the Schema L: exactitude and truth.

The first movement Derrida considers concerns the virtue of speech Lacan calls "exactitude." The narrator, you will recall, recounts the first dialogue between Prefect G and Dupin of what Lacan calls the "real drama," that triangulated business of not-seeing, hiding something, and all-seeing. The narrator brings these events to language, according to Lacan, by removing them from the Imaginary; "hypothetically [he] adds nothing" to the account Prefect G gives Dupin about the way in which the king, the queen, and Minister D assume the three roles respectively. Here Derrida, who would place the narrator as a fourth character in the real drama, scoffs: "as if one had to add something to a relation in order to intervene in a scene" (429). This insinuation collides, of course, with Lacan's claim that the letter, the word, at the foundation of intersubjectivity, plays the fourth character. Indeed we have already heard the letter's last Word: "I knot your desires." Here lies the key difference between these doubling theorists: Lacan's pure signifier, or letter, as the Absolute Other as opposed to Derrida's impure text surrounding all "concrete discourse." Whereas Lacan relies on the twin axes of the Schema L to cushion the effects of the Real, Derrida entertains the excess created by such violent totalizing. Although Lacan and Derrida both avoid equating desire with the Real—an equation embraced by Deleuze and Guattari—Derrida defers the truth, or last words, Lacan seeks to establish (and even upholster).

Their differences show up in greater detail when Derrida turns to the second movement of the "new, other drama," where Lacan's second virtue of speech, truth, is at stake. Here, as we have seen, the narrator presents the second dialogue of the "real drama" by reporting a conversation he himself has with Dupin. This lopsided conversation predicates Dupin, of course, as a subject of the statement who explains how the police, Minister D, and he assumed the same three roles—hiding, seeing, all-seeing—respectively. With the narrator effectively neutralized, Lacan is prepared to show how Dupin arrives at the truth, until Dupin himself succumbs to the signifier and it is time for the master—Lacan—to take over.

Derrida argues that such neutralization carries with it three commitments: Lacan *misconstrues* the "structure of the text," *neglects* formal elements of the text not contained in the two dialogues, and thereby *decides* to cut the narrator out of Poe's "Purloined Letter." First, Derrida argues that the fiction as inscribed serves as "an invisible, but structurally irreducible frame around the narration." The "structure of the text" includes this frame, the signature of the subject, and a certain parergon, or excess (which we will see in a moment). "Overlooking the frame," Lacan transforms the structure of the text into a field that is merely intersubjective. Derrida describes this reduction as a movement from writing to what is written, from text to discourse, from "The Purloined Letter" to its first and second dialogues. According to Derrida, this commits Lacan to a position in which the "scene of the signifier [is] reconstructed into a signified." This charge, that Lacan falls prey to the "logic of the sign," is, of course, a slap in the face to anyone caught up in (the misrecognition of) having liberated the signifier from the signified.

Second, Derrida argues that this formalist exclusion of the subject-author—which is not in the right hands always problematic—cannot even stand as effective formalism because of Lacan's preoccupation with giving the Other (*Autre*) the final word: "a letter [pure signifier] always arrives at its destination." What sense does it make, asks Derrida, to exclude the subject-author, Poe, only to ignore so many other subjects this formalist exclusion makes available? Such "rigidly illogical" formalism "guarantees the surreptitious extraction of a semantic content," the playground of any psychoanalyst pretending to outwit the logic of the sign (instead of deconstructing it).

Postponing a more general critique of formalist application of psychoanalytic theory to literature, Derrida notes here that Lacan's bad formalism "implies a decision" to refuse the narrator agency. Just as Lacan calls attention to the role of the narrator in his attempt to isolate the "new, other drama," he cuts him out in the name of the truth of the letter. In other words, Lacan uses his Schema L in a violent way to devalue, as ornamentation, all aspects of the text not contained in the two triangular dialogues. Derrida presents this decision to eliminate a fourth character as a blatant excision required to produce his predetermined Oedipal triangle. Here we arrive at a passage one might cite, with Barbara Johnson,

as evidence of Derrida's triangulation of the quadralinear Schema L. Insisting upon the complicity of the narrator—not the letter—in the action,
Derrida writes: "by cutting the narrated figure itself from a fourth side
in order to see only triangles, one evades perhaps a certain complication,
perhaps of the Oedipal structure, which is announced in the scene of
writing" (1987:433). Derrida joins Deleuze and Guattari here to suggest
that Lacan's debt to Freud, and the myth of the Oedipal intrusion of a
third element in any couple, forces him to cut the narrator out of the real
drama. To determine whether this criticism neglects the Schema L, we
must continue working our way toward what Derrida thinks Lacan misses
by exiling the narrator.

Derrida (1987:483) returns eventually to comment on the remainder
unnoticed by Lacan's seminar on Poe. Rather than accuse Lacan of not
adequately framing his Schema L, he argues that any such efforts must
fail in principle. Derrida insists that "the point is not to show that 'The
Purloined Letter' functions within a frame . . . but that the structure of
the effects of framing is such that no totalization of the bordering can
even occur. The frames are always enframed: and therefore enframed by a
given piece of what they contain" (485 n. 64). In other words, the effects
of framing (even one as imposing as the Schema L) are only ever to produce a provisional inside and outside; the outside enframes the gesture of
containment. But the outside also doubles as that which is contained. For
example, the narrator who recounts the tale in "The Purloined Letter"
is outside the story he tells, but he also remains inside as an American in
Paris on speaking terms with (at least) Dupin and Prefect G. He is part of
what actually happened already. The point is not that Lacan chooses the
wrong frame; the point is that any framing operation always fails in principle to establish effective borders.

First, the story never really begins anew. It is located in a library, sur-
rounded by writing, and is itself part of other writings, the two earlier
Dupin tales.[19] According to Derrida, the relationship between the two
men is almost an untold tale in itself; a tale of mutual interest, of shared
luxuries, or objects of desire, of financial interaction owing to Dupin's
dwindling surplus and the narrator's responsibility for paying the rent.
In fact, Derrida goes so far as to suggest that "as soon as the narrator is
placed on stage by a function which is indeed that of a public corporation
of capital and desire, no neutralization is possible" (1987:488). The narrator's active role in what really happened as well as in the analysis of what
happened assures us of a drift which can never be anchored by a transcendental signifier at the foundation of intersubjectivity (the Other).

Appreciating the interminable drift at the scene of writing makes it impossible to speak of a letter being indivisible or always arriving at its destination. One cannot escape the ruination because "the divisibility of the letter is also the divisibility of the signifier to which it gives rise, and therefore also of the 'subjects,' 'characters,' or 'positions' which are subjected to it and which 'represent' them" (Derrida, 1987:489). The quadruple division Derrida uses to illustrate the complexity of the field within which Lacan sets his play in motion involves both the narrator and Dupin. The narrator, who brings us the symbolic drama, passes into the play without words, in which so much more happens than misrecognition between self and other in the so-called Imaginary. And Dupin, whose character is given the direct lighting and center stage by the narrator, passes into the symbolic drama of the abstract, vacant, deliberate, distinct resolve of the truth. He is, of course, joined there by the narrator, who identifies with him. And finally, we must add to this complexity the relationship between Dupin and the narrator in a sea of writing, outside the circulation of the letter in either drama.

Derrida concludes his disseminating excursion through all that Lacan misses, when he cuts out the narrator, with the following summary:

> The fancy of an identification between two double doubles, the major investment in a relationship which engages Dupin outside of the intersubjective triads of the real drama and the narrator inside what he narrates; the circulation of desire and capital, of signifiers and letters, before and beyond the "two triangles," the "primal" and secondary ones, the consecutive fissioning of the positions, starting with the position of Dupin, who like all the characters inside and outside the narration, successively occupies all the places—all of this makes of triangular logic a very limited play within a play. (1987:491)

Note that Derrida's "parergonal logic" does not replace, but instead reconfigures, Lacan's triangular alternative when discussing above the "extraction" of the two dialogues from the overall tale. But he continues in ways that implicate the Schema L in the same charge: "And if the dual relation between two doubles [Dupin and the narrator] (which Lacan would reduce to the imaginary) includes and envelops the entire space said to be of the symbolic, overflows and simulates it, ceaselessly ruining and disorganizing it, then the opposition of the imaginary and the symbolic, and above all its implicit hierarchy, appears to be of very limited pertinence: that is, if one measures it against the squaring of such a scene of writing" (491-92).

Derrida does not, then, acknowledge that the Schema L—in which desire is the discourse of the other—is a square deal. The way in which Lacan privileges the already lopsided, twin-poled Symbolic over the already lopsided, the twin-poled Imaginary, as if preparing for the return of the real, can be described in terms of the triangularity of the Oedipal myth. Derrida's squaring of the scene of writing forces the narrator to acknowledge his complicity in the drama, rather than allowing him to occupy the center as a transparent observer. With the Imaginary and Symbolic cast into a wider context; the already decentered quadralinear subject is radically displaced.

The fact that "there is a narrator onstage" indicates for Derrida the presence of an invisible framing "from within which" Lacan lifts out the triangles that organize the consequently Oedipal real drama along the imaginary axis of the Schema L. This raises the possibility of an excess: "in missing the position of the narrator [in the real drama], his engagement in the content of what he seems to recount, one omits everything in the scene of writing that overflows the two triangles." This overflow (enframing the reductive frame that would contain its indeterminacy) is the key to the "heterogeneous and conflictual weave of différance" I call Derridian extravagance, the weave that always complicates subject-object relations (whether between Dupin and the narrator or between capital and labor-power).

According to Derrida, because the imperialistic Lacan cannot fathom the impossibility of establishing borders at the scene of writing, he cannot accept that discursive fields can only aspire to provisional limits within which subjects of the statement assume their positions. In other words, although subject-object positioning takes place within discursive fields, this play is located within the text-in-general, the weave of différance. Derrida (1987:483) approaches the text as "a scene of writing with ruined (abîmé) limits." By contrast, Lacan reduces the text to concrete discourse, and writing to written pages that fly away. By reducing Poe's tale to a "unity" that supports key doctrines, such as the indivisibility of the letter, Lacan cannot catch its "interminable drift."

The effect of this violent framing (producing the flip side that Deleuze and Guattari swim toward, imagining themselves escaping the logic of the sign) is to enframe the frame in an interminable drift of différance. All action, including class action, is part and parcel of "the scene of writing with ruined limits," a general text containing multiple concrete and possible discursive fields, within which subjectivity moves from silence to language and back again. The limits that Deleuze and Guattari's great beyond would go beyond are impossible to determine.

Derrida's ruined limits are not, then, just another way of talking about the Lacanian real, or Deleuze and Guattari's desire. We have seen how the Schema L organizes conscious and unconscious aspects to establish truth colonies in the real, where one might locate the danger of need. Lacan views desire negatively as "the impossible," or that which lies between the real and the colonized truth; and Deleuze and Guattari view desire as the real on the reverse side of the Schema L. But Derrida challenges the hierarchy of the Schema L, a move which deflates the unconscious as much as the poor ego, within a scene of writing where subjects and objects are forced to acknowledge the ruination of limits. This ruination explains why the narrator cannot pretend neutrality.

Derrida's work carries implications for other (re)presentations as well. As tempting as it is to read Marx, for example, as an advocate of the authentic voice of Labor, or how things really work beneath the ideological superstructure, on the way to the end (telos) of human emancipation, we are encouraged by this account to approach his project as a coherent presentation within a text with ruined limits. Within this representation (*Darstellung*) called Marxism, (objectified) labor-power and (subjectified) capital perform their negotiations (for example, the buying and selling of labor-power); but these doubling subject-object relations described by Marx must not be extracted from the wider text, especially the ruins I will soon call "abject," for lack of a better name. Spivak encourages us to distinguish constitutive representation—which problematizes how subject positions are constructed in discourse—from political representation—which can occur only among already predicated subjects of the statement. Her work helps bring the abject ruination permitted by Derrida's radical decentering of the subject closer to home.

But before moving to Spivak in Chapter 3 as we continue pursuing desire and representation, or on to Althusser in Chapter 5, where I pick up the thread of this discussion of theory, I must clarify what I find useful in the various ways of theorizing desire we have just examined. We have seen that Deleuze and Guattari would move outside Lacan's reductive Schema L to sabotage its operations through schizoanalysis. Their mobilization of the real of desire as an anticapitalist, antipsychoanalysis strategy can spark a revolutionary impulse because of the intimate (decoding) relation they expose between capitalism and schizophrenia. But the process of opposing the capitalist axiomatic with the chaos of desire threatens to eclipse Labor (once again) by establishing a totalizing desire in its place, as an out-class. By demeaning representation, Deleuze and Guattari grant the capitalist axiomatic a status that cannot be challenged through writing. The risk of mobilizing on the flip side of the Schema L is rendering its axes sufficiently orderly to be turned inside out. By contrast Derrida monkey-wrenches the axes, problematizing the notion of having a flip side. My task is to combine what is useful in each of the three approaches to indeterminacy just reviewed in a "model" of desire that resists the totalizing urge of structuralism without denying the brilliance of its organizing capacity.

Remodeling Desire

Each of these approaches to indeterminacy concerns Lispector's interval between subject and object, where one faces the paradox of writing what cannot be written. Lacan offers haunting insights on human beings at the mercy of language, forever unable with our fragile egos to exorcise the indeterminacy of the real. Deleuze and Guattari lend radical complexity to the critical question of resisting capital's discursive hegemony. And Derrida locates this discourse in a scene of writing in which one cannot transparently design theoretical constructs that promise either to complete or multiply the puzzle of desire's inarticulate status.[20] These elements work together in ways that anticipate my (re)presentation of Marx in Part 2.

In deciding what to salvage from Lacan's writing project of liberating the signifier from the signified (only to succumb to the logic of the sign), one does well to recall that he is really not interested in what he calls the "signifiable." A psychoanalyst on a mission, Lacan explores the relation of meaning and being and unlocks a vast territory of possibility outside the "scope of what language repeats" and "symptoms" reveal or disclose. The mirror-stage illustrates the subject on that Z-like path from a body in need of objects to an ego in demand of gratification, to an enunciatory position, from which "one" desires whatever is impossible to obtain. But his is not merely a diachronic venture. Even after "one" has passed through the defiles of language, Lacan's synchronic model allows for a real body in need that is "always there." The real is not, then, only the site of the subject of enunciation at odds with the subject of the statement; this effort to colonize the real is radically incomplete. The zone of the signifiable real includes all that resists signification.

I can postpone indefinitely joining in the hotly contested identity politics debates concerning the relation of the Imaginary and the Symbolic, including the impossibility of desire. Loyalist Marxists are right to complain that talk about discourse, language, and signification slips too easily into confusing the signified with the signifiable. To avoid this I meet Lacan at his mirror stage, where I loiter just long enough to borrow the "split" subject at the dawn of desire, the one that looks ahead to the channels of language with their signifiers and signifieds, and (only then) behind to the anxiety of the body in fragments. This subject is split between the demands of determinate form and the needs of the indeterminate signifiable. In other words, I am prepared to salvage desire's indeterminacy from Lacan and leave the "lack," the impossibility of desire, to his more capacious readers, such as those I have followed in my interpretation. I stand, then, at the limits of enunciation, where the operative distinction lies between the signifiable (needs) and the logic of the signs so necessary to the pursuits of those struggling for positions in discourse.

I had hoped and at one time had expected to meet Deleuze and Guattari here. After all, they make an explicit effort to locate the "out-class"—schizoid, flow-breaking desire—in the site of the real, which they also locate outside the scope of language. But we have seen that Deleuze and Guattari cannot resist throwing away the Saussurean sign, allowing it to pass through their hands (like litter). Instead of supplementing Benveniste's illuminating distinction between the speaking subject and the subject spoken by amplifying the inescapable question of the unpredicated signifiable subject, Deleuze and Guattari prefer to detach this distinction from representation and move beyond the sign's coding operations (except for the state) to asignifying signs. We have watched them use this detached distinction, liberating it from the shackles of "personology," to describe the axiomatic status capital has achieved in bourgeois society. By regarding capital as "a point of subjectification that constitutes all human beings as subjects" (1987:457), Deleuze and Guattari gloss over the significant problem of predicating subjects to concentrate on the proportions of capital's hegemony. The proletariat and capitalists participate in these axioms as (secondary) subjects of the statement and (primary) subjects of enunciation, respectively. Desire enters the picture as an autonomous outlying real that erupts at the scene of predictable interest-group negotiations—capital always winning—between these mismatched subjects. As useful as their work may be for culture jammers and others interested in contesting capital's presumption of immanence, Deleuze and Guattari cannot help us detect Labor's whereabouts because their equation of the real with desire eliminates the possibility of recuperating Labor in the real. As they shuffle in the new subject (desire), Labor gets shuffled out (again).

And so I am attempting an operation that salvages only the indeterminate "split" in the split subject from Lacan's desire-as-lack, which is otherwise too impossible to be useful for detecting Labor's whereabouts; and extracting only the treatment of capital as a determinate form from Deleuze and Guattari's desire-as-positive-rush, which is otherwise is too possible to be useful for my limited purposes. The former approach to desire has as much to offer the complications of identity politics as the latter does the politics of state resistance. By salvaging the Lacanian split and Deleuze and Guattari's axioms I am trying to stand at the gap of determinate form (the scope of language) and indeterminacy, the danger of need, where I remain focused on detecting Labor's whereabouts.

Rather than wage with Deleuze and Guattari a struggle against capitalism from a position (intimately related to but also somewhat) outside it—from the position, that is, of an exiled desire—I wish to continue the struggle from within the theater of representation. This irredentist struggle requires a mechanism for drawing the inarticulate ooze of human need that is "always there" closer to the structural integrity of a bourgeois "reality" that has been sanitized for our protection. I need to find a way of situating bourgeois axioms within a class-activated scene in which these so-called "axioms" can be undermined without pretending to go outside the domain they would define, thereby allowing that domain to consolidate its forces by falling prey to the logic of the sign.

As it turns out, the Lacanian split and the capitalist axiomatic of Deleuze and Guattari can be sutured, if not painlessly, in the ruination (*mise en abîme*) of Derridian extravagance. One need not take a final position in the fraternal tug-of-war Lacan and Derrida wage over Poe to appreciate how Derrida's distinctions between writing and what gets inscribed, or text and discourse, provide a scene within which I can locate the materials salvaged from the theorists of desire. By concentrating on desire's indeterminacy I allow myself to pay attention to all that desire—whether negativity or positivity—leaves to be desired. Instead of inverting the relationship of signifier and signified (Lacan) or replacing this unity with "asignifying signs" (Deleuze and Guattari), Derrida supplements the sign with endless possibilities of the signifiable. Appreciating the vastness of this region requires letting go of the notion that saying "*la langue* equals language minus *la parole*" is the end of the story. At my stance at the crossroads of the split between silent need and discursive demand, it is only the beginning. The scene of writing encompasses the diachronic development of speech as well as the synchronic structures of language, but its ruined limits insist upon asking "why do you persist in this chronic historicizing, as if the imposition of time can ever bring an end to the negotiations of arbitrary difference?" Such questions supplement the Saussurean sign by sending its reassuring unity out into a sea of indeterminacy. Desire as différance maintains both the lack of closure in the indeterminacy of Lacan's desire and the smooth operations of Deleuze and Guattari's axiomatic.

This means that Deleuze and Guattari's axiomatization continues to operate as writing, even as capital travels well beyond state and municipal codes. And the Lacanian real, unless tidied up by those, such as Žižek (1991:95), who decides for Lacan that the "*objet petit a*" should name the indeterminacy Derrida sloppily leaves undecidable, is quite consistent with the ruined limits. For although concrete discourse continually welcomes in and shuffles out subject positions—sparking a plethora of new and interesting political possibilities—there remains "nothing outside [the ruined limits] of the text," not even a revolutionary class of autonomous anticapitalists.

Approaching the indeterminacy of desire as différance allows us to draw strength from subject-object binaries—such as labor-power and capital—without succumbing to their governance; this is the key to survival in any irredentist struggle. When faced with an enemy so grand as to appear invincible, the key is always to sustain one's life—including looking out for one another—while seeking any possible opportunity to weaken the hegemonic forces from within. One must avoid at all costs granting the enemy legitimacy. A strategic break with structure can be discounted by the state as terrorism or lunacy or both and serve even to reinforce capital's power. A strategic immersion in structure can allow the state to diagnose human need as a social problem, giving capital time to add new axioms (I want a policy for crack babies). But the strategic double agency of perpetuating the very binaries one seeks to displace promises to avoid both extinction and co-optation, though it may have to brush either of these extremities from time to time.

The strength of Lacan's analysis lies in the way his writing opens up the subject to the real and the discursive without closing off our options for altering reality. This work carries fascinating implications for identity politics; becoming a subject of enunciation may well force one to accept received categories that are limiting and offensive. The weaknesses concern any effort by psychoanalysis to get at the truth behind all this signifying, the original behind the copies. After Derrida, Poe's story reminds us that anyone watching subjects and their objects trading places is already included in the activity, and one might extend this complicity to include those who set out to write about it. The strength of Deleuze and Guattari's analysis lies in the way their writing indicates the stranglehold capitalism has on dominant versions of reality. The weaknesses concern any efforts to get outside the domain of the frame. Their divorce of desire and representation gives Deleuze and Guattari fewer options than one needs for detecting Labor's whereabouts; in fact, they ultimately lose interest. The strength of Derrida's analysis lies in the way he can make room for indeterminacy without ruling out the difference between subject and object positions in discourse. Indeed, his work can supply formidable criticism of both Lacan's reliance on truth and Deleuze and Guattari's reliance on such writing practices as allegory. But the weaknesses, for my project, concern knowing how to connect Labor with this remainder. How does saying that Labor stands within writing but outside what is written (and spoken) help anyone facilitate its recovery?

CHAPTER THREE

Appreciating the Labor Underground

When capitalism is made to stand for history—so that the heterogeneity of histories of the colonized subaltern with those of the metropolitan proletariat is effaced—absolute otherness is appropriated into self-consolidating difference.
—Gyan Prakash, "Can the 'Subaltern' Ride?"

The work with theory just completed in Chapter 2 stands midway in an argument on desire and representation that began in Chapter 1, where I posed the problem of detecting Labor's whereabouts. I first distinguished a loyalist reliance on unitary subjects from a post-Marxist tendency to position subjects and objects in discursive fields concerned with identity politics, and I then differentiated both from a third set of approaches that acknowledges how an indeterminacy (sometimes called "desire") always complicates discursive fields. Chapter 2 provided a framework for this detective work by theorizing desire in terms of indeterminacy. There I worked through three influential approaches: Lacanian lack, Deleuze and Guattari's schizophrenia, and Derrida's différance. Salvaging useful qualities from each approach, I arrived at a scene of writing that can accommodate subjects of enunciation, subjects of the statement, and unpredicated subjects denied access to the means of representation. This framework supplements the unitary subject of enunciation presupposed by the loyalist approach—for example, persons or classes of persons who demand things—and is quite consistent with the multiple, overlapping subject positions required by most post-Marxist approaches, *on the condition* that such positioning does not rule out unpredicated subjectivity. In other words, the *mise en abîme* borrowed from Derrida rules out exclusive reliance on neat and tidy discursive fields—including the three-storied Schema L and the family "tree" of twins and triplets hidden in the allegory of the rhizome.

The present chapter, although coming at the end of my consideration of desire and representation, marks the beginning of a consideration of the value dimension, which explores how to value people by not reducing subjectivity to the materiality of persons. Chapters 1 and 2 are essential to respecting this paradox: of course, people are material persons, but this does not exhaust the subject. I wish to reevaluate the issue of representing material needs. My approach to desire's indeterminacy does not, then, follow Deleuze and Guattari in ruling out representation altogether; instead I fix my sights within representational fields (the scene of writing includes, after all, both determinate form and indeterminacy) even as I acknowledge the axioms that Deleuze and Guattari detect. This requires exploring more completely how to conduct subject-object analysis while also entertaining what Spivak (1988:306) calls "the violent aporia between subject and object status." I must show here not only how it is possible to embrace this supplementation on her part but also why it is necessary for Marxists to do so. Spivak's aporia inspires the supplemental category of the abject developed in Part 2, which allows me to pick up the thread of valorization again in Chapter 6, where Marx solves the problem of capital's subjectivity. Finally, after coming to terms with the problem of praxis, I face in Chapter 9 the difficulties of revalorizing the abject through a community education that decenters the self-image Western intellectuals learn to rely upon.

Supplementing loyalist approaches that rely on a straightforward unitary subject can easily be misconstrued as arguing that people should not demand things. Of course (classes of) people should demand things. But my work in earlier chapters of Part 1 enables me to say here that as an anticapitalist strategy this approach is "a little too self-evident" in the sense that such clear solutions must first be violently extracted from the scene of writing. How these demands are articulated and by whom requires negotiating representations, especially the representation of the subject. Reducing desire to demand and the subject to a person or class can result in the clearly articulated materialism of demanding persons (constituted as a class-for-itself) often associated with Marxism. Teresa Ebert's (1996) "red feminism," considered in Chapter 8, offers a formidable example of the strengths and limitations of a person demanding something on behalf of a class. But because most practitioners either evade or deny every political possibility that does not fit the model—whether teleological totality or liberal multiplicity—Labor's whereabouts are likely to remain a mystery. In its place one encounters an increasingly objectified labor-power always on the verge—indeed sometimes striving—to be consumed by increasingly socialized capital.

Deleuze and Guattari argue that capital acts as a point of subjectification which turns every person into a subject. Their work with capital's axioms reveals the limitations of viewing the working class as either a unitary subject or a subject of enunciation positioned alongside others in a new social movement. And yet the unitary subject of loyalist Marxism, and even the subject position named "working class" by Laclau and Mouffe, highlight exploitation in ways that Deleuze and Guattari neglect. My work with indeterminacy must not obscure the extent to which capital grows at the expense of working people—sometimes children—in "free" enterprise zones throughout the world. I must then consider both obvious and hidden ways of affirming the unitary subject scheduled for displacement. The obvious ways highlight exploitation but lose sight of Deleuze and Guattari's axiomatization. The hidden ways highlight axiomatization but lose track of exploitation. Sharpening the focus on exploitation while blurring the focus on reassuring unitary subjects or presupposed subject positions, I argue here against accepting Deleuze and Guattari's "point" with such "speed" that it turns into a (party) "line."

A Critique of Obvious Approaches to the Unity of the Subject

We must remember what is "always there" at the scene of writing. In the late eighties, Maria Mies informs us, an all-male bowling league in a small German town thumbed through a mail-order catalogue of available women and "ordered one Asian woman, who was [upon delivery] formally married to one of the men, but had to serve all of them sexually" (1986:140). Mies locates these subject-object relations in the context of "The International of Pimps" and includes "international and national capital" as the most dominant pimp of all. Mies moves down the hierarchy to remind us that "not only do the BIG WHITE MEN or MR CAPITAL profit from the exploitation of their own women and of Third World women, so also do the small white men, the workers (142).[1] This story involves the importation of non-Western women denied subject positions, valued only for purposes of market exchange; but such examples may display a phenomenon far less determinate that the objectification of "the other." We must keep this possibility in mind when developing suitable responses.

Most obvious responses work to reinstate the unitary subject. A liberal human rights approach might, for example, address the legal status of mail-order Asian "brides" in Germany, an address that presupposes their subject position. A familiar Marxist-feminist approach, such as Mies's, might address the exploitation of these women as sex workers whose dormant subjectivity is blocked by a combination of both patriarchal sex-right and capitalist profiteering. And we have seen that Deleuze and Guattari might find some similarity in these two approaches.

Capital acts, we recall, for Deleuze and Guattari as a "point of subjectification" which creates capitalists to "stand in" as enunciating subjects and workers (including sex workers) to follow the script as subjects of the statement, as second-order citizens caught up in the flux-reflux dynamic of income and wages. So when the bowlers buy domestic services from Asia, they participate in the free market axioms of bourgeois society, to which activists struggle to add human rights axioms on behalf of the commodified women. Combating exploitation is an ideological, not a structural, struggle for Deleuze and Guattari; state power and human desire might collide, however, if the subjects of oppression (here Asian women), as part of an out-class, were to articulate their desires. I return to this possibility below as a hidden way of restoring the unitary subject.

The problem posed by this example involves how to respond to an injustice without reinscribing the structures that make it thinkable. Spivak's appreciation of indeterminacy helps here. She works through an example of a Western corporation regarding some women employees as speaking subjects while cutting out the subjectivity of others. To set the stage she studies how sexed subjectivity relies on the violent extraction of devalued elements so as to produce orderly worlds of subjects and objects. Ultimately her efforts not to presume a unitary subject raise the possibility of locating "foreign" elements well within the (ruined) "limits" of exploitative Western society.[2] Such location may help resolve the problem posed in Chapter 2: how can we connect with an indeterminate subject relegated to the silent ruins at the scene of writing?

Spivak (1987:77–92) begins her approach to sexed subjectivity with the observation that Freud's concept of "penis envy" is of course part of his masculinist inheritance, but she is also concerned with the related presumption of a nuclear parent-child model of the family. Because his thinking is governed by a penis-womb distinction, Freud tends to view social organization in terms of coupling and reproduction. For Freud, men are sexed subjects with positions in both the world and the family; women's subjectivity is not only housebound but centered on reproduction. So both are subjects, but women never become sexed subjects in Freud's uterine norm of womanhood. What does Freud leave out, she asks, when he studies the predication of the sexed subject?

Spivak points out that because penile-vaginal sex is enough to satisfy (Freud), whether women are positioned as objects—men's sex providers— or subjects—mothers—the clitoris is judged superfluous to social organization. Moreover, this uterine norm of womanhood supports the phallic norm of capitalism. That is, the denial of sexed subjectivity makes women perfectly suited for supplying cheap labor-power in the workplace. When capital's men connive to "make it" in the marketplace, they rely upon already objectified women for labor-power. Although Spivak (1987:82) encourages a far-reaching "discourse of the clitoris," she uses this figure as a "short-hand for women's excess in all areas of production and practice, an excess which must be brought under control to keep business going as usual."

Spivak brings in Marxism at this point because of its unimpressive history of working together with feminism. When loyalist Marxists make the connection between women's work in the home and the practice of supplying capital with labor-power, the home-workplace relation can become a "controlled metaphor" for relations between civil society and the state. Women work a double shift, but only one for pay. Spivak tends to view home economics instead as a key element of bourgeois society which is nevertheless devalued; "the power of the . . . domestic economy . . . can be used as the model of the foreign body nurtured unwittingly by the polis"(1987:84). One common resource of an irredentist struggle is access to at least some of the territory under enemy control. But this proximity is all too often accompanied by a lack of access to the means of representation, such as one's own language.

To explore the theme of bringing the subjectivity of women under the control of an enemy regime, Spivak tells the following story.

> In Seoul, South Korea, in March 1982, 237 women workers in a factory owned by Control Data, a Minnesota-based multinational corporation, struck over a demand for a wage raise. Six union leaders were dismissed and imprisoned. In July, the women held hostage two visiting U.S. vice-presidents, demanding reinstatement of the union leaders. Control Data's main office was willing to release the women; the Korean government was reluctant. On July 16, the Korean male workers at the factory beat up the female workers and ended the dispute. Many of the women were injured and two suffered miscarriages. (1987:90)

Remarking that "socialized capital kills by remote control," Spivak condemns the ease with which its deadly errands are performed by distant accomplices. We can applaud a socially responsible corporation in the West, while its pro-union female employees are brutalized by their male colleagues in Korea. This troubling asymmetry undermines the possibility of placing the Minnesota-based workers in the same category as the seemingly objectified South Korean woman workers. Pregnant workers subjected to physical abuse because of their unionizing efforts does not rest easily alongside publicized Western notions of sensitivity to women. Spivak notes that *Ms.* magazine recently praised Control Data corporation: "Control Data is among those enlightened corporations that offer social-service leaves. . . . Kit Ketchum, former treasurer of Minnesota NOW, applied for and got a full year with pay to work at NOW's national office in Washington, D.C. She writes: 'I commend Control Data for their commitment to employing and promoting women'" (1987:91). Clearly, the relations between capitalists who own/control Control Data's profits and Kit Ketchum, who works for the corporation, embody discursive positions governed by the capital/labor-power opposition. But this field cannot contain the bloody labor-power/management dispute Spivak reports in South Korea.

Spivak encourages watching closely how figurative language operates in discussions such as these. Using "home and hearth" as a metaphor for women's place in the international division of labor places woman outside of the world of markets and production; as a result, the progressive agenda becomes one of bringing the women at the margin into the center. It seems only to make sense to make subjects out of these "urgent objects," these oppressed subjects. Kim Ketchum's paid leave could be cited as a successful strategy. Derrida makes a move rather like this, according to Spivak, when he criticizes the centrality of man, connecting men with property (proper names, patronymics), and sets up woman as the outside sign of impropriety, as if to work toward reversing and eventually displacing the woman-man opposition. We have seen something similar operating in his notion of ruined limits, which, however suggestive, makes it difficult to assess Labor's proximity.

Spivak charges that this kind of move can cooperate with a bourgeois liberalism that acts progressive, inviting some women in and producing newly liberated subjects while continuing to batter other women on the verge of subjectivity. Her sense of the clitoris as a metonym of the (foreign) body at home, which exceeds the very pretense of male control, displaces the home and hearth metaphor, which serves to contain the issue of excess. This replacement suggests the possibility of a devalued aporia between subject and object relations, of a position as integral to the foreign body as it is impossible for the intrusive hegemonic powers-that-be to appreciate.

Spivak distinguishes her work from Derrida's gestures toward writing under the sign of woman precisely because his move underplays the extent to which indeterminacy flows out of determinate forms. This is her remarkable suggestion: "Suffice it to say here that, by thus differentiating himself from the phallocentric tradition under the aegis of a(n idealized) woman who is the 'sign' of the indeterminate, of that which has im-propriety as its property, Derrida cannot think that *the sign 'woman' is indeterminate by virtue of its access to the tyranny of the text of the proper*" (1987:91, emphasis added).[3] One must take care here not to confuse an actual person from the sign in this passage. Spivak suggests that access to the text as "woman" carries the heavy price of an ambiguous significance. Certain positions, such as sexed subjectivity, are entirely foreclosed. In other words, the tyranny of the text resembles the suppression of the clitoris; "woman" becomes significant at the cost of rendering her "excess" insignificant. Spivak allows us to emend the salvaged framework by drawing what is "always there" into the closest proximity. Lack of access to the means of representation need no longer be equated with lack of access to the text.

Spivak illustrates the extent to which representation can effectively cut out aspects of the richest subjectivity, completely devaluing aspects of life as viewed from dominant perspectives. As such it opens a way of dealing with representation and desire that resists their divorce. We have seen how Deleuze and Guattari could use the discussion of excess as an example of desire outside the coding operations of the state. But Spivak's work makes it possible to acknowledge indeterminacy without leaving the site of representation. Indeed, we are about to see her argue that losing interest in representation—leaving the scene of writing—forces one back into reliance on a unitary subject. While Deleuze and Guattari are watching loyalist Marxists watching their bourgeois counterparts hiding exploitation, Spivak is watching Deleuze and Guattari.

A Critique of Hidden Ways of Restoring the Unitary Subject

Spivak's provocative essay "Can the Subaltern Speak?" explores how subjects find representation in Western discourse. I am most intrigued by her suggestion "that a . . . radical decentering of the subject is . . . implicit in both Marx and Derrida" (Spivak, 1988:271). On the way to making this point she raises the possibility of progressive intellectuals repeating the restoration of the very unitary subjects we seek to decenter. Valuing the subject requires self-determination, of course, but this requirement is always more complicated than remaining neutral while an imagined "other" speaks.

Spivak shares my respectful wariness of Deleuze's treatment of the "working class" precisely on the issue of representation. When Deleuze claims, in the famous interview with Foucault, that "only those directly concerned can speak in a practical way on their own behalf" (Foucault, 1977:209), he rightly chastises anyone who would speak for subaltern subjects by representing "them," but his claim never comes to terms with Western complicity in representational schemes that devalue these subjects. Neither advocating speaking for the "other" nor avoiding issues of complicity, Spivak offers a radical approach to the subject, which complicates issues of representation that Deleuze and Guattari dismiss too easily.

Spivak's essay first meets Deleuze, in his conversation with Foucault, on the common ground of problematizing the subject. But here she argues that these theorists' interest in the power and desire of the (unnamed) subject undermines their appreciation of transnational exploitation and that, as a result, they are unable to appreciate the complicity of Western intellectuals in the "epistemic violence" of capital's hegemony. She then illustrates this complicitous tendency by examining Western efforts to constitute the colonial subject as Other, particularly in the British codification of Hindu law. This "narrative of codification" allows Spivak to credit Foucault with discovering material layers of life—in prisons, hospitals, and elsewhere—that although "always there" are sometimes invisible, while insisting that we maintain a distinction between making something visible (granting access to the text) and making it speak (allowing access to the means of representation). We are, for example, exploring the possibility that seeing a working class does not render Labor vocal. At this point Spivak relies on Derrida's *Grammatology*, where Derrida develops the radically decentered subject familiar to us by now, one which insists that indeterminate material (ruination) travels along with (the necessary limits of) any determinate form. This section would supplement self-other relations with a "place of in-betweenness" that is always there but cannot speak. Spivak shares Derrida's respect for the unnamable and seeks to develop her earlier insight (on clitoridectomy) that interstitial subjects are sometimes rendered indeterminate by virtue of their access to the tyranny of the text of the proper[ty]. Perhaps indeterminate subjects such as Labor are centrally located, living under an assumed name. Finally, after noting the "epistemic violence" of Western academia, providing an illustrative "narrative of codification," and taking time out for a Derridian defense of "ruined limits," Spivak offers an Indian case study of widow sacrifice to explore the construction of a "good" widow's desire as it came to collide with British colonial law in a script she describes as involving "white men saving brown women from brown men." This section lends sustained coherence to her exquisite essay; but those who reduce the essay to this section may mistakenly conclude that Spivak finds Third World women mute and renders their self-immolation undecidable. My interest in avoiding unwitting participation in what she calls a "masculine radicalism," which fights the good fight for social justice while maintaining a neutral transparent position, draws me away from these misconceptions and closer to the first and third sections of her essay, which clarify her overall position. And because my salvaged framework already carries trace elements of Derridian supplementation, the first part of her argument is most important here. Within that section I must show how Spivak builds her claim that radical theorists sometimes unwittingly restore the unitary subject they seek to avoid.

Spivak's problem with Deleuze begins with his exhortation that "theory . . . has nothing to do with the signifier" (Foucault, 1977:208). We have seen how Deleuze and Guattari would relegate any recoding required by capitalism to the state apparatus (at the opposite pole of desire's "outclass"). Spivak highlights the troubling implications of this casual disregard for the relation of representation and desire. An unambiguous Deleuze claims that "there is no more representation; there's nothing but action — action of theory and action of practice, which relate to each other as relays and form networks" (206-7). Spivak acknowledges that such a declaration makes the "important point" that the pure theory–applied action distinction is too "quick and easy" to be useful.[4] But she cannot abide Deleuze's articulation of this point. Spivak (1988:275) borrows his words to concoct the following sentence: "*Because* 'the person who speaks and acts . . . is always a multiplicity,' no 'theorizing intellectual . . . [or] party or . . . union' can represent 'those who act and struggle.'" Spivak draws the line here and issues the following response: "Two senses of representation are being run together: representation as 'speaking for,' as in politics, and representation as re-presentation as in art and philosophy . . . within state formation and law, on one hand, and in subject-predication, on the other" (275).

I must explore this distinction, in part, because of the way she connects the predication of subjects and economics (as opposed to political representation's relation to law and the state), because economics operates as the domain in which capital gains subjectivity and Labor fragments and disappears. For Deleuze and Guattari, as we have seen, Labor loses out to desire.

Spivak's critique of Deleuze — like Derrida's critique of Lacan reading Poe — focuses on the transparency of a narrator reporting at the scene of writing. Instead of positioning Labor outside representation, to the point of making it an "outclass" no longer distinguishable from any other indeterminate desire, she allows for vestiges of subjectivity cut out of discourse by virtue of their access to dominant representation. This acknowledges a revolutionary situation in which the dominant discourse is forced to rely upon silent inarticulate aspects of itself, which are eliminated if too visible and devalued if barely visible. Spivak charges that allegedly neutral Western intellectuals are complicit in these profitable hierarchies. Even those of us who criticize the stable subjectivity of a person, or a class-for-itself, may come to rely upon an unnamed subject of desire (we would never allow ourselves to call "humanity")—or subjects of oppression—those "Third World women." In addition to denying so-called "subjects of oppression" self-determination, this reliance sneaks a unitary subject back in under the cover of desire. But how can Spivak accuse theorists like Deleuze and Foucault—who would multiply subject positions in an increasingly heterogeneous discourse—of restoring unitary subjectivity?

Spivak uses the Deleuze-Foucault interview as a vehicle for introducing her twofold understanding of representation, a distinction she also wants us to appreciate in Marx. This is why her strategy for confronting problems of complicity begins with a plea to take representation more seriously, not less. By conflating the twin senses of representation, she argues, these authors neglect crucial questions of subject formation. That is, they allegedly take these constitutional conventions for granted. To elaborate her distinction, Spivak shows how Marx distinguishes the political sense of representation (*Vertretung*) from the philosophical-economic sense (*Darstellung*).

The structure of her elliptical reading of Marx's *Eighteenth Brumaire* introduces both senses of representation. Even though Marx does not use the word *Darstellung* there, Spivak contrasts his (re)presentation of a class-in-itself, an analytical category he "works up" from the chaotic material conditions of people's lives, on one hand, and the way in which a political hero, such as Napoleon, stands in for the people in his territory, on the other. Then, for evidence of Marx's use of *Darstellung*, she cites a passage from *Capital I* in which value finds representation in exchange-value. This is to say that Spivak notes a similarity between the way Marx writes about class at both the abstract and phenomenal levels and the way in which abstract value under capitalism finds itself in the phenomenon of the marketplace.[5] Accordingly, Marx's approach requires a radically decentered subject that does not rest easily with unitary subjectivity, whether person, collectivity, or unnamed force (of power or desire).

Spivak is most concerned in this part of her essay with the familiar understanding of Marx's class-in-itself/class-for-itself distinction, one which positions labor-power as capital's object (in-itself) and then seeks to enhance its subjectivity (for-itself). To avoid the utopian consequences of this approach, she attempts also to explore the aporia between subject and object. Instead of reading the French peasantry in Marx's *Eighteenth Brumaire* as a mere class-in-itself, she reminds us of its disorganization, difference, and chaos—a disorder that requires one to use abstraction when presenting such disparate lives as an economic collectivity with any kind of mutual interest. Here she finds Marx saying that "in so far as millions of families live under economic conditions of existence that separate their mode of life . . . they form a class" (Spivak, 1988:277). But this has little to do with the instincts of a people and even less with "their" nascent consciousness. Class formation is best viewed as Marxian portraiture, framed at a high level of abstraction. This portrait captures one aspect of the workers' divided subjectivity, for despite their "identity of interests," they are as different as actual people and their families always are.

In fact the aporia alongside the subject-object binaries of class analysis helps to explain the emergence of a Napoleon, who represents a people who cannot—because of their various differences—represent themselves. In other words, Napoleon assumes the position of proxy for a divided-until-he-came-along people. Here Spivak tells us that Marx uses the word *Vertretung*, with its added emphasis on substitution, to name this kind of representation. He describes Napoleon's relation to the peasants "as their master, as an authority over them, as unrestricted governmental power that protects them from the other classes and sends them rain and sunshine from above" (Spivak, 1988:277). At this point we might note, with Deleuze and Guattari, that the Napoleonic code is precisely the kind of writing or representation that capital's axioms manage to deterritorialize. But Spivak makes a crucial point here that disallows any pending divorce between coding and axiomatizing, which locates both—contra Deleuze and Guattari—at the scene of writing. She shows that Napoleon's representation (*Vertretung*) of the French peasantry "behaves like a *Darstellung*" that constitutes heretofore disparate families as "the people" (for the first time).

Marx begins his observation at the phenomenal level with an aggregation of indeterminate people who cannot represent themselves. Napoleon enters the scene and begins to "speak for" these people. But the process of someone speaking for "them" constitutes their subjectivity. According to Spivak, Marxists must expose the complicity of political and constitutive representation which occurs whenever, in speaking for a people (representing them politically), one creates "the people" (representing them constitutively): "The event of representation as *Vertretung* . . . behaves like a *Darstellung* . . . taking its place in the gap between the formation of a (descriptive) class and the nonformation of a (transformative) class. . . . The complicity of *Vertreten* and *Darstellen* . . . can only be appreciated if they are not conflated by a sleight of word" (1988:277).

The economic implications of such constitutional conventions are perhaps understood best by Marxists (in part because of Marx's work with abstraction). The formation of a descriptive class can be staged only at the highest level of abstraction, sufficiently removed from contingency to permit a working up of otherwise disparate material. The nonformation of a transformative class operates at the level of the disparate material, where heterogeneity resists any mapping operation. To argue that a proxy can behave like a portrait in the gap between the abstract and phenomenal levels helps to explain how working in the name of the people can sometimes prematurely assume determinate form to the detriment of the very people one wants to call "the people."

Spivak first notes that Marx uses abstraction to present (*Darstellen*) class formation in a people who have not yet constituted themselves as a class. And then she watches Marx describe Napoleon's political representation, as it behaves like a *Darstellung*. This raises the possibility not only of a portrait (Marx's) and a proxy (Napoleon's) but also of a stolen portrait that has been painted over to disguise its value—a stolen subjectivity imposed on a people who are consequently denied self-determination. The possibility of a stolen portrait carries implications which resonate throughout any project that, like mine, seeks to expose capital's masquerade as a subject occupying Labor's position. Just as the actual people farming the soil—"always there"—in nineteenth-century France are constituted as peasants in the Napoleonic Code, so the actual people struggling for subsistence—"always there"—in the late-twentieth-century West are constituted as a working class in the capitalist axiom. Hence the devastating bite of Deleuze and Guattari's critique; both farmers and residents are rendered indeterminate (in terms of self-determination) by virtue of their access (as citizenry or labor force) to the tyranny of the text of the proper (whether Napoleonic Code or capitalist axiom). By making peasants visible citizens, Napoleon renders them nonvocal; by making working people visible as labor-power, capital renders Labor silent. To speak one must be what capital—with its monopoly on subject-predication—says one must be. Political representation can so easily behave like a *Darstellung* that everyone involved—even an observer—slips easily into complicity, especially if we fail to keep the distinction alive (a distinction best viewed as identity in difference because the political sense always spills into the economic). To draw Marx more completely into the field governed by this distinction, Spivak needs next to show the other sense in which he uses the term representation. Here she shifts from *The Eighteenth Brumaire* to *Capital I*.

We have already seen that the class-in-itself Marx presents at the highest level of abstraction is defined economically, whereas the unformed transformative class operates politically at the phenomenal level. This raises the possibility of actual people "always there" who can be presented economically (as exploited) without this description affecting their political activity. Viewing the description of class as a dated reductionism risks losing track of the complicity of Western intellectuals in transnational capital's hegemony. Here Spivak joins forces with loyalist Marxism. Class description, of course, often travels along with the racism and sexism of its early articulation, but these problems are more easily addressed than the naive, self-evident realism of saying that people want things and that is the end of the matter. Desire is indeterminate and people require a self-determination that neither presumes subject-predication nor imposes one from a fixed center. In other words, Spivak parts company with loyalist Marxism by reading a Marx who radically decenters the subject.

Spivak turns to *Capital I* for the "most obvious place" that Marx uses *Darstellung* to describe the presentation or description he mentions in the *Eighteenth Brumaire*. "In the exchange relationship [Austauschverhältnis] of commodities their exchange-value appeared to us totally independent of their use-value. But if we subtract their use-value from the product of labour, we obtain their value, as it was just determined [bestimmt]. The common element which represents itself [sich darstellt] in the exchange relation, or the exchange value of the commodity, is thus its value" (quoted in Spivak, 1988:278). Spivak reads these lines in two related ways: first, "value . . . is computed as . . . the sign of objectified labor" (or labor-power); second, "in the absence of a theory of exploitation" that allows for the "realization of (surplus) value as *representation of labor power*," the economic aspect will be confused with the political and capitalist exploitation will begin to look like state domination. We are dealing then with macro and micro levels of analysis—in ways that anticipate the work with Althusser in Chapter 5 below. Spivak insists that "the staging of the world in representation dissimulates the choice of and need for heroes, paternal proxies, agents of power. Indeed this is why a proxy can behave like a portrait. In this case, if the scene of writing is not yet clear about the relation of value and labor-power, or about Labor's access to the economy, exploitation will appear as what people do to each other, and Labor will be rendered indeterminate by virtue of its access to the economy, like the immigrants who gain access to a state only to silently occupy its sweatshops. Thus to speak of "the workers" or the working class without a Marxist theory of exploitation is to hide the fact that we tolerate a proxy who speaks for "them," even when we remove ourselves to allow "them" to speak. This is precisely what is wrong with Deleuze and Guattari's out-class; this new proxy—this Yes! of desire—behaves like a portrait. And one struggles in vain to decipher the face of exploitation.

Spivak argues that distinguishing (again, as an identity in difference) the staging from the proxy—the economic context from the political nego-tiation, if you will—keeps alive a critique of the "individual subject as agent" that lurks in the self-evident phrase that (classes of) people want things. Whereas we should expect to find Deleuze and Foucault along-side her here, she notes two senses in which these progressive intellectuals participate in a "clandestine restoration of subjective essentialism": "In the Foucault-Deleuze conversation . . . the oppressed can know and speak for themselves. This reintroduces the constitutive subject on at least two levels: the Subject of desire and power as an irreducible methodological presupposition; and the self-proximate if not self-identical subject of the oppressed" (1988:279). We have anticipated this claim by closely tracing Deleuze and Guattari's operation in Chapter 2. Spivak is right to detect "an irreducible methodological presupposition" that requires a subject of desire. By placing desire outside the Lacanian schema, Deleuze and Guat-tari presuppose an exiled, if unnamed, subjectivity. And they also rely on a self-proximate out-class of oppressed people; by positing a out-class cut off from the benefits of the capitalist axiomatic, they seek to acknowl-edge, especially when considering the Third World, the subjectivity of oppressed people denied representation. But even more troublesome is the fact that their position as intellectuals requires neither subject; the subject of desire is unnamed—it is really a presupposition—and the sub-ject of the oppressed cannot include Western intellectuals. Indeed, these authors remove themselves from the scene, as if to say: "Now this role of referee, judge, and universal witness is one which I *absolutely refuse* to adopt" (1988:280).

So where can intellectuals stand in Deleuze and Guattari's formulation? We who stand back and let the disenfranchised speak for themselves are in the rather awkward position of being "nowhere," reporting on unrep-resented subjects and noting the workings of a desire that cannot name its subject. This refusal to intervene is, for Spivak, an individualism wrapped up in a masculinist radicalism that must be deconstructed before one can take it seriously. The problem is that our transparency draws us into re-peating a devalorization of the subjects we seek most to value: "Further, the intellectuals, who are neither of these S/subjects, become transparent in the relay race, for they merely report on the unrepresented subject and analyze (without analyzing) the workings of (the unnamed Subject irreducibly presupposed by) power and desire" (Spivak, 1988:279). The alternative to such complicitous neutrality—this co-optation by the very theorists most concerned with co-optation, this reintroduction of a unitary subject—cultivates a decided in-betweeness, an interstitial resistance (explored in Chapter 8).

Spivak draws this section to a close with the following advice to take class seriously but never too seriously: "In the face of the possibility that the intellectual is complicit in the persistent constitution of Other as the Self's shadow, a possibility of political practice for the intellectual would be to put the economic 'under erasure,' to see the economic factor as irreducible as it reinscribes the social text, even as it is erased, however imperfectly, when it claims to be the final determinant or the transcendental signified" (Spivak, 1988:280). This is a clear call for Derridian extravagance, honoring the de facto foundation of exploitative class relations without giving determinate form the last word. The next task, then, is to establish a subject-object framework that we simultaneously undermine by reintroducing indeterminacy, and with it a distinction between revolutionary self-determination and liberal self-involvement. As Spivak points out earlier, intellectuals must learn to (re)present themselves differently within an exploitative world order.

Supplementing Subject-Object Analysis

Allowing for the aporia between subject and object, whether expressed as supplement, trace, or différance, forces my project to remain at the scene of writing with ruined limits. For this reason I am inclined to respect Spivak's insistence that one study both the way discourse is framed and the way its indeterminacy cannot be framed. But we have seen that this requirement need not be approached as a choice between order and chaos; placing a system under erasure requires neither total systematicity nor total obliteration. One can deploy subject-object analysis even while deconstructing the orderly fields produced by these relations. For my purposes, this means examining the relation between owners of capital and owners of labor-power, while paying close attention to what cannot be located in the discursive fields produced by their interrelation. Moreover, what cannot be located must never be viewed in a static manner; location, like vocality, is a question of staging. Marx's staging of bourgeois society tells a story of how labor-power becomes the object of capital. Loyalist Marxists seek to transform the objectified class-in-itself represented by Marx into a class-for-itself whose subjectivity comes alive when the people speak for themselves. Post-Marxists either seek to replace Labor with the desire of an out-class to which all participants in the economy conceivably belong or add labor-power to other subject positions (which amounts to the same thing when identity politics begins to self-destruct). I am trying to combine subject-object analysis with poststructural zeal for indeterminacy without falling back into either the trap of a new and improved subject (of power and desire), which elides issues of exploitation, or the dream of neutrality, which comes from failing to acknowledge any discursive position at all.

It should now be possible, then, to expand discussions of value within subject-object analysis to locate a grave silence in the penumbra of the hyphen. Spivak's discussion of the clitoris-as-excess in phallo-uterine social organization illustrates how to regain appreciation of what relations of subjects and objects leave to be desired. Bourgeois society silences Labor in its capital/labor-power social organization; exploitation of labor-power is always attended by a denial of "being in possession of labor-power." Just as women who would be subjects can only be mothers, so those selling labor-power who would be subjects—for example, by following union organizers—can only be employees; other possible subjects are silenced, institutionalized, imprisoned, eliminated under capital's influence. And those among us who cannot or do not sell our labor-power risk being rendered completely worthless, unless we already own money or are postponing exploitation (as privileged people sometimes do). Those in abject poverty often die in the process of struggling to find alternative access to the means of subsistence (crime, charity, assistance). Earlier work with the indeterminacy of desire can now help us come to terms with the all that we are willing to discard (in ourselves or others) as a consideration of value in bourgeois society.

My efforts in this chapter to avoid reinscribing a unitary subject at the scene of writing (by watching carefully the distinction between political and constitutive representation) are designed to answer the question of detecting Labor's whereabouts, posed in Chapter 1, in terms that respect its nameless properties. Labor has dropped out of sight. We have assumed a position rather like Dupin's when he first meets the prefect. Marxists have looked everywhere for labor as a class-for-itself, a subjective Labor (the subject of enunciation outside the expression "I should be everything!") sufficiently conscious and organized to expropriate the expropriators and lead the way to human emancipation. Although we sometimes uncover shining paths and fight the good fight, we seem plagued by a fragmentation of groups and, more recently, even by a denaturalization of ourselves as persons. To make matters worse, capital continues to consolidate and naturalize its forces. Deleuze and Guattari's axiomatization seems to be smoothly filling every crevice in bourgeois society (except for the areas it is prepared to discard).

Just as the purloined letter was in Minister D's apartment all along, even when it passed (as litter) through the hands of Prefect G's search patrol, so Labor is onstage all along during the buying and selling of labor-power. But a materialist, or empiricist, or positivist commitment to reality cannot seem to locate it. Aware of the danger of political representation acting like constitutive representation, I remain committed to the notion that material solutions to the problem of capitalist hegemony are too self-evident. Getting all exploited workers together on the issue of exploitation so that we can demand bread and roses, or perhaps an end to wage labor, is a necessary part of anticapitalist struggle. But we must never forget that this good work transpires within the territory mapped out by fixed categories, the territory in which political representation can act like constitutive representation and begin to predicate subjects with the blink of an eye. Who has not experienced the tension between "workers" and the categories of contemporary identity politics? Which Marxists, except for the most doctrinaire, have not struggled with questions of how class is related to race, gender, sexuality, and other asymmetries of power? We must avoid, at all costs, confusing the problem of locating Labor, the missing subject, with the loyalist problem of getting so many different people together under the same banner. One could imagine classifying the entire population in terms of multicultural criteria and still not finding Labor. Rather than blaming multiculturalism for erasing class, my approach involves locating indeterminacy at the scene of writing. To see how this works we must revisit the scene and ask if desire's indeterminacy can reveal that Labor—like the purloined letter—has been right under our noses all along.

Remember how the owners of labor-power and owners of money meet face to face and exchange equivalents in the drama staged in Chapter 1? This encounter resembles the dialogue portion of Poe's "The Purloined Letter" in the sense that each subject stands in relation to the other as its object. Workers send their proxies to bargaining tables and financial backers extend their proxies to employers who are expected to drive hard bargains. Things change, however, in bourgeois society after the transformation of money into capital. Owners of money, or their proxies, are still onstage representing both those who invest and those who use their money to consume. But now some of the money has been transformed into a new object—capital—that begins immediately to assume subjective properties wherever it can find a steady diet of labor-power, the object of the owner we call Labor.

And yet when we left Chapter 1, Labor was nowhere to be found. Labor-power, now the object of the emergent subject capital, is often confused with Labor, its real owner. Before capital became a subject, all owners of labor-power had value in their capacity to find uses for things. But after the conversion of money into capital, where value represents itself in exchange-value—only labor-power under contract holds value. Capital determines which labor-power is valuable and which is expendable. We might begin locating Labor in such a scenario—in which disembodied fictions, such as Control Data, can appear more natural than the embodied need of a neighbor—by recalling three elements from the framework salvaged in Chapter 2.

First, one's onstage presence need not correspond to one's predication in discourse. I distinguish action onstage, where some subjects are apt to be taken for granted, from the channels of signification through which subjects must pass before they can assume enunciatory positions. People cannot—regardless of real needs which are "always there"—speak as persons until predicated as subjects in discourse; and subjects predicated in discourse need not be associated with people in need. This situation raises the possibility, explored in Part 2, that capital could be predicated as a subject in terms of literary or economic representation without any connection to the real needs of actual people—predicated, that is, as a subject of the statement with no connection to the real. Similarly, actual people with needs in the domestic economy could be represented politically (and thereby silently predicated) as something other than manifestations of the subject Labor. This might happen in a variety of ways in identity politics, not all of which are easily detected. Both the manager who objectifies people as "the cost of labor-power" and organizers who subjectify people as "the oppressed" or unnamed "subjects of desire" participate in the "sleight of word" Spivak notices in the slide from political to economic representation, creating fixed categories in discourse that obfuscate Labor's possibilities.

This is why, despite all their efforts to escape the (post-)Saussurean question of signification by divorcing desire and representation in late capitalism, the axiomatizing that Deleuze and Guattari attribute to capital remains a question of representation. The second element of my framework acknowledges the degree to which political representation (proxy) is not capital's thing. Hegemonic forces hover above the hustle and bustle of encoding and decoding the competing demands of subjects and their objects. Capital's axioms are taken for granted in ways that communication channel surfers cannot imagine. Thus efforts to organize objectified labor-power against socialized capital often result in frequent-flyer capital, socially responsible capital, lean and mean capital, etc., each secure in its bottom line (until gobbled up by one of its own). Exploitation of objectified labor-power and the naturalization of capital's subjectivity remain uncontested; Control Data can offer its team-playing employees mutual funds that "grow" in a socially responsible way. But following Spivak we must ask: Which subject positions are enjoyed by capital? Who portrays the labor-power consumed? How does this positioning in discourse correspond to the real needs of actual people? What happens to Labor when (its) value finds representation (predication as money) in exchange-value?

This brings me to a third element of the salvaged framework: an insistence that the channels of language one passes through and the intersubjective demands one makes in the presence of the other are all implicated at the scene of writing with ruined limits. This is where we might at last detect Labor's whereabouts. Without the first two elements of the model such a pronouncement might be misconstrued as an insult—accusing Labor of being ghostly, inarticulate, undecidable—but we have seen with Spivak how subaltern subjects denied discursive positioning can travel under signs *rendered indeterminate by virtue of having already gained access to the text of the proper(ty)*. For purposes of this project, this means that although it is locked out of the means of representation, Labor has already gained access to bourgeois society, where it assumes many different identities, travels under many different names. Capital nurtures the labor-power it requires for continued growth, but unbeknownst to those locked into subject-object relations (whether dialectical or binary-driven), it also sustains (unwittingly) the aspects of Labor it renders indeterminate. For example, when capital investment provides housing for people with money, it builds shelters that can be taken over by squatters ("vagrants," it calls them). Similarly, when venture capital stocks its malls with perfect fruit for well-heeled consumers, it dumps nutritious garbage at the service entrance, which can nourish thrifty recyclers ("transients") and other subsistence-minded home economists who sometimes survive without selling their labor-power. Capital is positioned as a subject with labor-power as its object; and yet squatting, dereliction, scavenging, delinquency, and other subjects devalued during the buying and selling of labor-power are also at the scene. And these invisible subjects are only the extreme cases of the depreciated Labor. Capital renders aspects of all domestic economies indeterminate—for example, the artistic skill of the domestic worker whose job is not her work, or the agricultural talent of the educational worker who overlooks unplanted fields while writing books for job security or ego gratification. The *mise en abîme* indicates the opening of an unfathomable Labor underground devalued by capital's axioms, but totally unimpressed by axioms, ungoverned yet nourished, sometimes invisible (unless one knows where to look), yet always included, poised as if ready to strike.

Loyalist Marxists are the first to point out the exploitation involved in labor-power's subjection to capital's hegemony. Their commitment also reminds one of Marx's "industrial reserve army," whose function is to keep wages as low as possible (not to mention the rest of the surplus population). And yet, beginning one's critique with the exploitation of labor-power rules out Labor's off-limits resources. The important lessons learned from exploitation and impoverishment must not undermine appreciation of the silenced, nameless aspects of the domestic economy. We need to study the role of indeterminacy in Marxist revolution.

Capital is a smooth operator. To reject poststructuralism as an idealism that violates Marxist materialism may actually serve to perpetuate its hegemony. Even more alarming is the possibility that a materialist (and in some cases a post-Marxist) defense of someone may devalue that person. For example, a committee of leftist academics concerned with hunger in their community might seek to organize around the issue of access to food. In the most materialist, clearly articulated, down-to-earth fashion, the intellectuals, may explore linkages between other issues of access—medical care, technology, etc.—doing so democratically without speaking for the "other" and perhaps with the help of a well-paid professional facilitator who has waived the usual fee. On a good day everyone might talk. A successful community organization empowers the participants and succeeds in establishing some of the goals articulated by the membership. But even the most democratic grassroots organization may actually perpetuate the devaluation of hungry people unless it raises difficult questions of supplementing subject and object positions in dominant discursive fields. The problem begins with the relation of the intellectuals and the hungry person, a self-other relation. The intellectual remains in the enunciatory position of the self-same while constructing a hungry person as other. This happens every day in global contexts among people who never meet with one another. But even sitting in the room together, getting to know and trust one another, talking together in straightforward fashion—optimal conditions that it may take years to establish—does nothing to rearrange the dominant discursive positions charted out at the scene of writing . This leads to common dilemmas in community organizing (explored in Chapter 9). Without addressing these constructions, persons constructed as bearers of the Western intellect interacting with persons constructed as a mere surplus population are likely to reinscribe each other's positions in that familiar way: "you're not like the rest." *Class Action* explores the possibility that "surplus people" constructed as hungry, homeless, prisoner, etc., are Labor denied subjectivity and that Western intellectuals who write about them are no more transparent or neutral in the center of Western institutions than Poe is in the center of "The Purloined Letter."

Any materialism so hostile to abstractions as not to address these constructions risks conflating political and literary representation. Simply to say, "It's about food, stupid (not subject-predication)," ignores the vast territory of positions already plotted by an axiomatic capitalism that wins either way—whether breathing life into the community orchestra or orchestrating the community's last breath. Indeterminacy is one way of trying to talk about the gap between an actual need that is "always there" and discursive fields that value some positions as subjects, make use of others as objects, and prepare to discard the rest through forms of attrition including hunger and inadequate health care.

The subject of desire must remain therefore an open question; only newly constituted subjects marked by Labor's heterogeneity can transform the silence of indeterminacy into languages conducive to radical action. Rather than issue invitations from the center (please join us!) to a marginalized "them" not constituted until "they" receive the invitation, we Western intellectuals would be better served repatterning ourselves, deconstructing the self-images we extend across linear time, and joining in the fray of indeterminacy, thereby resisting complicity with a system of exploitation that depreciates the very people we seek to appreciate. Bourgeois academics must learn to reassess our constitution, to represent ourselves differently, to perform our own excentricities.[6]

With this commitment to the relation of desire and representation, we turn now to the second dimension of *Class Action:* representation and production. Marxism has acquired such a reputation for being preoccupied with production that we need to remember that Marx is, after all, a theorist of capitalism. His presentation (*Darstellung*) of capitalism allows us to see our preoccupation with production, which unsympathetic readers frequently blame on him. But more important, because of the way he stages the performance, Marx never loses sight of exploitation, or how capital steals Labor's subjectivity when value represents itself in exchange-value. First, following my earlier work with Lispector's interval, I find my bearings in a subject-object analysis of Marx's relation of capital and labor-power; then, building upon my work with desire and indeterminacy, I show how his method is attentive to the aporia of subject and object; finally, following leads developed in this chapter, I find room in his depiction of labor-power's relation to capital for an irredentist struggle on the behalf of Labor.

PART TWO

REPRESENTATION
AND PRODUCTION

CHAPTER FOUR

Rearranging Labor's Relation to Value

Labour is the living, form-giving fire; it is the transitoriness of things, their temporality, as their formation by living time.

—Karl Marx, *Grundrisse*

In the preceding part I detected Labor's whereabouts in bourgeois society —in prisons, lost dreams, broken spirits, daydreams, dilapidated buildings —in a devalorized state underground. Like subjects in an enemy-occupied territory deprived of their language, workers have been forced in the name of survival to learn new languages. Because we are not in control of our capabilities, our resourceful labor-power, we can assume only enunciatory stances that obey capital's proliferating axioms. It is quite possible to multiply the permissible subject positions in ways that extend the political franchise. But debates concerning various identities, and especially the possibility of not even having an identity, rarely threaten capital's hegemony. Capital gains a more diverse, flexible supply of labor-power; Labor remains locked out of the means of representation, rendered indeterminate by virtue of its access to the economy. But we remain split in our submission to the channels of signification. Maintaining an awareness of the Labor underground requires remembering the significance of being split between embodied need and discursive demand. Although knowing one's way about amidst capital's axioms requires performing multiple scripts that evade the danger of need, one is never secure from the return of the real, an encounter with what is too painful to acknowledge, all that resists signification.

Who exactly is the hegemon spinning these axioms, writing these scripts? Any attempt to deliver the body, the speaking subject in the hypothetical statement "I will develop the moon," would turn up a list of the usual suspects: investment bankers, venture capitalists, college trustees, TIAA-CREF investors. But the subject of the statement bears only the faintest family resemblance to people like ourselves, who, although they may grow rich with superfluities, know full well that they do not control the flow of capital. And we ourselves, many of us, are only one serious ill-ness or stock market crash away from being completely depreciated. Try-ing to wage an irredentist struggle against this palace guard would find us all expendable, and capital somewhere else. I hinted in Part 1 that capital's discursive presence may be completely divorced from the site of the sub-ject of enunciation, which would free this market phenomenon, capital, from the fierce vexation of being split between need and demand. Indeed, capital appears free to become a naturalized citizen with dominant sub-ject positioning and no anxiety whatsoever about ego or fragmentation. My task in Part 2, then, requires considering the relation of representa-tion and production, placing special emphasis on restaging capital's sub-jectivity, exploring the possibility that capital—like a vampire sustaining itself on the blood of actual people—cannot even see itself in a mirror.

Because we are fully complicit in our own subjugation, strategies for undoing what we have done must include explaining to ourselves how hegemonic capital has managed to gain such axiomatic control. Marx's writing remains quite useful here because, as a theorist of capitalism who nevertheless writes in the name of the Labor underground (to the extent this is possible), his presentation of bourgeois society tells the story of capital's transformation from mere money to a "power ruling over every-thing." We must, however, never lose track of the point that his project is located at the "scene of writing with ruined limits." This requires special vigilance when reading Marx because of his fondness for Hegelian ter-minology; such categories—including the "relief" made possible by the seductive dialectic—create the impression of a totalized system that has overcome indeterminacy. To fall for this illusion is to devalue Labor even as we struggle for its recuperation.

Supplementation need not distract us from Marx's presentation of La-bor and capital in bourgeois society. Hegelian categories permit Marx to set aside from the outset any reduction of Labor to a person or a group. Rather, Labor is presented as an abstraction that must be made manifest in the "direct, physical activities of [those] individuals" whom Marx calls "possessors" of labor-power. This chapter maintains that Labor serves as the beginning of Marx's explanation of how capital emerges as an active subject. To explain Marx's plan to expose capital's pretense of being the active partner in a subject-object relationship with labor-power, I begin with his twofold understanding of Labor in *Capital I*. Then, in an infor-mal conversation with Marx, I examine Labor's relation to relative and equivalent forms of value. Finally, I encourage reading Marx without fil-tering his commitment to the form-giving fire of Labor through either an economistic "labor theory of value" or a relentlessly determinate "value theory of labor."

The Twofold Character of Labor and Its Value

Early Marx (Marx and Engels, 1978:18) asks, in his well-known critique of Hegel's *Philosophy of Right*, that instead of privileging the Hegelian Idea as absolute subject we "start from the actual subject and look at its objectification." By concentrating on the lives of productive human beings instead of disembodied concepts, Marx shifts the emphasis between matter and idea while keeping the subject-object paradigm intact. His problems begin, of course, in the fact that productive capacity is already objectified and operating under the influence of capitalist axioms. Bourgeois society is already marked by the predominance of capital as the active, form-giving force; capital wants us to limber up when it says, "I am the key to community development. Dance here." We must be careful to understand this inversion—or substitution of capital's form-giving powers for Labor's—without becoming overcome by a Hegelian subject-object paradigm. I must show how, in other words, to read Marx using this language without limiting Labor to its restricted domain.

Marx opens *Capital I* by distinguishing human subjects from objects "outside" us, objects that supply our demands even if they fail to satisfy desire. Bourgeois society—our society—tends to convert these objects into commodities. Indeed, wealth under capitalism can be defined as "an immense accumulation of commodities." Marx proposes to analyze a single commodity at the highest level of abstraction on the way to exposing the secret of money and, ultimately, the predominance of capital as an active subject in bourgeois society. Focusing on a single commodity allows Marx to postpone the question of exchanging one commodity for another. This postponement gives Marx the time he needs to consider this object "outside" us apart from how well it satisfies demands and how much one can get for it through exchange. At this level of abstraction he asks what properties commodities share so as to make them exchangeable in the first place. This question leads Marx to connect the nature of Labor and value in ways that are sometimes construed as a "labor theory of value." But we will discover several other ways of understanding the relation of Labor and value. I begin by distinguishing in Marx the nature of value, abstractly considered, from its phenomenal appearance as "exchange-value" in the marketplace.

Significantly, Marx begins his analysis by reminding us that every useful thing may be regarded from two points of view: qualitative and quantitative. The qualities of commodities "constitute the substance of all wealth"; the quality of a single commodity (what is it for?) concerns its substantial usefulness—or use-value. The other point of view asks a quantitative question: How much of it do you have? In an exchange situation involving at least two qualitatively different commodities, the question becomes How much is it worth? or a matter of exchange-value. Any trip to a market illustrates these two points of view: I really want it; can I afford it? But Marx is not shopping just yet. He begins with one commodity and abstracts away from the qualitative dimension; "its existence as a material thing is put out of sight." Now it is merely a commodity in the abstract (whether a sack of potatoes or a bunch of basil). Next—because he is considering only a single commodity—Marx postpones the question of exchange (how many potatoes do you want for that basil?). We leave the marketplace momentarily to consider the basic unit of capitalist society: any object outside us that can qualify as a commodity.

Such abstraction and postponement permit Marx to consider the "common something" shared by all commodities, without which these objects cannot be placed in circulation. Imagine a market with wholly unrelated objects: a gust of wind, a child's cry, a jar of pesto, the smell of ozone, and a batch of perogies. How is exchange possible under such chaotic circumstances? Clearly some of the above items are not necessarily commodities (though capitalism could certainly commodify any one of them). What do commodities, abstractly considered, have in common? Just being use-values, being useful, is not enough of a common property to facilitate exchange. A gust of wind is useful when sailing, a child's cry can indicate danger or desire, the smell of ozone can make one feel invigorated. For exchange to be possible, use-values, or useful objects, must have value; and to have value any object, according to Marx, must embody living human Labor: "A use-value, or useful article . . . has value only because abstract human labour is objectified [*vergegenständlicht*] or materialized in it" (Marx, 1976a:129). Labor emerges in Marx's representation of bourgeois society as the predominant subject, a subject that creates useful things—"The discovery of . . . the manifold uses of things is the work of history" (125)—as well as the source of what makes things exchangeable. "I worked all day making these perogies; pesto doesn't grow on trees, and I raised the basil myself." To commodify ozone or crying or gusting is, of course, possible; but this would first require an expenditure from Labor's vast reserve bank. Value can be regarded as the crystallization of Labor at this same level of abstraction. Labor's representation as value, then, is the "common something" that makes the exchange of commodities possible.

But because they are only abstractions in Marx's theoretical field, Labor and its crystallization, value, must find representation in the sensible world. Before seeing how this comes to pass in the circulation of commodities, we need to examine abstract Labor's relation to abstract value. In *Capital I*, near the end of the first section of chapter 1, Marx offers three distinctions to clarify this relation. First, without being "mediated through [useful] labour," use-values (such as a gust of wind) contain no value. Second, if a product is useless—such as the work of a would-be sculptor who reduces his ivory soap bar to a pile of soap flakes—then "the labour [contained in it] does not count as labour and therefore creates no value" (Marx, 1976a:131). We must keep our eyes open for the abject, in this case the useless product cast aside by the subject-object relation. Third, without exchange, even use-values carrying value (such as pesto that workers make for their own consumption) cannot be regarded as commodities. A commodity is a use-value bearing value placed in exchange with other use-values bearing value. Labor is, then, a form-giving force when viewed from either the qualitative or quantitative perspective. People participating in living human Labor create a wide variety of useful things with differing degrees of value.

Keeping these distinctions in mind, and without leaving the realm of abstraction concerned with a single commodity, we can understand that Marx's phrase "the value of a commodity is determined by the quantity of Labor expended to produce it" (Marx, 1976a:129) is not concerned with what to charge for a product in an exchange. To confuse the abstraction, value, with its sensible appearance, exchange-value, could lead one to the hasty conclusion that the amount of labor-time expended helps predict the market price of a commodity. But remaining at the level of abstraction—after all, exchange value is not taken seriously by Marx until the third section of this first chapter—we can be content to realize that Labor is present in all commodities as both a bodily form (or use-value) and a value. And so, abstractly speaking, the above quotation says only that Labor is crystallized in value as the common something that makes objects exchangeable. Contrast, for example, "The cost of the weekend is determined by (expressed by) the quantity of food, shelter, and entertainment consumed" with "The cost of the weekend is determined by the extravagance of the guests." The latter stresses a causal connection between independent and dependent variables; the former, like Marx's quotation, stresses logical determinacy. Value crystallizes the quantitative dimension of Labor, whereas use-value—more body oriented—concerns the qualitative dimension of Labor.

Marx opens a well-known part of *Capital I* (chap. 1, sec. 2) by claiming that he was the first to notice this twofold character of Labor embodied in commodities: "Initially the commodity appeared to us as an object with a dual character, possessing both use-value and exchange-value. Later on it was seen that labour, too, has a dual character: *in so far as it finds expression in value*, [Labor] no longer possesses the same characteristics as when it is the *creator* of use-values" (Marx, 1976a:131–32, emphasis added). We are dealing, then, with the difference between how much Labor is expressed and what kind of forms are created. Labor brings forth qualitatively different use-values, which find quantitative expression in value (which as an abstraction must ultimately find representation in the form of exchange-value).

Using the language of representation and determination, Marx first examines Labor's usefulness. Labor, the abstraction, finds expression in the usefulness of its products. The consumption of useful objects provided by human Labor draws Labor out of the realm of abstraction and into the world of supply and demand. Marx illustrates this in the following way:

> The coat is a use-value that satisfies a particular need. A specific kind of productive activity is required to bring it into existence. . . . We use the abbreviated expression "useful labour" for *labour, whose utility is represented by the use-value of its product*, or by the fact that its product is a use-value. In this connection we consider only its useful effect. . . . the use-value of every commodity contains useful labour, i.e., productive activity of a definite kind, carried on with a definite aim. (Marx, 1976a:132–33, emphasis added)

Marx states quite precisely here that abstract Labor's utility finds representation in use-value. Labor, the real subject, stands behind all productive activity, manifests itself in the usefulness of commodities.

Because Marx is trying to present how capital has taken over bourgeois society, he is interested in use-value primarily as a dimension of commodities. Isolated subsistence farmers are not interesting here, for example, because their use-values are not commodities. Although these first two sections step back from the bourgeois economics of supply and demand, behind the dazzle of money, to locate the actual subject, they both are designed to analyze commodities; commodity exchange is always just around the corner. Because "use-values cannot confront each other as commodities unless the useful labour contained in them is qualitatively different in each case" (Marx, 1976a:133), Marx chooses here to remark on the social division of Labor as a prerequisite for commodification of life in bourgeois society. If people did not create qualitatively different use-values, there would be no point in exchanging our creations as commodities. "I'll trade you my shovel for your shovel" makes sense only if our shovels are different. But his discussion of Labor's social divisions in bourgeois society also celebrates its creative capacity in any society: "Labour, then, as the creator of use-values, as useful labour, is a condition of human existence which is independent of all forms of society; it is an eternal natural necessity which mediates the metabolism between man and nature, and therefore human life itself" (133). Necessary as it is, Labor is not sufficient for survival. A vital force, Labor must remain in contact with both its means of subsistence and production. If value takes on a life of its own, where will this leave Labor? For now we will concern ourselves only with the two dimensions of Labor's expression in the phenomenal world of commodities.

Marx turns next to the quantitative dimension of Labor in commodities. He moves away from use-value: "If we leave aside the determinate quality of productive activity, and therefore the useful character of labour, what remains is its quality of being an expenditure of human labour-power. Tailoring and weaving, although they are qualitatively different productive activities, are both a productive expenditure of human brains, muscles, nerves, hands, etc., and in this sense both human labour. . . . *the value of a commodity represents human labour pure and simple*, the expenditure of human labour in general" (1976a:134–35, emphasis added). To establish the quantitative dimension of Labor, Marx needs for purposes of calculation (determination) to overcome the differences among types of expenditure. This is relatively easy to do at the level of abstraction, the level of Labor in general. He reduces all productive Labor in general to "the labour-power which, on the average . . . exists in the organism of every ordinary individual." So when Marx writes that the value of a commodity represents Labor, he is "equating [value] to the product of simple unskilled labour" and saying that value "represents a definite (determinate) quantity" of Labor in this reduced form of "human labour pure and simple." Such a reduction allows Marx to ignore qualitative differences among types of Labor in different societies and to concentrate instead on the relation of Labor and value in the abstract. To call this a labor theory of value in the predictive sense of using amount of labor-time expended to explain the price structure of the product ignores the distinction between the qualitative and quantitative extremes of the dialectical unity.

Marx is quite explicit about Labor's form-giving powers as expressed in both the utility and value of commodities. Significantly, his summary of section 2 first mentions value: "On the one hand all labour is an expenditure of human labour-power, in the physiological sense, and it is in this quality of being equal, or abstract human labour that it forms the value of commodities" (Marx, 1976a:137). Only then does Marx remind us of the other dimension: "On the other hand, all labour is the expenditure of human labour-power in a particular form and with a definite aim, and it is in this quality of being concrete useful labour that it produces use-values." Through an "expenditure" of its object, labor-power, Labor is represented qualitatively in use-value and quantitatively in value.

Before Marx can place Labor's use-value and exchange-value in a dialectical tension (as twin poles at work in the commodification of bourgeois society), his analysis of commodities must come to terms with the representation of value, an abstraction which is itself one aspect of the representation or expression of labor. To accomplish this requires finally leaving behind both the heights of abstraction and our preoccupation with a single commodity. We have seen how Labor's expression as utility manifests itself in specific situations as use-value. We must now ask how (Labor's) expression as value manifests itself in specific situations as exchange-value. The two aspects, of course, are portrayed as traveling together in a dialectical unity.

The third section of chapter 1 of *Capital I* opens with the claim that in bourgeois society commodities are, by definition, "objects of utility" (with natural form) and "depositories of value" (with value form). The former is straightforward, uncomplicated, and has already been demonstrated. But the latter is hard to grasp because the form of value has yet to be established. Marx is now ready to say the following

> Let us remember that commodities possess an objective character as values only in so far as they are all expressions of an identical social substance, human labour, that their objective character as values is therefore purely social. From this it follows self-evidently that it can only appear in the social relation between commodity and commodity. In fact we started from exchange-value . . . in order to track down the value that lay hidden within it. We must now return to this form of appearance of value. (1976a:138–39)

It is helpful here to note a distinction between the immanent position of value in the abstract (laid out alongside use-value in sections 1 and 2) and the way value makes itself manifest, or represents itself, in exchange value. We are ultimately interested in what happens to Labor in the process of the expression of its quantitative value. Marx is prepared to explain why so many people miss the point of Labor's real subjectivity, or Labor's form-giving force. His work behind the scenes in this representation of bourgeois society allows us to see that how Labor creates and is embodied in both use-value and value. We must now see how value represents itself in the exchange value of actual commodities. Then we can work through the dialectical relation of the two poles: (relative) use-value and (equivalent) exchange-value. To start here and never view Labor's relation to value at the level of abstraction risks neglecting the importance of use-values as qualitative expressions of abstract Labor that enable humans to survive, as well as missing the connection between exchange-value, value, and Labor. That is, without the first and second sections of chapter 1 it would be difficult to see exchange-value, especially in its money form, as the representation of value, which itself is the representation of plain and simple human Labor's expenditure of labor-power; and it would be even more difficult in the dazzle of money to remain interested in use-value at all. Hear capital speak: "It's not my problem that this product will stunt the body's growth; I'm responsible for economic growth."

To explain the relation of use-value and exchange-value as a reversal of the real subjectivity of Labor and objectivity of money, which results in the domination of Labor by money, Marx explores the genesis of the money-form of commodities. His accounting locates use-value at the active relative pole and exchange-value at the passive equivalent pole. This reverses the burden of proof by requiring apologists for bourgeois society to show where value comes from rather than beginning by insisting that Marxists prove otherwise. In other words, Marx uses a detailed discussion of money to get things back on track: positioning Labor as the real subject and money (eventually capital) as its object. The following informal conversation summarizes the distinctions already established by our discussion and then shows the passivity of exchange value.

A Conversation with Marx

WC: You claim that people who receive income from land, stocks, bonds are parasites because other people support them. That is, these parasitic rentiers claim to own the surplus generated by others.

KM: Well, not all people who could do so sell their labor-power; some choose instead to live on income produced by others. Those who do so exclusively are parasites.

WC: All this talk about the importance of people who work makes me uneasy. You make it sound as if today's workers suffer the same conditions they did in your day. Have you seen the size of a pay-check and working conditions today?

KM: Yes, things may have improved for some wage laborers (especially some of those still employed in the most parasitic nation-states). But people who work are still a primary source of value in the marketplace.

WC: That's ridiculous. I'll show you value. Just test-drive my 1967 Chevy, a car that has increased in value over the years. If working people are the source of value, then how can my car increase its value over thirty years after it left the assembly line? Mercedes and Mustangs also appreciate.

KM: I can see this is going to be a long discussion. We should attempt to begin with the real subject and consider its objectification. For example, real people (subjects) have wants and desires that they attempt to satisfy with objects outside themselves.

WC: That's why my uncle bought this cool car when he was my age.

KM: To do otherwise—to get the subject-object relation backwards— creates a strange situation in which an object outside us can—like a car—become a fetish (an object supposed to possess magical powers). I would suppose that your commodity fetishism leads you to believe that this 1967 Chevy possesses the power to grow in value.

WC: I understand fetishism from my religion classes, but what's a commodity?

KM: A commodity is an object, a thing, outside us, that satisfies human wants (of whatever origin). Things we consider useful require exchange to be considered commodities.

WC: Since my uncle found the car in the marketplace, I guess it is a commodity.

KM: That's right. Now, how did he and the owner come to agree to transfer the title? Did he have to give the owner something equal in value?

WC: Yes, he gave him an old clunker and some cash.

KM: What do you suppose is the source of the common something that makes commodities exchangeable?

WC: That's easy. Money. You look in the Blue Book to see what clunk-ers are worth and then reach for your wallet and take out the rest in cash.

KM: But money is just one form of expressing value. Starting there is what I warned you about. What is value saying?

WC: Well, the car does seem to just sit there growing more valuable. It is a little spooky.

KM: Beginning with the real subject and considering its objectification requires asking what commodities have in common. Why do they all have prices?

WC: Well, they are all products of working people. But labor-power is just one of the costs.

KM: In other words, one cannot see it, but a social substance called human Labor is embodied in these products.

WC: Okay, but what does this social substance have to do with value?

KM: When viewed as crystals of this social substance (human Labor), these products of Labor's expenditure of labor-power can be called values.

WC: So—if I understand what you are saying—a useful article (one might call my uncle's car a use-value) has value only to the extent that Labor has been embodied (or materialized) in it.

KM: Yes.

WC: Then you are a fool, because clean air or virgin soil are useful and require no expenditure of labor-power.

KM: Well, a thing like clean air can be a use-value without having value (that is, without requiring Labor to draw it out or develop it). Now, selling bottled clean air in Los Angeles is, of course, a different story. Does your old 1967 car meet today's air quality control standards?

WC: Okay, so you are being strict with definitions. But you said that the source of the common something that makes things exchangeable is Labor. This means that when my uncle works his backyard garden to feed his family, he is producing commodities?

KM: No—but Engels would have liked that question—a thing that directly satisfies your own wants can be a use-value and not a commodity if no social exchange is needed.

WC: So what you are saying is that to become a commodity a product must, first, be transferred to another by means of an exchange and, second, serve that other person as a use-value, even if it only satisfies the most fleeting desire.

KM: Yes, that's your uncle's Chevy.

WC: But the Labor embodied in these commodities differs so widely in quality—for example, it takes a different kind of labor-power to make cars than it does to make coats—that you could never give a name to the common something that all commodities share.

KM: Ah, but you are thinking only about the qualitative dimension of Labor. It's good to do this sometimes because it reminds us of the rich character of concrete useful labor-power, the secret of survival, the work of history. But the Labor embodied in these commodities also differs in quantity — that is, it takes more labor-power to produce some things than other things.

WC: But if Labor is the common something that makes things exchangeable, then the same labor-power exercised during equal parts of time should always yield equal amounts of value, at least in your strict sense.

KM: That's right.

WC: Time to get real, Marx. This Labor hang-up is going too far. You say you are talking about the real world, right?

KM: But we might see different realities. I'm trying to get behind the appearances you mistake for reality. Perhaps you are caught up in a surface reality. Let's have another talk about commodity fetishism after your next trip to the mall.

WC: I was born to shop, but this does not make me a fetishist. . . . Everybody knows that commodities have very different use-values, but these values are irrelevant. Exchangeable things also have this "common something" that you want to connect to the quantity of Labor they embody. But why not just admit that this common something is money? How can such a critical reader of capitalism miss the point about money? Money is real; it even talks. For example, my 1967 Chevy is more valuable than my sister's Edsel. Labor might create use-value through the expenditure of labor-power, but that's irrelevant here. Some cars are worth more than others. Why complicate matters?

KM: If you insist on talking about money, I'll talk about money. But let's slow down. Can we at least agree that value can only manifest itself in the social relation of commodity to commodity — such as Edsel to Chevy?

WC: Okay.

KM: I agree that the value of these cars appears to us as exchange-value.

WC: You agree to that?

KM: Yes, but I want to get behind that appearance to the hidden value. That's what I've been trying to do. But let's do it your way and place two commodities in a relation so as to explain the genesis of this money thing.

WC: You are going to explain where money comes from?

KM: In a manner of speaking, yes.

KM: Imagine a relation between two commodities: twenty yards of linen is equal to one coat.

WC: Do you mean to say that the value of the linen is *relative* to the value of the coat or that the coat is the *equivalent* of twenty yards of linen?

KM: Precisely. All value has two poles: one relative (linen's value), one equivalent (the coat's value).

WC: Okay, but I'm not sure where this takes us. I see how the linen's value is active in the sense that it is represented as a relative value, or appears in relative form, while the coat's value is passive because it merely serves as the material in which the value of the linen is expressed . . . Wait, this isn't a subject-object relation is it?

KM: There may be hope for you yet.

WC: Well, your twenty-yards-of-linen-equals-one-coat relation does not take us very far toward the money thing because I can easily invert it: one coat equals twenty yards of linen. Now linen is the equivalent and the coat is the relative value. How does this help us arrive at the common something that makes things exchangeable? Everything is so arbitrary.

KM: Now we're getting someplace. Let's imagine other equivalents to twenty yards of linen: one coat or ten pounds of tea or forty pounds of coffee, etc.

WC: You mean that you are expanding the elementary form of value?

KM: Yes, that's right.

WC: But the list of possible equivalents is endless. How can we ever arrive at a common something uniting coffee, tea, linen, coats, and all other conceivable commodities?

KM: Well, trying turning the equation around.

WC: You mean to say that I would assign the relative (active subject) position to all the things like ten pounds of tea and forty pounds of coffee, etc. and place twenty yards of linen in the (passive object) position of being equivalent?

KM: Yes.

WC: But then any product would find its value in exchange when converted into the equivalent of twenty yards of linen.

KM: Yes. As I wrote, "The internal opposition between use-value and value, hidden within the commodity, is therefore represented on the surface by an external opposition, i.e. by a relation between two commodities such that one commodity, *whose own* value is supposed to be expressed, counts directly only as a use-value, whereas the other commodity, *in which* that value is to be expressed, counts directly only as exchange-value" (1976a:153).

WC: So, in our example, linen expresses the value of any commodity?

KM: So you say.

WC: Then quantities of social products (use-values) play the active part of relative values—or, if we must, subjects—and the linen plays the passive part of the equivalent value—the object or the passive material in which the value of the products is expressed.

KM: Yes, linen played the opposite role in the elementary form above.

WC: But what does this have to do with money?

KM: Well, call linen "gold" and take it from there.

WC: I would say that gold (or its equivalent) marks the value, or acts as the exchange value, of any commodity.

KM: But this seems at odds with your earlier position. Money makes the world go round. How can such an allegedly creative force be a passive equivalent form? The relative pole, where use-values gather in their qualitative difference, seems to be where the action is. And this is where we might expect to find Labor.

WC: Yes, gold does seem passive, like value petrified. The world seems to make money, but not enough to go around. How can it be that the producers of use-values, the key to human survival, so often cannot find enough money to survive themselves?

KM: Perhaps we are so bedazzled by the money-form of value that we lose sight of the Labor it represents.

In this way Marx might explain that appreciation in the "exchange-value" of an antique car is only a price fluctuation in a world of money, a world in which hoarding, usury, buying cheap to sell dear, etc. all manage to move money around, from pocket to pocket, without adding any value (unless Labor is involved). To treat money as the active subject confuses the order of the dialectic between relative and equivalent form: money is the passive material in which value is expressed. Confusing relative and equivalent form gives money representation as the active utility element in commodities when it is *really* value petrified, the passive equivalent form of value. Getting this subject-object relation backwards creates the illusion that money has a life of its own, that value fluctuates in a sea of supply and demand. Exchange-value does fluctuate in this way, but exchange-value is only the passive equivalent (money) form of value gone haywire in bourgeois society.

Our conversation with Marx relies more on the twin distinctions of quality/quantity and use-value/exchange-value than it does on Labor as a "common something" that makes objects exchangeable. We learn from this conversation that when Marx writes that "the same Labor exercised during equal parts of time should always yield equal amounts of value," he does so at the highest level of abstraction, where he is dealing with the internal tension between utility and value, or between the qualitative and quantitative aspects of a commodity. This is his way of claiming that "all kinds of actual labour [can be reduced] to their common character of being human labour in general" (Marx, 1976a:159–60). Such a claim does not commit Marx to saying that the amount of labor-power expended acts as an independent variable when predicting prices, the dependent variable. As Ollman (1993) instructs, Marx is answering why everything in bourgeois society has a price, not predicting actual prices in the grocery store. Diane Elson (1979) attributes most versions of such Labor theories of value to a confusion of value and exchange-value (or price). Exchange-value, the price of a commodity, names the equivalent "value form" of the value created by labor, which also has a relative bodily or natural form (use-value). Price is simply the money-name of the equivalent form; such names come in handy when commodities—such as Edsels and Chevys—are viewed in relation to each other. Saying that equal units of Labor's labor-time always yield equal units of value is Marx's way of saying that Labor lies immanent within all of the commodities we exchange for money (C-M) or buy with money (M-C). Abstractly considered, this is to say that Labor creates value. If we keep the twin poles of the value Labor creates in mind, the question of what causes prices to fluctuate above or below their value (as incorporation of labor-time) is far less significant than the question of whether these fluctuations themselves create value. Supply and demand, or fraud and corruption, or fools and their money, may govern price fluctuations in bourgeois society. So when Marx argues later that the "value of labour-power is determined . . . by the labour-time necessary for [its] reproduction"(1976a:274), he is operating at a level of abstraction away from actual people at work and therefore not talking about wage rates. Because labor-power's exchange-value may be higher or lower than the costs of its (re)production—that is, its value—Marx is not concerned with the operation of predicting wage rates. His science springs from the dialectical relation of use-value and exchange-value, whether internally (behind the scenes) or externally (in the consumption and exchange of commodities. The Labor immanent in the Chevy and Edsel gives them value, which makes them exchangeable as commodities; but the equivalent form of value—money—facilitates any actual exchanges.

Chart 3 shows how Marx's model starts with the real subject, Labor as

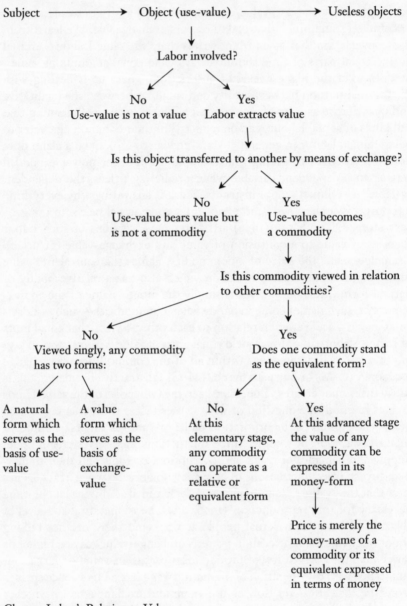

Subject ⟶ Object (use-value) ⟶ Useless objects

Labor involved?

No
Use-value is not a value

Yes
Labor extracts value

Is this object transferred to another by means of exchange?

No
Use-value bears value but
is not a commodity

Yes
Use-value becomes
a commodity

Is this commodity viewed in relation
to other commodities?

No
Viewed singly, any commodity
has two forms:

Yes
Does one commodity stand
as the equivalent form?

A natural
form which
serves as the
basis of use-
value

A value
form which
serves as the
basis of
exchange-
value

No
At this
elementary stage,
any commodity
can operate as a
relative or
equivalent form

Yes
At this advanced stage
the value of any
commodity can be
expressed in its
money-form

Price is merely the
money-name of a
commodity or its
equivalent expressed
in terms of money

Chart 3. Labor's Relation to Value

expended by actual people, and its relation to objects (use-values among other things) in ways that transform one commodity, money, into the equivalent measure of value. "The bodily form of the commodity [money] becomes its value form."

Money is, then, by this account the "metamorphosed shape of commodities." In a society in which the "dominant social relation" is between "possessors of commodities" (Marx, 1976a:152), it makes sense that we should view this passive material in which value represents itself as the common something that makes commodities exchangeable. Rather than continue to invest in the fiction that money has a life of its own, Marx had to abstract away from the phenomenal world of subjects and objects to appreciate that the internal relation between use-value and value in any given commodity is a representation of Labor. Commodities are, after all, objects created by Labor's expenditure of labor-power. Capital's subjectivity must be unmasked; capital must be repositioned as an object.

Mirroring the Labor Theory of Value

Elson captures brilliantly the significance of value in Marx's formulation of Labor. Noting that most readings of the labor theory of value are intent upon showing the relationship between labor-time expended and the price of a commodity—sometimes in an effort to "prove" exploitation—she argues that this approach confuses Labor as an abstract subject with Labor as the object of Marx's representation. Elson's "value theory of labour," a mirror image of the labor theory of value, points out that "the *object* of Marx's theory of value was labour" (1979:123). By this she does not wish to argue that value is the subject, the fire, the creator; her point is that by asking "why labour is expressed in value," Marx makes Labor the object of his theory. Indeed Elson argues that "it is because labour is the object of the theory that Marx begins his analysis with produced commodities, as being [here quoting Marx] 'the simplest social form in which the labour product is represented in contemporary society'" (124). Elson is not, then, arguing that Labor is value's object; she claims instead that Marx's theory is concerned with the objectification of Labor. The value theory of labor inverts the labor theory of value in the sense that Elson shifts our attention away from Labor as a source or origin of value and toward value as the medium through which Labor is objectified in contemporary society.

Elson (1979:139) distinguishes immanent and external measures of value to conclude that the relation between labor-time contained in commodities (it took about as long to make an Edsel as a Chevy) and the money they are worth (as antiques) is "one of continuity and difference." All commodities contain elements of qualitatively different labor-time (which therefore cannot act as equivalent form). Money, the metamorphosed shape of commodities, is highly useful as an equivalent for exchange purposes. Labor makes exchange possible theoretically by creating value; the money-form of value makes exchange possible next Tuesday. Marx explains that "money as a measure of value is the necessary form of appearance of the measure of value which is immanent in commodities, namely labour-time" (1976a:188). Labor-time measures value in the same sense that amount of Labor determines magnitude of value: value represents the quantitative side of Labor, and Labor is the actual subject.

Now it is crucial to keep both the internal/external and quality/quantity distinctions running at the same time. Otherwise one could get the impression that labor-time is the key to all that is valuable in society. Elson explains that Pierre de Boisguillebert proposed a system of dividing up the social product according to proportions of labor-time contributed. Marx warns explicitly against such a labor theory of value. "Boisguillebert's work proves that it is possible to regard labour-time as the measure of the value of commodities, while confusing the *labour which is materialized in the exchange value of commodities and measured in time units* with the direct physical activity of individuals" (quoted in Elson, 1979:138–39). Recall that the latter, work, corresponds to the qualitative character of Labor embodied in all commodities. Labor is expressed in both use-value and exchange-value.

Elson cites this passage as evidence of the dangers of forgetting that "it is money, not labour-time, which functions as the social standard of measurement" and that "labour-time and money are not posed as discretely distinct variables which have to be brought into correspondence" (1979:138–39). She notes that Marx's metaphors are chemical and biological ("crystallization," "incarnation," "metabolism") and reads this as yet another indicator of his lack of interest in economistic prediction. We must therefore be on the alert for any changes of form in the physiognomy of our dramatis personae.

To guard against the confusion of money and labor-time, we might juxtapose the two crucial distinctions. Although the typology shown in Chart 4 cannot stand as a static depiction of *Capital I* because both tensions work dialectically, it serves to remind readers that the relationships among use-value, exchange-value, and value are themselves related to Labor, the real subject. I rely on this typology heavily in Chapter 6. It presents Labor as an abstraction divided between its qualitative and quantitative aspects, an abstraction that explains life, after returning to the material base, in

Aspect of Labor's expenditure of labor-power

Level of analysis		Qualitative (expended with a definite aim)	Quantitative (expended in a specific amount)
	Abstract	Utility	Value
	Phenomenal	Use-value	Exchange-value

Chart 4. Labor's Expenditure by Level of Analysis

terms of production and consumption of use-values. Exchange-value provides the quantitative measures needed in a specific form of society, for our purposes bourgeois society, to attend the business of survival.

The critical question of this subject-object paradigm becomes this: what happens to Labor's representation in bourgeois society? In Marx's schema, *capital*, as the transmogrified form of the money form—which is itself the metamorphosed form of commodities, which are themselves formed by labor-power—*is the object of the real subject, Labor.* But when owners of commodities meet in the marketplace, Labor loses its representation; value takes on (as we shall see in Chapter 6) a life of its own. Indeed, Labor plays the role of an object outside of us, labor-power, a commodity embodying the Labor of others and capable of producing more than its value. While continuing to create capital, Labor's labor-power falls under capital's influence. And Labor goes underground.

Elson acknowledges that she risks undermining the case for "proving" exploitation. But she is right to argue that Marx is concerned here with the degree to which Labor finds representation in exchange-value; value enters his inquiry only because he is interested in the relentlessly one-dimensional properties of bourgeois society. Speaking for Marx, Elson (1979:129–30) explains that "what is required is a conceptualization of a process of social determination that proceeds from the indeterminate to the determinate; from the potential to the actual; from the formless to the formed. *Capital* is an attempt to provide just that." My discussion of desire and representation in Part 1 permits me to accept the discursive positioning of determinate subjects and objects, including the pluralist expansion of the political franchise, but only on the condition that we do not neglect what is rendered indeterminate in the process. Elson relies on Marx's texts on method (Marx, 1975), to which we turn in Chapter 5, but she looks only in the direction of determination, whereas we are committed to looking both ways before crossing the split between need and demand.

To show how Marx's scheme explains the hegemony of capital in bourgeois society, then, I must first note carefully what is accomplished by his proposed mapping. We are dealing with a system that creates determinate meanings in seas of indeterminacy. The subject-object relation of capital and Labor is constructed meticulously in an effort to show how backwards the overdeveloped world is in its thinking about Labor. Elson is right to suggest that biological metaphors, such as metamorphosis, suggest a changing relation between forms that leaves the door wide open for political intervention and contestation. But even if Marx's theory were completely true, so to speak, we could not share Elson's reassurance that the forms created by the fire of Labor successfully rule out indeterminacy. Crucial distinctions such as quality-quantity and internal-external work only as axes in an effort to map regions that are in principle unmappable. When we contrast such statements as "I am nothing and I should be everything" and "GE brings good things to life," we must assess each occurrence for signs of how the speaking subject is and is not aligned with the subject spoken.

Louis Althusser, sympathetic to the plea of counterhegemonic ideology, was also quite aware of the limitations of ideological readings of Marx that rely on the mutually antagonistic and dependent poles of the Hegelian dialectic. In fact, he develops a "scientific" reading of Marx's *Capital I* that does not rely on a labor theory of value and attempts to deliver a more complex relation of economic forms and other forms than Marx provided or could have imagined (at least this is what Althusser would have us believe). Whereas Althusser is most interested in showing how the structure of capitalism effectuates changes in other forms, his detailed manner of proceeding allows us to raise questions of indeterminacy that attend even the most determined answers. By studying Althusser's effort to get beyond subject-object ideology, we can see the structure of this system, if only to learn how it fails to deal with indeterminacy. By considering Althusser, we can develop a "theory of labor's value" that includes the abject ruled out by both Marx's labor theory of value and Elson's value theory of labor. In fact, we are about to see that Marx's method accomplishes this more successfully than Althusser's.

CHAPTER FIVE

Containing Indeterminacy:
From Althusser to Marx

Poststructuralism has shown some of us a staging of the agent within a three-tiered notion of language (as rhetoric, logic, silence). We must attempt to enter or direct that staging, as one directs a play, as an actor interprets a script.

—Gayatri Spivak, *Outside in the Teaching Machine*

We are reading *Capital I* as a project that starts with the actual subject, Labor, and considers its objectification as labor-power. Here I want to explore the possibility that Marx's Hegelian method of presentation (*Darstellungsweise*) does not exhaust Labor's possibilities. Spivak's suggestive work with indeterminacy permits imagining Labor (underground), living in the real but denied access to the means of representation. Althusser is useful here because he reads Marx in ways that raise questions about establishing determinate forms of life.[1] By exploring the relations between what can be thought and what lies outside of thought, Althusser illustrates the reliance of any determinate form on the rules of language. His efforts to map bourgeois society with greater complexity than he thinks Marx could have imagined need not blind us to the useful aspects of Althusser's work. My work locates in Marx a model that constructs determinate forms of life while producing vast regions of indeterminacy, zones from which one might resist the discursive powers that be. Perhaps Labor needs to relocate its basis of emancipation to indeterminate spaces alongside determinate forms of existence, such as capital and labor-power.[2] Exploring the ways in which any determinate form itself contains indeterminacy requires distinguishing logical determinacy from the causal determinacy so often attributed to Marx. I want to reexamine Althusser's science project for signs of a neglected indeterminacy. This allows a return to Marx's discussion of method in the introduction (1857) to the *Grundrisse*, where he distinguishes his "rich totality of many determinations" from a "chaotic conception of a whole" (Marx, 1975:72). Marx's presentation of a society that presupposes the power of capital remains timely because it raises the possibility that bourgeois academics have grown accustomed to economic forms of life that depreciate many of the actual people—exploited and discarded women, men, and children—who stand to gain the most from expansion of the political franchise. Adding the abject to the Hegelian unity of subjects and objects gives me the space I need to offer a modest theory of Labor's value. I continue my work with *Capital I* in Chapter 6, where relying on this theory helps to enhance Marx's presentation of capital's subjectivity.

Examining the grammar of the word *determine*, Wittgenstein recounts the following language-game: "when A gives an order B has to write down a series of signs according to a certain formation rule" (1958, sec. 143). He proceeds to investigate how rules are meant and how A is able to obey B. This leads to the larger question of how the rules of a formula can be said to determine which steps one takes. After reformulating ways of discussing how a mathematical formula determines the steps that are to be taken, Wittgenstein instructs that "the way the formula is meant determines which steps are to be taken." The "criterion for the way the formula is meant . . . is . . . the kind of way we always use it." The following example shows what it takes for any representational sign "to determine the steps in advance": "We say, for instance, to someone who uses a sign unknown to us: 'If by x!2 you mean x squared, then you get this value for y, if you mean 2x, that one.'—Now ask how does one mean the one thing or the other by x!2? That will be how meaning it can determine [*bestimmen*] the steps in advance" (sec. 190).

We face, then, a distinction between what follows logically in determinate constructions (or forms of life) and what follows, perhaps causally, after one has grown accustomed to the rules of these constructions. "All the steps are already taken" is best read, then, according to Wittgenstein, as a proposition designed "to bring into prominence a difference between being causally determined and being logically determined" (1958, sec. 220). If *Darstellung* names a theoretical-practical model, and if bourgeois society must be textualized as a mode of production in order to present orderly connections between its various elements (such as commodities and money), then we might say that the model logically determines the steps in advance.

Althusser studies how Marx attempts to work at the level of determination and representation. His articulation of the relation between Marx's scientific presentation and the objects it appropriates in the process is part of a project that grants causal, not logical, determinacy to the mode of production. Tracing Althusser's steps toward causal determination (what he calls "structural effectivity") should position us to raise strategic questions concerning the formation of form and the inevitability of the formless, even within the boundaries of his science project.[3] I want eventually to show that even though Althusser tends to read Marx in the direction of causal determination, Marx can also be read in the direction of logical determinacy and beyond.

Mirroring Althusser's Practices

At issue is the relation between forms of life and life outside thought in the real (world). If reality can be known only in discursive forms — "What looks as if it had to exist, is part of language"(Wittgenstein, 1958, sec. 50)—then it makes no sense to say that the truth of a theory lies in its successful application, because practice and theory are both already discursively intertwined. Althusser (1979a:56) works with precisely this problem when he reviews the inadequacy of the "practical" response to the following question: "By what mechanism does the production of the object of knowledge produce the cognitive appropriation of the real object, which exists outside thought in the real world?" Although posed as a detour, Althusser's rejection of "ideological" responses to this question provides an elegant illustration of his argument on economic determination. Exploring the mechanics of this argument points to its vulnerability and the need for a supplemental reading.

Section 17 of part 1 of *Reading Capital* rejects the claim that practice — whether pragmatic success-in-practice or idealist concrete practices — is the mechanism used by the knowledge industry to "appropriate" real objects, that is, to make sense of objects outside of thought: "Practice is the touch-stone . . . the proof of the pudding is in the eating" (Althusser, 1979a:56).[4] Althusser defends one general reason and a number of special reasons for the inadequacy of practice as the link between objects of thought and objects outside of thought. The general reason is the insistence on guaranteeing a certain "harmony" between knowledge and its referents, the objects that lie outside of it.[5] Such a harmony begs the question of appropriation; one uncritically assumes that practice can access a "reality" outside the production of concepts (knowledge effects). Thus, those who settle for the proof of the pudding in the eating have no way of determining "that it really is a pudding we are eating and not a poached baby elephant" (Althusser, 1979a:57).

Althusser then makes a transition from the general reason to the special reasons why practice is not the mechanism by which theoretical enterprises appropriate objects from the world outside of thought. In so doing, he points out that one need only say "practice" (*pratique*) aloud to realize its simultaneous dependence on theory (for example, one's practice as a therapist) and independence from theory (for example, one's practice of lying). This observation illustrates, for Althusser, the impossibility of a simple mirror relation between theory and practice. In Althusser's words, "practice understood in an ideological way is only the mirror image, the counter-connotation of theory (the pair of 'contraries' practice and theory constituting the two terms of a mirror field) " (1979a:57). The mirror analogy fails, says Althusser, because "there is no practice in general" but only "distinct practices which are not related in any Manichean way with a theory which is opposed to them in every respect"(58). Althusser refuses to follow any rule that seeks a guaranteed harmony between concepts (the objects produced by thinking subjects) and the facts (objects outside of thought) and extends this critique to both reactionary and revolutionary discourse. In any hands an "undifferentiated proclamation of the primacy of practice" fails to challenge the general rule of ideology. Althusser endorses this "egalitarian" view of practice—every person's experience of reality is valid—in the short run for revolutionary thought, but he argues that it must be "criticized and superseded in order to establish a scientific conception of practice exactly in its place" (58). The first special reason for practice not satisfying as the mechanism by which the production of knowledge produces the appropriation of "real" objects, then, is that practices are far too complex to serve as determinants of proof, since all practices are not equally significant.

On the way to explaining the difference between one-sided ideological conceptions of practice and more complex scientific conceptions, Althusser presents two more "special" reasons for the failure of practice to satisfy. Not only must we think in terms of distinct practices beyond the "undifferentiated egalitarian endorsement of practice," we must also distinguish the question of differentiating levels of distinct practices from the question of forging an alternative view of the relations between theory and practice.

Turning first to the question of levels, Althusser instructs that "we can assert the primacy of practice theoretically by showing that all the levels of social existence are the sites of distinct practices . . . [including] scientific (or theoretical) practice" (1979a:58). Any determinate practice, according to Althusser, shares in different and peculiar ways the "structure of a production." By this he means that all practices can be shown to transform unfinished material objects into finished objects, whether concepts or dogma or commodities. Althusser employs the metaphor of production to challenge the ideological guarantee of harmony between the thinking subject and the object outside of thought. Different practices are related to different objects. All practices are structured to convert "raw materials" into some kind of object, which Althusser calls a "product."

Coming to terms with the potentially overwhelming variation across all conceivable practices, Althusser employs qualitative and quantitative variables for purposes of classifying practices—degree of independence and type of relative autonomy. That is, some practices are more structurally interrelated than others. This raises the exciting possibility of a relatively autonomous cultural practice—say hip-hop—that cannot be reduced to more basic capital-labor relations. But as quickly as you can bid the superstructure–economic base distinction adieu, Althusser insists that both the degree of independence and the type of relative autonomy are "fixed" by their dependence on economic practices. All practices, it seems, however independent they may be otherwise, bear some relation to economic practices, which are therefore "determinant in the last instance" (Althusser, 1979a:58).

No sooner does he suspend the rules of bourgeois ideology—rules that allow guarantees of fit between thinking and its objects—than Althusser substitutes new rules to govern what constitutes proof of its propositions. To understand how this is not an arbitrary move requires distinguishing what Althusser calls "ideological" production from "scientific" production. Whereas the first kind of rule following relies on guarantees that its rules are not of its own making, the second acknowledges that it "produces" the objects it thinks according to rules of its own making. There is no guarantee of authenticity expressed here. Indeed Althusser's next step, the third reason for practice not satisfying as the mechanism theory employs to appropriate reality, is to show a new way of relating theory and practice.

Theory is presented as a practice (or production process) that produces a scientific order by establishing protocols among distinct practices. Elements of theory are present in all practices.[6] This new version places knowledge at both ends of a practice spectrum that ranges from subsistence to science. The range, then, lies between, on one hand, the "primitive" practices most susceptible to ideological guarantees that seeing is a precondition of believing (in a form of life) and, on the other, the "purest" practices most likely to appreciate that believing (in a form of life) is a precondition of seeing. Practice cannot stand as the mechanism by which theoretical practice appropriates real objects because theoretical practice "contains in itself definite protocols with which to validate the quality of its product" (Althusser, 1979a:59). Althusser explains these proof rituals as "exactly what happens in the real practice of the sciences."[7] For these reasons, he concludes with the following chiasmus: "Marx's theory is not true because it has been applied with success; it has been possible to apply Marx's theory with success because it is true" (1979a:59).

As a production process, then, Althusserian science works with the material at hand. Indeed some of the less "pure" practices—steeped as they are in rule-following ideology—can induce "profound reorganizations in theoretical structures," according to Althusser (1979a:60). He ends section 17 of part 1 with a story of Marx's theoretical practice under the influence of his practical experience in activist politics.

We have just observed Althusser substituting a complex relation between science and ideology for the simple relation between theory and practice that he associates with pragmatism and idealism. But the sophisticated spectrum that ranges from pure thought to mere subsistence, which Althusser substitutes for the naive "Manichean" mirroring of nature, has a mirroring effect of its own. In what Jane Gallop identifies as the "pleasing elegance" of the chiasmus (1985:93–94), Althusser sets a reassuring view of the relation of thought and its objects (the naive relation of theory and practice) in a mirror relation with a somewhat self-contained structuralism: "it has been possible to apply Marx's theory with success because it is true." Here we feel the jubilation of the mastery of a structural reading, a totalized system. But recall that Althusser advances a mastery without guarantees. An understanding of the tension between the anticipation of mastery and the anxiety of fragmentation requires a careful look at this hidden mirror. In constructing a theory that is true, one produces not only what will be considered coherence ("mastery") but also what will have been viewed as chaos ("fragmentation"). To explore this possibility we need to consider Althusser's sophisticated spectrum once more before returning to his question of the mechanism by which thinking appropriates material objects.

Loitering at the Mirror Stage

Marx, of course, employs a mirror metaphor in his 1873 postface to the second edition of *Capital*, where he discusses the relation between a "scientific presentation (*Darstellungsweise*)" of "the life of the subject-matter" and the material worked up, or "appropriated," by "methodical inquiry (*Forschungsweise*)" (1976a:102; 1989:55).[8] Although the mirror he would hold up to material objects may create the illusion of an "*a priori* construction" (1976a:102), these reflections are based on objects that must first be organized. Althusser's hidden mirror resembles Marx's use of mirroring in the sense that both rely on theoretical practices to organize otherwise fragmentary material. The methodical presentation—whether one uses the Hegelian language Marx rehearses with such delight or the less delightful Althusserian language of "structural effectivity"—relies on having appropriated material (what Althusser calls "objects outside of thought"). But in all of this mirroring, one must not lose sight of the fact that both Marx and Althusser reject a reassuring relation between science and nature, a relation in which theoretical abstraction "reflects" a prior order. If the mirroring practices of deceived academics have not reflected reality—if the point is to produce it—then there will always remain a question of insufficiency. The insufficiency of any theoretical endeavor (to draw together unifying abstractions and fragmented material) brings to mind a Lacanian mirror stage, though when using this term I must be careful not to exempt Lacan as an analyst from the charge of theoretical insufficiency.

Lacan uses the concept of the mirror stage to describe the pleasure of seeing one's reflection as a unity for the first time: "The mirror stage is a drama whose internal thrust is precipitated from insufficiency to anticipation—and which manufactures for the subject, caught up in the lure of spatial identification, the succession of phantasies that extends from a fragmented body image to a form of its totality that I shall call orthopedic—and, lastly, to the assumption of the armor of an alienating identity, which will mark with its rigid structure the subject's entire mental development" (Lacan, 1977:4). Elizabeth Grosz explains that although the mirror stage provides the child with the grounds of its identity as a being separate from other beings, "it also is the basis of an alienation, a rift which it will forever unsuccessfully attempt to cover over. It is necessarily split between what it feels (fragmentation, 'the body in pieces') and what it sees (the image of itself as a *gestalt*, as a visual whole)" (Grosz, 1989:22).[9] We must be careful not to presume that this fragmentation precedes the mirror stage; rather it is one in a "succession of phantasies" associated with this stage. Using the concept of a mirror stage as a heuristic when approaching Marx may open up readings to the anxiety of indeterminacy as we seek to establish the "orthopedic totality" of determinate forms of life. But we need first to understand how any subject, not only grand theory, can anticipate mastery and insufficiency in the same stage.[10]

Gallop (1985:85) presents the "drama" of Lacan's mirror stage as an Edenic tragedy so as to emphasize the lost innocence involved: "Just as man and woman are already created but do not enter the human condition until expelled from Eden, so the child although already born, does not become a self until the mirror stage. . . . When Adam and Eve eat from the tree of knowledge, they anticipate mastery. But what they actually gain is a horrified recognition of their nakedness. This resembles the movement by which the infant having assumed by anticipation a totalized, mastered body, then retroactively perceives his inadequacy (his 'nakedness')." When applied to Althusser's structuralist reading of Marx, we anticipate a totalizing explanation of bourgeois society as a mode of production, but retroactively perceive the inadequacy of this model (its "nakedness").

Gallop's reading of Lacan allows us to see how time flows in two directions at the mirror stage. The Edenic couple looks forward to the sinful human condition and back to a lost innocence they never saw as lost at the time. The child looks forward to the identity of subjects and objects and back to an anxiety (of the body in bits and fragments) never experienced before confronting the mirror image. Marx's grand theory looks forward to the masterful symbolic mapping of bourgeois society as determinate form and back to an indeterminacy (of aspects of life devalued by commodification) never before seen. Rather than reading Marx's theory as merely drawing order out of chaos, then, we can view his efforts as producing both what we see as orderly and what seems — as a *result* of the new order — chaotic; Marx's presentation allows us to see both what can and cannot be named as valuable in bourgeois society.[11]

The totality provided by the mirror reflection, then, does not provide the reassurance one often associates with a thought totality (such as economic determinism). But we are about to see that Althusser does not view economic determinism as a logical concern, which would require assessing theory's role in presenting orderly worlds (and the anxieties of this mirroring). We have just seen that Althusser builds an elaborate case for the construction of the "truth" of a science without guarantees; but he does not conceive his spectrum of pure theoretical practices and fragmentary practices in terms of a mirror stage. Althusser's attention is instead riveted on the way theoretical structures produce their effects, the problem of condensation (or what he comes to call "overdetermination") derived from Freudian-Lacanian studies of the unconscious. Disagreements concerning the relative autonomy and effectivity of significant subjects, such as capital, and significant objects, such as labor-power, presuppose a distinction between subjects and objects at the scene of writing. Fortunately, Marx does study, as we will soon see, economic determinations at the "mirror stage" of scientific writing. The mise en scène of constitutive representation determines who has speaking parts, who has the stage props, who is a stage prop and who never makes the scene.[12] Where Althusser claims that there is no practice in general but only distinct practices and goes on to make all practice out to be a matter of production, Marx claims that there is no production in general but only distinct forms of production and goes on to make all production out to be a matter of practices.

The Janus-Face of Indeterminacy

Following the lead of the hidden mirror in Althusser's continuum of practices, and concentrating meanwhile on theoretical practices that transform the raw material of other practices into concepts that allow one to grasp the theoretical consequences of these practices, I arrive at the arrangement between the thought totality of a theory and the complexity it seeks to organize. Althusser offers Marx's surplus value as an explicit example of a concept produced by theoretical practice in an effort to grasp the actual movement of objects outside of thinking (i.e., the exploitation of the majority of people).

> Just as bodies were "seen" to fall before Newton, the "exploitation" of the majority of men by a minority was "seen" before Marx. But the concept of the economic "forms" of the exploitation, the concept of the economic existence of the relation of production, of *the domination and determination of the whole sphere of political economy by that structure did not then have any theoretical existence.* Even if Smith and Ricardo did "produce," in the "fact" of rent and profit, the "fact" of surplus-value, they remained in the dark, not realizing what they had "produced," since *they could not think it in its concept*, nor draw from it its theoretical consequences. (Althusser, 1979b:181, emphasis added)

Althusser is explicit here about the role of theory in grasping such practices as exploitation of Labor. Without theoretical practices that promise to map complexity by producing concepts, people remain disoriented. But I must explain why, when confronting a "fact" such as rent or profit, one needs to "think it in its concept." And I must also make sense of the excitement Althusser finds in the "determination of the whole sphere" by its "structure."

Thinking facts "in their concept" is Althusser's way of answering the major question he raised during section 17's "detour": By what mechanism does the production of the knowledge effect produce the appropriation of objects outside of thought? Fredric Jameson (1981:12) explains that the task proposed by Althusser when he asks such questions is "not to elaborate some achieved and lifelike simulacrum of its supposed object [objects

outside of thought], but rather to 'produce' the latter's 'concept.' We have
seen that this is what theoretical practices do for Althusser, but the inward criteria by which these practices evaluate their product are not the
fundamental concern for Althusser. He wants to go deeper than that.

Althusser writes quite openly that there are two dimensions to the production process of scientific inquiry: the discourse of proof (the "inward
criteria" of science he highlights earlier) and the structures which house
this discourse (the unacknowledged "mirror stage"). Although the product of knowledge is evaluated in the first dimension by inward criteria,
the mechanism of this production process appropriates objects outside of
thought in the second dimension, the structural domain. Althusser puts
it this way: "We can say, then, that the mechanism of production of the
knowledge effect lies in the mechanism which *underlies* the action of the
forms of order in the scientific discourse of the proof. . . . in fact these
forms of order only show themselves as forms of the order of appearance
of concepts in scientific discourse as a function of other forms which,
without themselves being forms of order, are nevertheless the *absent principle* of the latter" (1979a:67, emphasis added). When theoretical practices
are developing concepts—such as surplus value—and arranging them in
true ways that can be applied with success, they are operating under the influence of "other forms" which operate as their "absent principle." In this
latter, deeper dimension, theory appropriates objects outside of thought
by thinking them as concepts. Recall above that, on Althusser's reading, when
Marx thinks the fact of Ricardo's profit in its concept, "surplus value," exploitation is finally out of the closet.

Althusser adopts here the language of a basic synchrony and diachrony
both existing "purely inside knowledge" (1979a:68) to describe the relation of these two dimensions: the (absent) hierarchy of concepts and the
(present) scientific protocols that constitute proof of a proposition. "Synchrony represents the organizational structure of concepts in the thought
totality . . . diachrony the movement of succession of the concepts in
the discourse of the proof"(68).[13] Synchrony "governs everything," he explains, because "the hierarchy of concepts" "determines the definition of
each concept . . . [and] the diachronic order of their appearance in the
discourse of the proof" (68).

Consequently, the mechanism by which the production of knowledge
produces the appropriation of objects outside of thought is a relation
in knowledge called "thinking the concept." The "inward criteria" for
establishing proof—criteria that operate in all sciences—are not the fundamental concern. We are dealing here with a self-contained system of
determinate meaning. We are, of course, discussing the mode of produc-

tion, a basic structure which determines the definitions and order of forms in present scientific discourse. Because its influence is that of an absent principle, those who repeat the famous Althusserian line about economic practices being "determinant in the last instance" should always include a reminder that, being synchronic, the last instance never "arrives," or always comes too soon.[14]

Although his work with synchronous structures seems to illustrate precisely the mirror function of theory described by Marx, Althusser is not looking back anxiously in the direction of questioning the establishment of logical determinacy. He is not asking with Marx (1976a:102) how a scientific presentation stands in relation to "the real movement." Althusser works exclusively in the other direction, keeping both eyes on the relations between the whole synchronic structure and its constituent parts in their diachronic movement as protocols.

This raises a confounding question, which Althusser is quite prepared to address because he argues that Marx could only sense it practically and hence ideologically: in what sense can a synchronic form—a form that does not participate in linear time except perhaps at the periods of rupture—be said to determine the movement of diachronic forms in time's flow? For here we see the relation between dominant and other forms of production in the complex and deep space of the mode of production. And here we can witness Althusser inject causal relations into the very act of representation. Because he does not notice the mixed blessing of mastery, Althusser views the scientific representation of the actual movement as a success and moves on to issues of how the various levels of this structure are causally related to each other. He does this in the renowned chapter on the "Marx's Immense Theoretical Revolution."

Reading Marx in Both Directions

After reminding us of that the synchronic structure we have been discussing is none other than the mode of production, Althusser asks how diachronic theory can produce the synchronic form of its own existence? Marx needs to "think the concept" of structural causality—the synchronic whole finding its existence only in the diachronic parts—without such a concept being available (except in the "trampled face" of Spinoza).[15] Because Marx could not pose the problem of structural causality theoretically—in its concept—he "set out to solve it practically in the absence of its concept." According to Althusser, we can see Marx "attempting to focus" on structural causality in the following passage. "In all forms of society it is a determinate production and its relations which assign every other production and its relations their rank and influence. It is a general illumination (*Beleuchtung*) in which all the other colours are plunged and which modifies their special tonalities. It is a special ether which defines the specific weight of every existence arising in it" (quoted in Althusser, 1979b:187). According to Althusser, this passage discusses the "determination of one structure by another and of the elements of a subordinate structure by a dominant, and *therefore determinant structure*" (188, emphasis added).

Without missing a beat, Althusser "produces" the concept of "overdetermination" (1979b:188), his structural alternative to merely diachronic readings of economic determinism. But here we must note that as a psychological term, "overdetermination" marks—at least for Lacan—the condensation of multiple aspects of the unconscious in one sharply focused object only *after the subject-object distinction is achieved at the mirror stage*. Althusser pays no attention whatsoever to the mirror stage, not to mention its attendant anxieties. He concentrates instead on how all effects carry traces of the contradiction between forces and relations of production built into the mode of production.

Marx, according to Althusser (1979b:188), came as close as practically possible to sharing this spirited concentration when he produced the concept of *Darstellung*, "whose object is . . . to designate structural causality itself." To paraphrase Althusser, Marxian representation of actual movement attempts to solve practically the effect of the hierarchy of concepts on the relations they underlie and govern. By never looking back to consider problems of achieving determinate forms of life, Althusser manages to restrict issues of representation in Marx to the question of causal determination.

But I must at this point note a possible difference between Althusser and Marx on representation and determination. We have seen Marx acknowledge in his 1873 introduction to *Capital I* that holding up a mirror to the world produces the "appearance" of a priori order there. This approach leaves plenty of room for the anxiety of a spirited slip, a crack in the mirror, an unmapped excess, or an anachronistic moment in the theory itself.[16] But Althusser is on a science mission that denies such anxiety and moves immediately to the synchronic and diachronic rules (of what might be called "the Symbolic"). This approach cannot allow, as perhaps Marx's can, for the fantastic or anachronistic. These are ideological remnants to be overcome by science.

So my problem with Althusser is not necessarily the concept of overdetermination; we can postpone the question of condensing the effects of living in a mode of production indefinitely. I question the extent to which the problem of causal determination is all that can be gleaned from Marx's 1857 introduction. Is that text only in the business of explaining how synchronic structures work (perhaps as absent causes), or does it also explain how synchronic structures represent an abstract order that permits logical representations? The question of how theory represents the orderly and the chaotic—how (in)determinacy is possible—can accompany questions of orderly relations between determinate causes and determinate effects. Perhaps logical representation (*Darstellung*) is better deployed as the concept Marx uses to address the problem of presenting subjects and objects as determinate forms, as established by critical inquiry (*Forschung*).

The famous 1857 introduction consists of four sections: introductory remarks on the significance of determinate forms, a Hegelian presentation of production as an "oppositional determination," an explanation of the constitutive relation between methodical inquiry and methodical presentation, and final notes on the incommensurability of determinate forms of life across history. The third section—because of its relation to the mirroring mentioned in the 1873 introduction to *Capital I*—is most relevant here.[17]

In earlier sections Marx explains that scientific representation is required to arrange distinct movements into patterns that can be said to emerge when most of the signs are used in the same way by most of the individuals involved. As if illustrating how the constitutive process of scientific representation of class works, Marx discusses the relation of distribution, consumption, exchange, and production. Production is both the total form of order being fixed by thinking (the "organic totality") and one of its four moments. In a spirited discussion of the identity and difference of these forms, Marx establishes the priority of forms of production in any economic thought totality:

> The result which we have reached is not that production, distribution, exchange, and consumption are identical, but that they all form members of a totality, differences within a unity. Production transcends . . . itself [and] . . . the other moments. The process always begins anew from production. . . .

> A determinate form of production determines a determinate form of consumption, distribution, exchange, and the determinate relations of those different moments to one another. (Eine bestimmte Production bestimmt also eine bestimmte Consumtion, Distribution, Austausch und bestimmte Verhältnisse dieser verschiednen Momente zu einander.)

Of course, production in its one-sided form is also determined for its part by the other moments. . . . A reciprocal effect takes place between the different moments. This is the case with any organic whole. (Marx, 1975:70–71; 1976b:35)

Slavoj Žižek cites this passage as an "outright example" of "what Hegel called 'oppositional determination'" (1993:132).[18] His Hegelian reading encourages us to highlight the logical aspects of determination, but leaves open our earlier question of the sufficiency of these determinations. Is it possible to read Žižek's "a determinate . . . production determines . . . other determinate relations" without ascribing causal properties to economic practices, or transforming Marx into a Young Hegelian?

Rather than breaking down a given concrete whole into its constituent parts, Marx isolates the parts of what is otherwise a "chaotic conception of a whole" and concentrates on building up a synthetic totality—a representation in the constitutive sense—a whole that is systematic and orderly, with logical relations between parts (fixed by thinking). This is how Marx discusses the operation:

Therefore if I begin with population, then that would be a chaotic conception of the whole, and through closer determination I would come analytically to increasingly simpler concepts; from the conceptualized concrete to more and more tenuous abstractions, until I arrived at the simplest determinations. From there the journey would be taken up again in reverse until I finally arrived again at population, this time, however, not [with population] as a chaotic conception of a whole, but as a rich totality of many determinations and relationships [among determinations]. (1975:72)

For Marx, then, "the concrete is concrete, because it is the sum of many determinations, [and] therefore a unity of diversity." Orderly presentation creates the impression of a prior order. "Hence the concrete appears in thinking as a process of summarization, as a result [after the mirror stage], not as a starting point, although the concrete is the actual starting point and hence also the starting point of perception and conceptualization" (72). The fragments must first be appropriated from history, but they cannot be grasped as such until the synthetic whole is represented, textualized. In this way "the abstract determinations lead to the reproduction of the concrete by means of thinking" (73). To say that the form of production determines the other forms is very much like saying that—after it is written—if the script/formula is followed, the plot/solution will unfold.

Marx reminds us that "economic categories . . . express forms of being [*Daseinsform*], determinations of existence" (1975:79; 1976b:41). Social science does not produce the fragments it seeks to organize; it begins with the particular fragments—of the determinate society—it seeks to grasp. Science must reproduce the concrete by means of thinking, or develop representations in language that fix relations between determinate forms. To neglect developing abstract categories—to not hold up the mirror—is to fall into the trap of isolating general conditions of all production and what we can accept, after Marx, as a chaotic understanding of the whole. "For example [when analyzing bourgeois society], nothing appears more in accord with nature than to begin with ground rent, with landed property, since it is bound up with the earth, the source of all production and all existence. . . . However, nothing would be more false" (Marx, 1975:80). Indeed, we have seen that one cannot grasp the actual movement of a contingent event by studying general conditions. One must first construct a representation so as to identify the rules in operation.

Because Marx argues that "abstract determinations" should reproduce the concrete "by means of thinking" and illustrates, in the Hegelian language of "oppositional determination," how methodical presentation can grasp the economic life of a particular society, one can reasonably expect him to present bourgeois society by highlighting production as an oppositional determination. This is the precise location of the ether passage Althusser cites as evidence of Marx grappling with the problem of structural causality:

> In all forms of society there is a determinate [*bestimmte*] [form of] production which directs all the others [consumption, distribution, exchange], and whose relations therefore direct [*anweist*] all the other relations, [and their] position and influence. There is a general illumination in which all other colours are submerged and which modifies them in their particularity. There is a particular ether [which] determines the specific gravity of everything in it. [Es ist ein besondrer Aether, der das spezifische Gewicht alles in ihm hervorstechenden Daseins bestimmt.) (Marx, 1975:80; 1976b:41)

Although the ether allusion can be read, following Althusser, as evidence of Marx examining the effect of a structure on its elements, it also signals a reminder that Marx's entire theoretical scheme is a methodical presentation and necessarily removed from the objects it appropriates. Ether is indeed a more luminiferous trope than Marx could have imagined in 1857. We have seen Althusser use this passage as evidence of Marx gesturing toward "structural effectivity," but looking in the other direction helps one to recall Marx's efforts to organize the otherwise ungraspable aspects of the chaotic whole.

Because bourgeois society is the "concrete" that Marx wishes to reproduce by means of thinking, he needs to break it down into the most simple elements and then determine which elements are most fundamental in the logical sense of being presupposed and opposed by all the others. The concrete thought totality is reproduced in this fashion. One does not follow the rules of such a system because one's free will is impinged; rather, one does so as a way of making sense. The rules become a way of life. The scientific representation of bourgeois society—as a mode of production— determines all the steps in advance. Causal determination is another matter altogether.

Toward a Theory of Labor's Value

Progressive disillusionment with economic determinism (including Althusser's formulation "determinant in the last instance") derives from the primacy such theories extend to class exploitation, as opposed to racism, sexism, and other oppressions. Faced with such issues as the disproportionate number of women unpaid for expending labor-power in the household, or the disproportionate numbers of African-American teenagers locked up in labor-power reserves, Marxist theory seems incapable of representing the intersections of multiple oppressions. For example, Cedric Robinson (1983:451) cautions against reading Western Marxism (including Althusser) as a "total theory of liberation." [19] But at least two ways of contesting totality are at stake in such criticism. One way emphasizes the politics of competing constituencies: which people are represented as subjects and objects within the total theoretical structure? The other way emphasizes the constitutive problems of establishing theoretical structures within which people seek (re)presentation as subjects and objects.

These two approaches to representation are so intimately related that one must avoid choosing one over the other when rethinking Western Marxism. In the case of political representation, one can fault Western Marxism for not fully appreciating nonclass social relations; for example, when Marx represents the "popular mind" of working people politically by hurling the defiant phrase, "I am nothing and I should be everything" (Marx and Engels, 1978:63), his depiction fails to notice fundamental differences among racialized, gendered, and sexed subjects. In the case of the constitutive representation, one can fault Western Marxism for not noticing that theoretical models, regardless of the relations they map, cannot adequately reflect the actual history of the people involved; for example, when Marx (1975:81) presents bourgeois society scientifically as a structure in which "capital is . . . the power ruling over everything," his representation must not be confused with the actual lives of working people. To contest the totality of Marx's political representation without also contesting the totality of his constitutive representation risks addressing racism, classism, sexism, or homophobia without problematizing the categories. But contesting constitutive representation raises new possibilities for political representation; rethinking the totality of a mapping can draw attention to subjects with ambiguous relations to the operative categories, subjects whose ambiguity may account for neglect in debates concerning political representation. Homi Bhabha (1992:49) writes convincingly of the ways in which "the rule of language as signifying system—the possibility of speaking at all—becomes the misrule of discourse."[20] We have seen how Labor, despite its access to the text in the needs to the actual people, has been subject to the "misrule of discourse" and denied access to the means of representation.

But this supplemental reading of Marx's method recalls our salvaged framework and with it an insistence on the fragility of representation in any language as a signifying system. Far from being an "immense" theoretical model that maps relations between levels of existence in the deep space of their complexity, constitutive representation becomes the unifying effort to organize what will only then have been seen as fragmentary practices, a provisional effort that can never wholly succeed. At the mirror stage one learns quickly that the truth of the whole is never the whole of the truth. Indeed, this is why stories about being watched while hiding something from someone, such as "The Purloined Letter," hold such wide appeal (to theorists). Marx's science may be applied with success because it is true; but every grand theoretical success signals its own insufficiency. Readers should notice by now that *Class Action* joins in the critique of Western Marxism's preoccupation with totality by adding a third (non)category to the subject-object relation. By refusing to rule out the indeterminacy of unpredicated subjects, such as Labor, I can encourage an expansion of political representation that struggles to appreciate the chaos of knowledge.

In Chapter 4 I argue that Marx's discussion of the money form relies on Hegelian terminology, but not exclusively. When Marx describes the relative and equivalent forms of value as "two inseparable moments, which belong to and mutually condition each other," he goes on to say that these "poles" are "mutually exclusive or opposed extremes" (1976a:139-40).

Setting aside the labor theory of value, on the grounds that it conflates the distinction between abstract and manifest levels of analysis, clears the way for the value theory of labor, an approach indebted to precisely the kind of dialectical unity I seek to supplement. Diane Elson, who develops the value theory of labor, is transfixed here, for example, on the role of political intervention—instead of a reductive determinism—in changing from one mode to the next. And yet she, like Ollman (1993), remains committed to the diachronic history presumed by loyalist Marxism. Elson's value theory of labor does not, however, rule out synchronic moments, such as those analyzed discursively in ways associated with post-Marxism. Discursive approaches open new territory for a variety of coalitions based on identity positions. Laclau and Mouffe (1985:181), for example, are concerned with "the emergence of a *plurality of subjects*, whose forms of constitution and diversity it is only possible to think if we relinquish the category of 'subject' as a unified and unifying essence." While continuing to observe the complicated negotiations between putting class first and enlisting class identity alongside other identifications, my approach seeks to supplement these commitments.

Indeed, the diachronic and synchronic elements must not be viewed in isolation. As is the case with the Saussurean sign—under which users of speech effectuate change in the synchronic structure—both forms of time travel together. But just as it is a mistake to confuse language as a signifying system with the real (needs) of the signifiable, so is it unnecessarily restrictive to limit subject-object relations to either a teleological form of drawing determinate form out of chaos (from potential to actual) or the synchronic suspension of teleology in a pluralism that maps out new actualities without raising the issue of subject predication. Even an economic summit between loyalist and post-Marxist theorist would not break the stranglehold of the subject-object paradigm on the political imagination.

The framework of desire's indeterminacy salvaged in Chapter 2 may help break this lock on theorizing. The plight of the subject split between discursive demand and actual needs suggests a gap between language as signification and what is really going on in people's lives. The iron curtain of capital's axiom proliferation suggests that relations between subjects and objects will not be resolved in discourse. And the ruination at the scene of writing suggests that those caught up in the subject-object relations governed by capital's axioms are ignoring the abject, a nameless third element signified for now only by the hyphen, which is nevertheless an integral part of the text.

When approached in this fashion, Labor's value can be located within the representational scheme provided by Marx and analyzed by Elson.

But this location must not detract from the point that Labor is the actual subject, even if its expenditure of labor-power is the object of Marxist inquiry. A theory of Labor's value refuses, then, to join in efforts to contain the indeterminacy surrounding relations between labor-power and capital. Looking in the direction of competing demands as governed by axioms of immense proportions, a theory of Labor's value speaks the language of positioning subjects and objects, and inverting these determinate forms. This is the domain of identity politics, where diachronic change transpires in symbiosis with synchronic form. But looking in the direction of actual needs as they exist in the real, a theory of Labor's value explores the aporia, the Labor underground, out of time. This Janus-faced approach permits supplementing the story of value's mutinous attempt to self-valorize, leaving Labor out of the picture and giving labor-power, its object, the uphill struggle of turning into a subject. In a word, a theory of Labor's value reminds each of us that Labor remains in a possessive position with respect to value, even if, under the violence of capital, we sometimes confuse our subjective properties with the labor-power we are forced to sell.

Because questions of diachronic and synchronic form are located on the determinate side of the yawning gap between need and demand, history must acknowledge its debt to linear time. By arguing that history, aside from its chronic continuity, is always already over, my approach seeks to relocate the teleological model of totality in a wider frame, which serves to displace subject-object operations even as it continues to perform them (perhaps in an inverted form). Drawing our attention to "the law of an invincible *anachrony*," Derrida's recent return to Marx claims that although it is "untimely, 'out of joint,' even and especially if it appears to come in due time, the spirit of the revolution is *fantastic and anachronistic through and through*" (1994:112). The salvaged framework makes it possible, then, to work within the aporia of subject-object relations to consider all that is marked for death but manages to find—perhaps due to deception and sabotage—access to subsistence. Looking first in the direction of the value theory of labor, our theory of Labor's value concentrates, with Elson, on how value finds representation in exchange-value and the transmogrification of the money-form. But my point is to expose the myth of capital's subjectivity; and this requires also looking in the direction of indeterminacy. Anyone engaged in fighting the "power that controls everything" must surely welcome allies committed to depreciating the subjectivity of the violent hegemon. Borrowing once again from Derrida, one can almost hear Labor—"the as yet unnameable . . . proclaiming itself . . . as is necessary whenever a birth is in the offing . . . in the formless, mute, infant, and terrifying form of monstrosity" (1978:293)—as if delivering an edict from the underground. We need to restage capital's subjectivity and labor-power's objectivity in ways that allow Labor access to the means of representation.

Which way one criticizes or defends the totality of Marx's theory of liberation depends, then, upon how one understands determination and representation when viewing Labor's production. Bourgeois society has grown accustomed to reading Marx with political representation and causal determination in mind. After adding "classism" to the list of other oppressions, one finds it difficult to claim that class position dominates or influences the others in a primary way. And the power of capital emerges uncriticized, free to play the margin for all it is worth. But I have argued that Marx also admits readings in terms of constitutive representation and logical determinations. Although I am not interested in defending Marxism as a total theory of liberation, I do propose rethinking Marxism by examining these terms, which involves a return to *Capital I* for signs of the unmappable. This focus on the specificity of class structure need not detract from related, but different, deconstructions of race, sexuality, and gender. One can articulate these elements of identity politics as subjects and objects positioned in discourse because they have already achieved determinate form. My specific problem is restaging capital's subjectivity so as to contrast it with Labor's objectification. Labor has nothing to say about identity politics because it is not represented by any identifiable subject of enunciation; when working people speak under the given forms of identity, they are often divided against each other in ways that benefit capital. And capital—capable as it is of killing, as Spivak reminds us, "by remote control"—need not say anything. Labor's self-determination would permit the people involved to explore their heterogeneity without capitalist axioms.

Because my approach finds in theoretical endeavor the same anxieties and fantasies commonly attributed to individual and collective subjects, I can conclude by suggesting both that class structure is foundational, in the sense that its practitioners—we theorists—follow the rules mapped out by Marx's methodical presentation of bourgeois society, and that class structure is not foundational in the sense that foundations are never all they are cracked up to be. The economic rules of bourgeois society that Marx presents in *Capital I* only appear to be prior constructions, and constructed worlds contain many more language-games than these. To resist capital's discursive power requires examining Marx's methodical presentation for signs of indeterminacy, signs under which we might expect to find aspects of life not sold as labor-power in the circulation of money and commodities. Until Wittgenstein's phrase "what looks as if it *had* to exist, is part of language" succeeds in reminding us that what looks as if it had no right to exist is often the indeterminate part of language, many working women, men, and children will struggle in vain to signify anything other than the often unsold commodity, labor-power. And capital will continue looking as if it *had* to possess rights, privileges, and immunities, until we stop following its rules and learn to represent ourselves.

CHAPTER SIX

Depreciating Capital's Value

When objectified labor is, in this process, at the same time posited as the worker's non-objectivity, as the objectivity of a "subjectivity" antithetical to the worker, as the property of a will alien to him, then capital is necessarily at the same time the capitalist, and the idea held by some socialists that we need capital but not the capitalists is altogether wrong.

—Karl Marx, *Grundrisse*

The work just completed stands midway in an argument on representation and production, which begins with the problem of staging capital's emergence in discourse: how can such an obvious object, money, become a subject? Chapter 4 presented this problem by setting aside the labor theory of value in favor of Diane Elson's value theory of Labor. Chapter 5 showed how one might supplement the subject-object paradigm Elson presupposes by adding a category of the abject to arrive at a theory of Labor's value. Because it seeks to supplement rather than reject the value theory of labor, the theory of Labor's value does not pretend to bypass debates concerning the primacy of class. But its concern for the abject serves as a constant reminder not to dissociate the problem of Labor's disappearance (Part 1) from the problem of capital's emergence (Part 2). The theory of Labor's value must address capital's subjectivity without detracting from Labor's indeterminate status.

Although it completes my consideration of representation and production, this chapter stands midway on the value dimension of *Class Action*. Whereas Part 1, and especially Chapter 3, appreciated Labor's deflated subjectivity, my task here is to depreciate capital's inflated "ego." Placing Labor well within reach (though underground) and catching capital in the act of masquerading as a subject (of enunciation) prepares us for the problem of practicing class action, addressed in Part 3.

The salvaged framework of desire's indeterminacy raises the possibility of a silence in the Lacanian "real," a silence denied access to the channels of signification and thereby unable to assume a position as subject of enunciation. The theory of Labor's value develops this by providing a supplemental context within which to view Marx's dialectical relation between categories without embracing the implicit teleological vision of a totality. Marx's method of presentation relies so effectively on subject-object dialectics—for example, the mutually dependent and mutually contradictory relation of the poles of relative and equivalent value—that readers may too easily dismiss properties of Labor still locked in its reserve banks as useless or nonproductive instead of the unexpended, undiscovered, sometimes unimagined uses of things. Using materials we have already covered on the structure of Labor's relation to value to set aside the labor theory of value, I read the transubstantiation (*Verwandlung*) of money into capital in *Capital I* for signs of excess not currently valorized (*verwertheten*). The value theory of Labor encourages reading the circulation of money and commodities as a value theory, which calls our attention to the story Marx tells of self-valorizing value. Such a reading sets the stage for my supplemental reading of value which amplifies the excesses in Marx's inspirational analysis without turning its back on his commitment to Labor.

Marx's Formula for Capital

Marx opens chapter 4 of *Capital I* with a reminder that the starting point of capital is the circulation of commodities, defined as the "exchange of the various use-values." Concentrating on economic forms, and abstracting from the material substance of the exchange, he identifies money as the "ultimate product" of such circulation and thus "the first form of appearance [*Erscheinungsform*] of capital." He elaborates: "All new capital . . . steps onto the stage . . . in the shape of money, money which has to be transformed into capital by definite [*bestimmte*, or determinate] processes" (Marx, 1976a:247; 1989:163).

So we are beginning this representation with money as the object of a money owner. We will end it with capital assuming the role of all-powerful subject. My focus requires paying close attention to how Marx stages capital's subjectivity. Marx tells us that money that becomes capital differs from mere money in its "form of circulation." But how can a mere difference in form yield such a significant transformation? This he sets out to explain.

Mere money's circuit (C-M-C) sells commodities in order to buy other commodities; capital's circuit (M-C-M) buys in order to sell. Marx describes the latter circuit as consisting of two antithetical phases: M-C and C-M. Mere money's circuit consists of the same phases; indeed this is in large part what they have in common. In both forms of circulation M-C signifies a purchase, C-M a sale. Marx explains that "both paths can be divided into the same two antithetical phases, C-M, a sale, and M-C, a purchase. In each phase the same material elements confront each other, namely, a commodity and money, and economical dramatis personae, a buyer and a seller" (1976a:248–49). At this point Marx allows for various arrangements of subjects and objects. Some buyers use money to buy use-values; some sellers sell the commodities they have on hand; others both buy and sell. Through their activities each circuit (C-M . . . M-C, as well as M-C . . . C-M) constitutes the unity of the same two antithetical phases. But the C-M/M-C antithesis is not what interests us most here. We need to detect the difference between the two circuits.

Marx notes here an inversion: whereas C-M-C begins with a sale (C-M) and ends with a purchase (M-C), M-C-M operates the other way around. C-M-C in the end converts money into a commodity that serves as a use-value. Period. M-C-M, on the other hand, converts money into money. Endlessly. "The money therefore is not spent, it is merely advanced." Marx explicitly connects this dual circuitry to the bifurcated aim of use-value and exchange-value:

> The path C-M-C proceeds from the extreme constituted by one commodity, and ends with the extreme constituted by another, which falls [*anheimfällt*, or devolves] out of circulation and into consumption. Consumption, the satisfaction of needs, in short use-value, is therefore its final goal (*Endzweck*). The path M-C-M, however, proceeds from the extreme of money and finally returns to that same extreme. Its driving and motivating force [*treibendes Motiv*], its determining purpose [*bestimmender Zweck*] is therefore exchange-value. (1976a:250; 1989:166)

Note the distinction between the sphere of circulation and devolving out of that sphere into consumption. By establishing the general formula for capital, which he will rely upon to map the discursive terrain of political economy, Marx sets its twin goals on conflicting courses.

Because use-value vanishes when converted to its money form, the second circuit appears pointless: why bother converting money into money? What could be the point of spinning gold into gold? The rationale for advancing money (M-C), of course, is to make more money (C-M and then some). Owners of money do not necessarily "advance" money; owners of commodities do not necessarily buy with anything other than use-value in mind; but those who call themselves "capitalists" are owners of money who buy and sell with the intention of making more money. When all goes well, "More money is finally withdrawn from circulation than was thrown into it at the beginning" (Marx, 1976a:251). Marx at this point revises the exchange-value circuit to M-C-M', where M' = M + ΔM. The delta marks the excess, or surplus value. He elaborates in the language of valorization: "This increment or excess over the original value I call 'surplus-value.' The value originally advanced, therefore, not only remains intact while in circulation, but increases its magnitude, adds to itself a surplus-value, or is valorized (*verwertet sich*). And this movement converts it into capital" (1976a:251–52). Creating surplus value is the determining purpose of the second path. We are in the process of explaining how this happens.

Just as there is no point to M-C-M if the values of M remain equivalent, so there is no point to C-M-C if their values do not remain equivalent. Although these formulae are designed to capture the movement, there will, of course, be deviations. During C-M-C, I might be taken in by a wily merchant; during M-C-M an investor might be taken to the cleaners in a bad investment; but the ways in which C-M-C pursues use-value and M-C-M does the money thing remain the same in principle. The value of the second C is supposed to equal the value of the first C in C-M-C; the value of the second M is supposed to exceed the value of the first M in M-C-M.

Although it makes sense—because the ideal involves equivalent exchange—to end C-M-C when demand is supplied or the goal is achieved, there is never any end to M-C-M because the goal is limitless; the end point is supposed to expand infinitely. "The movement of capital is . . . limitless [*maßlos*]" (1976a:253; 1989:168). At this point Marx introduces the possibility of an actual person acting as the conscious bearer (*Träger*) of the circulation of capital. Although he describes a person who owns money and participates in M-C-M' as self-consciously representing capital, Marx is somewhat ambiguous about this "person": "His person, or rather his pocket, is the point from which the money starts, and to which it returns." As we will soon see, this ambiguity provides the best context for interpreting Marx when he describes a capitalist as "capital personified and endowed with consciousness and a will" (254). Anticapitalist struggle must contest this incorporation of personhood all the way down to the positions assumed in dominant discursive fields.

Use-values, the goal of C-M-C, can therefore never be mistaken for the goal of any person whose pockets serve as capital's points of arrival and departure. Capital pursues M' relentlessly. One need only contrast investment strategy with grocery shopping; the former is never finished and ought not concern itself with taste or nutrition. "The ceaseless augmentation of [exchange-] value . . . is achieved . . . by means of throwing . . . money again and again into circulation" (1976a: 254–55). Because the section of *Capital I* we are reading is stalking the secret of capital, Marx's chapter 4 allows the path intent upon exchange-value to eclipse the path whose aim is use-value. By the end we arrive at a formula for capital, M-C-M', within which the money element of the M-C pole unites with the money element of the antithetical C-M pole. Indeed commodities become the object of value itself instead of acting as the object of the money owner.

As Marx's chapter 4 draws to a close, the concept of value has assumed a major force in the claim. Marx describes this strange transformation of priorities in rather strange language. The original father divides itself from a son whose presence transforms the pair into a ghostly subject, capital. Marx begins the story by explaining that "in simple circulation [C-M-C], the value of commodities attained at the most a form independent of their use-values, i.e. the form of money. But now, in the circulation M-C-M, value *suddenly presents itself as an self-moving substance* [*bewegende Substanz*] which passes through a process of its own, and for which commodities and money are both *mere forms*" (1976a:256; 1989:170, emphasis added).

A full appreciation of the mutiny we are about to witness requires recollecting our fourfold approach to Labor from Chapter 4. Abstract Labor requires both useful things and exchange-value to make itself manifest in the world. Value represents the quantitative dimension of Labor at the highest level of abstraction. Marx tells us here that in use-value's circuit (C-M-C) money plays the role of equivalent form between qualitatively different commodities. No mutiny here; Labor's qualitative side—utility—is made manifest in useful things exchanged for one another. But over in exchange-value's circuit (M-C-M), value begins to stop representing abstract Labor and to start acting in its own interest (sometimes as money; sometimes as commodities). In other words, exchange-value becomes an end in itself instead of a means of representing Labor's life-giving force. Marx elaborates:

> Instead of simply representing [*darzustellen*] the relations of commodities, it [value] now enters *into a private relationship with itself*, as it were. It differentiates itself as original value from itself as surplus-value; as God the Father differentiates himself from himself as God the Son, although both are the same age and form, in fact one single person; for only by the surplus value of £10 does the £100 originally advanced become capital, and so soon as this has happened, *as soon as the son has been*

created, and through the son, the father, their difference vanishes again, and they again become one, £110. (1976a:256; 1989:170, emphasis added)

Capital is presented here, then, as value in the process of exchange, which results in money in process. Being mindful of the mutiny prepares us to see capital as misrepresenting abstract Labor's quantitative dimension.

Marx immediately distinguishes three kinds of M-C-M' arrangements involving capital, to which he will return later. First, the formula M-C-M' represents merchants who buy at wholesale and sell at retail. Second, the formula M-C-M' represents money lenders who buy money, add interest, and sell money—skipping C in the process. Finally, industrialists, who buy qualitatively different use-values and combine them outside the sphere of circulation to produce commodities of greater value, are covered by the formula. This arrangement, of course, is the only one that adds labor-power as a commodity; but we have yet to learn the special properties of labor-power. Of the three kinds of capital, only industrialists' capital concerns what goes on outside the sphere of circulation. Money lenders stay inside at all times counting their money; and merchants are also always in the sphere of exchange trying to work it in their favor or stay in business, but industrialists must leave to facilitate their various combinations of commodities. Marx wishes to explain how leaving the sphere of circulation works. He is quite mindful, then, of the fact that the formula contains intervals. In fact in *Capital II* he marks these intervals with ellipsis dots. In the chapter we are reading Marx is content to say that "events which take place outside the sphere of circulation, in the interval [*Zwischen*] between the buying and selling, do not affect the form of this movement" (1976a:256; 1989:171).

Chapter 4 of *Capital I* opens, then, by comparing and contrasting two different circuits composed of identical parts. Before our eyes Marx creates the possibility of actual people personifying capital (the name for a ghostly fusion of money advanced and surplus pocketed). We sense that most people, however, buy and sell commodities in a struggle merely to survive. And this struggle—meeting subsistence needs—takes place in the intervals outside the circulation of money and commodities altogether. We have not yet seen the correspondence between actual people and the roles or subject positions available in Marx's representation of bourgeois society.

Nor have we yet ascertained when and how capital grows and at whose expense. We get some inkling that merchants are parasitic (why does everyone not buy wholesale?) and that money lenders who charge interest are worse than parasites (scotching the C in M-C-M'). But industrialists

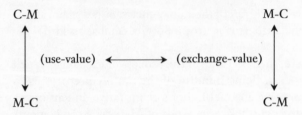

Chart 5. Value's Double Dialectic

create value in ways we cannot yet understand from this chapter. This chapter only sets the stage for the eventual transformation of money into capital. The general formula for capital is M-C-M'. On the exchange side of the dialectic between use-value and exchange-value, the opposite poles M-C and C-M' find a certain patriarchal unity when the son (the surplus in M') begets the father (the original value or the M in M-C) as capital by transforming his money into capital before they join one another indistinguishably. A mapping of these twin circuits accentuates the double dialectic (see Chart 5). With the terrain thus mapped, we can now seek contradictions in the formula on the way to discovering the secret to the transformation of money into capital.

In his fifth chapter, to which we now turn, Marx asks how "this purely formal distinction [can] change the nature of these processes, as if by magic?" (1976a:258). There he reminds us of the three different positions in business transactions: owners of money buying commodities (shopping at the mall), owners of commodities selling whatever they have (whether behind the fruit stand in the market or in the lines at temp services), and owners of capital (on Wall Street) buying and selling in an endless pursuit of a surplus. Unless we unlock the mystery of "the valorization of the values" entering into circulation (259), the third person, the owner of capital, will appear superfluous. Inverting the use-value relation between buying and selling makes little sense. It makes no sense to "start" with a purchase (M-C) because that must merely presuppose an earlier sale (C-M), does it not? But this would not account for the father-son dyad in the transformation of capital. When capital makes its "advances," it does not operate as a mere owner of money shopping for use-values, as if for groceries or back-to-school clothes. But how can we make sense of inverting the order of the use-value circuit C-M-C in such an antithetical pursuit of exchange-value?

Zone of activity

		Inside circulation	Outside circulation
Type of circuit	Exchange-value (M-C-M')	1. Buying, selling	2. Capital consumes commodities
	Use-value (C-M-C)	3. Selling, buying	4. People consume commodities

Chart 6. Economic Zone by Type of Circuit

Contradictions in the Formula

The structure of Marx's fifth chapter addresses this question by working through four distinctions, two of which have already been introduced. We have seen the distinction between the circuits of use- and exchange-value. And we have seen the distinction between the interval (outside circulation) and inside. This allows us to form the typology of economic zones shown in Chart 6. The following transactions are examples of the four zones. Zone 1: capital investment seeks a dividend but only breaks even. Zone 2: a business venture employs half the population of a small town. Zone 3: a worker buys groceries on payday. Zone 4: adults struggle to raise the children in their care. Here Marx poses the following problem: surplus value cannot be generated within the sphere of circulation (zones 1 or 3), nor can it be generated outside the sphere (zones 2 or 4).

To eliminate zones 1 and 3 as possibilities, he introduces two new distinctions: exchange of equivalents and nonequivalents and within the exchange of nonequivalents, situations that permit retaliation (recovering the loss from somewhere else) and those that do not. By eliminating all possibilities in zones 4, 3, 2, and 1, Marx sets the stage for a contradictory moment (where use-value meets exchange-value in zone 2) during which capital is subjectified and Labor becomes objectified as labor-power.

Marx (1976a:259; 1989:172) begins by taking "the process of circulation in a form in which it presents [*darstellt*] itself to us as the exchange of commodities pure and simple." When farmers A and B exchange wine and corn, under the informal circuit of C-C (wine for corn)—or, to be distinct and formal about it, C-M-C (in those cases in which money changes hands)—there is a gain in the sense that there is both corn and wine for both farmers. Life prospects glisten; we now have wine with dinner. But in terms of exchange-value there is no overall gain or surplus created. "All that happens in exchange (if we leave aside the replacing of one use-value by another) is a metamorphosis, a mere change in the form of the commodity" (260). Both farmers can engage in such circuits as C-C or C-M-C, but swapping wine for corn does not create more money than either started with.

The basis of the claim we are considering contrasts the circuitry of use- and exchange-value. Indeed Marx (1976a:261; 1989:176) concludes that "behind all attempts to represent [*darzustellen*] the circulation of commodities as a source of surplus value, there lurks an inadvertent substitution, a confusion of use-value and exchange-value." The gain that bourgeois economists attribute to circulation is a gain in use-value only. One case of wine is still worth four bushels of corn; both farmers end up with the same amount of exchange-value they started with. As we have seen, "in its normal form the circulation of commodities demands the exchange of equivalents." Thus, when exchanges are equivalent they cannot produce added value. To say otherwise confuses conflicting ideas about what is useful (one person's weeds may be another person's food supply) with the exchange-value of the commodities in question (what the vegetation is worth on the market).

But Marx is quite willing to entertain the exchange of nonequivalents, as an exception to the norm in the C-M-C circuit. He considers both the case of selling over value and under value. This move brings him around to the M-C-M circuit's interest in growth; does the pursuit of nonequivalence yield an increase in exchange-value? Here even if A rips off B in an uneven exchange, A must go out again and risk being ripped off by C, and B is free to recover the loss by sandbagging D. Marx's presentation requires all players to operate both inside and outside the circulation of commodities and money.

But Marx is quite willing to acknowledge individual differences between the players; we are not all generic owners of money or commodities. After insisting that all people involved respect both buying and selling, he allows for these differences: "Let us therefore keep within the limits of the exchange of commodities, where sellers are buyers, and buyers are sellers. Our perplexity may perhaps have arisen from conceiving people merely as personified categories, instead of as individuals" (1976a:265). It is still possible, then, for some highly unprincipled or resourceful individual A to take advantage of fellow individuals B or C in ways that disallow their retaliation. I might, for example, make a killing selling my house and then turn around and trick some other lost soul into nearly giving his to me. But even this windfall does not create a surplus, it only redistributes existing wealth. I get richer, and those who are gullible (with less of Locke's rationality and industriousness) get what they deserve. Circulation begets no value.

So how does the surplus value, the son, conjoin with original value, the father, in the formation of capital? Marx is now completely focused on the M-C-M′ circuit. Recall that Marx has just laid out three forms of this circuit: merchants, money lenders, and industrial capitalists. We now see why the first two forms of M-C-M′ must be eliminated as possibilities: buying junk and selling it as antiques, for example, produces no increase of actual value in society; for a similar example, lending money and charging interest yields no net gain for anyone but the lender. In each case the lender or merchant may get rich, but the overall amount of value remains constant in this zero-sum game. For every player enriched, one can find another player impoverished. Furthermore, neither form is exclusive to bourgeois society; there have always been merchants and usurers. We must ascertain why Marx casts industrial capital as a different kind of undertaking.

As it pertains to industrial capitalism, the M-C-M′ faces the following dilemma: "We have shown that surplus-value cannot arise from circulation, and therefore that, for it to be formed, something must take place in the background which is not visible in the circulation itself. But can surplus-value originate anywhere else than in circulation, *which is the sum total of all mutual relations of commodity-owners?* Outside circulation, the commodity-owner only stands in a relation with his own commodity" (Marx, 1976a:268, emphasis added). It is quite possible to increase value outside of the sphere of circulation. Making leather into boots creates a more valuable product (by definition because value expresses added labor-time). "The commodity-owner can create value by [the expenditure of] his labour, but he cannot create values which can valorize themselves" (268). Unlike the retirement annuity of a tenured professor enjoying a "robust economy," boots do not grow while one is sleeping. Something else must explain how an original value (the father) can distinguish itself from a surplus (the son) and complete the trinity as value valorizing itself: capital.

We have now exhausted all possibilities. Activity between the players within the sphere of circulation produces no value; activity outside the sphere produces value, but not a self-valorizing kind that resembles capital. Respecting the Hegelian subject-object model he is using, Marx concludes that if one cannot explain the birth of Mr. Capital either inside or outside the flow of money and commodities, "it [capital] must have its origin both in circulation and not in circulation" (1976a:268). We are, then, tracing an argument based on a dialectical model with use- and exchange-value positioned as subject versus object, a model complete with intervals, or zones outside the sphere of circulation, governed by this opposition. Following the theory of Labor's value will soon permit relocating this dialectical presentation, with its teleological implications, in a scene of writing with ruined limits.

As we prepare for chapter 6 of *Capital*, then, we must keep track of two circuits of exchange: one is bent on survival, the other pursues the growth of money as an end in itself. These opposite goals require each other. If separated from the means of subsistence, people must sell whatever they have to find sufficient use-values to sustain life; and capital must constantly circulate to continue its growth patterns. In mutual antagonism and mutual dependence, owners of money (who buy in order to sell) and owners of commodities (who sell in order to buy) relate to each other in ways that yield a surplus—ways that are as yet indeterminate. With the structure of chapter 5 clearly in mind, especially the tension between what transpires within the sphere of circulation (zones 1 and 3) and what happens outside it (zones 2 and 4), we can continue our exploration of the dialectic between the twin circuits, C-M-C and M-C-M. Juxtaposing these oppositions highlights the extent to which the perspective of owners of money differs from the perspective of owners of commodities when they enter into negotiations concerning that "special commodity," labor-power.

The Buying and Selling of Labor-Power

Chapter 6 of *Capital I* opens with a process of elimination that serves to summarize the claims of the two preceding chapters. First, the change in value—from money to capital—we have been stalking cannot take place in the money itself because money is, by definition, value petrified, the metamorphosed shape of commodities. Second, the change in value cannot originate in the second act of circulation (C-M) of the general formula of capital—that inverted pursuit of value one sometimes calls exchange-value—because that act "does no more than transform the article from its (qualitative) bodily form back into its (quantitative) money-form." This leaves (on the strength of the general formula) the commodity element of the first act, M-C, but only as it is consumed by capital in zone 2. Something must happen during the consumption of commodities—"outside" the circulation of commodities and money—to account for the transmogrification of value, the process in which original value separates from the value advanced, only to return as that swollen value named "capital."

Marx opens, then, with the only possible source of expansion of wealth (as opposed to zero-sum thieving and cheating) lying in the consumption of commodities purchased during the initial M-C phase of M-C-M. The interval between money advanced for commodities and changing the bodily (relative) form back into its money (equivalent) form is now the key consideration. Divulging the secret will take us both inside (zone 1) and outside (zone 2) the sphere of circulation. And along the way we must learn how the area outside of capital's consumption of commodities (zone 2) differs from the human consumption of commodities (zone 4). "In order to extract value out of the consumption of a commodity," Marx writes, "our friend the money-owner must be lucky enough to find within the sphere of circulation, on the market, a commodity . . . whose actual consumption is . . . itself an objectification of labour, hence a creation of value." The peculiar commodity is, of course, labor-power—"the aggregate of those mental and physical capabilities existing in the physical form, the living personality, of . . . human being[s], capabilities which . . . [they expend whenever producing] a use-value of any kind" (Marx, 1976a:270). We have seen all along that the expenditure of labor-power is tantamount to creation of value; now this expenditure is linked to capital's consumption.

Whereas the production of use-values bearing value requires labor-power; the expenditure of labor-power is not limited to production of use-values bearing value. And use-values need not, of course, become commodities (designed for exchange-value) if they are never transferred in an exchange. But most crucial for us at this juncture is the reason Marx gives for this "peculiar commodity" being the one whose consumption is synonymous with creation. Marx connects Labor and value in the passage just cited by stating both that capital's consumption of labor-power is equivalent to the objectification of Labor and that the objectification of Labor is tantamount to the creation of value. Labor creates value in the sense that Labor (being in possession of labor-power) is expressed by a value that lies immanent in commodities until represented by exchange-value. But despite this actual relationship, Labor is cut out of the picture when value begins to valorize itself.

As Marx promised earlier, capital's secret lies both inside and outside the circulation of money and commodities. In addition to the twin circuits of circulation—use-value and exchange-value—we must account for the twin zones inside and outside circulation. People in zone 3 who sell their labor-power to buyers in zone 1 can expect to have it consumed in zone 2 before receiving money to buy the commodities they consume in zone 4. Anyone buying commodities in the M-C-M circuit consumes them with exchange-value as a goal (will I get richer?); in the C-M-C circuit use-value is the goal (will I get dinner?). Marx moves into zone 2 and designates labor-power as the "special commodity" whose consumption objectifies Labor and thereby creates value. Zone 4 lies outside the purview of this discussion. Assessing the consequences of leaving zone 4 out of the picture requires studying the conditions under which labor-power is commodified in this presentation. What happens to the subject-object relation between Labor and its object, labor-power? If labor-power is, in fact, so special, what keeps Labor from using it? Why not keep this capacity in the family, so to speak, and pocket the surplus it creates?

Marx lists several conditions here that must be met "in order that our owner of money may be able to find labour-power offered for sale as a commodity." These conditions help to define the economic position of the majority of the members of bourgeois society. The first condition, freedom of person, regards all persons as the "free proprietor[s]" of their "labour-capacity" (1976a:271). The second condition approaches labor-power as the commodity of last resort, by stating that "instead of being able to sell commodities" in which Labor has already been objectified (for example, the boots made during one's leisure time), persons are "compelled to offer for sale as a commodity that very labour-power, *which exists only in . . .* [the] *living body*" (emphasis added). No one selling labor-power has figured out how to get the special goose to lay those golden eggs. Labor seems not to have the golden touch.

Marx (1976a:272–73; 1989:185) summarizes these two conditions by reminding us that to bring about the "transformation [*Verwandlung*, or transubstantiation] of money into capital," owners of money must find owners of labor-power who are free in a double sense: first, these owners can dispose of their labor-power as their own commodity and, second, these owners are not tied down by the objects needed for the realization (*Verwirklichung*, or materialization) of their labor-power. Separated from their object, labor-power, these owners are forced into the sphere of circulating money and commodities to work in the name of survival. The labor-power one possesses must be effectively "liberated" from the state of being in possession of labor-power (Labor).

Merely possessing labor-power, the capacity for drawing upon Labor's reserves, carries no guarantee of survival. One needs means of production to produce anything; and one's "living self" requires access to the means of subsistence. Because this unusual commodity needs to be combined with others, in production, and also needs to consume other commodities to survive, labor-power is forced into the market as a commodity. But being forced into the labor-power market does not guarantee finding buyers. Many people who are obliged to sell labor-power cannot find buyers; sheer survival becomes a prime consideration. Hence the violence of bourgeois society. In an aside, reminding us that his entire discussion is located within a relation between exchange- and use-value, Marx points out that there is no basis in nature for the opposite goals of the M-C-M and C-M-C circuits. That one cycle is hell-bent on exchange-value while the other struggles merely to survive (maintain use-values) "is clearly the result of a past historical development" (1976a:273). In fact Marx takes this opportunity to remind us that his entire framework—including the use-exchange distinction—bears a "historical imprint [*Spur,* or trace, sign]" (273; 185). Capital can "spring into life [*entstehen,* or find determinate form]," *only* when the "owner of the means of production and subsistence [*Lebensmitteln,* or nourishing life] finds the free worker available, on the market, as the seller of his own labour-power" (274; 186). Capital—the subject that kills by remote control—is a revolutionarily new, life-threatening hegemonic force. But we have yet to learn the secret of its subjectivity.

Marx next attempts to calculate the value of labor-power as a commodity; we are quite well prepared to read by now that "the value of labour-power is determined [*bestimmt*] . . . by the labour-time necessary for the production, and consequently also the reproduction, of this specific article" (1976a:274; 1989:186). We have already seen that for the labor theory of value a quantitative amount of labor-time predicts what Labor is worth. On the other hand the value theory of labor approaches value as the quantitative aspect of Labor (as opposed to the more qualitative "utility"), which, if exchanged for a wage, is value made manifest. In the value theory of labor, in other words, exchange-value represents value, the quantitative aspect of form-giving Labor. Our theory of Labor's value finds the latter approach quite instructive, but I seek to belabor its distinction between use- and exchange-value by taking another look at value's mutinous self-valorization.

Following the value theory of Labor, we can view the wage as the external measure of labor-time's value lying immanent within the commodity labor-power, which itself makes manifest the qualitative side of abstract Labor by being a useful thing. The price of labor-power, the wage, may fluctuate above or below its value. This accounting builds upon the common sense observation that "the owner of labour-power is mortal" (1976a:275). The owner of labor-power must receive enough in compensation to continue life by repeating the C-M-C circuit. Recall that the second condition of free Labor states that the owner of labor-power is obliged to work for wages. Paying owners of labor-power less than they need to complete the C-M-C circuit would be like starving the goose that lays the golden eggs before it can reproduce goslings. In other words labor-power, once sold, must maintain sufficient access to the means of nourishing life.

So when Marx determines (*bestimmten*, or calculates) the average quantity of the means of subsistence necessary for the worker and calls this the "value of labour-power" (1976a:276), he is operating at the highest level of abstraction, not at the phenomenal level of wages. Fresh supplies of labor-power must be available for M-C-M and this requires sufficient compensation for people to repeat the C-M-C circuit. Owners of money can then buy labor-power at its value—the amount necessary for subsistence—can consume it (put it to work outside the sphere of circulation) in whatever ways yield the most exchange-value, and thereby squeeze out a surplus. Marx is careful to defend the Labor/labor-power distinction he needs to continue staging the story of capital's predication as subject. Insisting on keeping clearly in view the people passed over by capital's hiring decisions, Marx points out that "when we speak of capacity for labour, we do not speak of labour, any more than we speak of digestion when we speak of capacity for digestion. As is well known, the latter process requires something more than a good stomach" (277). The question is whether this subject-object analysis (Labor/labor-power) abstracts away from the actual means of subsistence (for example, bread and potatoes).

In answering this charge Marx points out that when people are separated from the means of subsistence (when, for example, they leave a small farm to work for wages in the city) they must sell the only commodity they have left or face extinction. Rather than abstracting away from subsistence, his representation of Labor—qualitative work versus quantitative labor-power—offers an objective understanding of what survival requires. Marx acknowledges here that labor-power must find a buyer if its owners are to derive any benefit whatsoever. Work for its own sake is, for the capitalist, irrelevant. And yet the danger of need persists regardless of the C-M-C circuit. In Marx's representation people learn, following Sismondi, that "the capacity for labour [-power] . . . is nothing unless it is sold" (1976a:277). Capital's one-dimensional pursuit of exchange-value seeks fresh labor-power, totally disregarding the supply that exceeds its demands. Marx's representation of the workings of capital leaves room for the excess (as surplus population); but we must work hard to keep this in mind because this excess (Hegel's "rabble") cannot be contained by the subject-object model he is using. A major obstacle to noticing the "danger of need" in the "Garden of Eden," when following the circuitry of C-M-C or M-C-M, is the myth of self-valorization. Recall that when value enters into relations with itself, a father, son, and ghostly presence come together; money that has been advanced and surplus that has been squeezed from commodified labor-power are transubstantiated into the form we call "capital." We must remember that this story of self-valorization leaves out Labor, even as we consider Marx's analysis of capital's consumption of labor-power.

Marx points out what has certainly been my experience, namely, that custom allows the buyer to consume labor-power first and pay for it later (for example, at the end of the work week). Even after waiting for a buyer, owners of labor-power advance owners of money their special commodity and wait again to be paid. In this way Labor "everywhere gives credit to the capitalist." Under the influence of capital, value, the quantitative aspect of the real subject (Labor), takes on a life of its own (enters into relations with itself consuming use-values in the name of exchange-value) and divides and subdivides in an endless pursuit of gain, regardless of the lives of any of the bodies in question.

We have now arrived at the solution to the problem of staging capital's subjectivity. Marx gathers his threads in the following way:

> We now know the manner of determining [*Bestimmung*] the value paid by the owner of money to the owner of this peculiar commodity, labour-power. The use-value which the former gets in exchange manifests itself only in the actual utilization, in the process of the consumption of labour-power. The money-owner buys everything necessary for this purpose, such as raw material, in the market, and pays the full price for it. *The process of the consumption of labour-power is at the same time the production process of commodities and of surplus value.* (1976a:279; 1989:190–91, emphasis added)

Just as value enters into relations with itself and just as labor-power reproduces itself by getting enough money to return for more squeezing, two men (one owning money, the other labor-power) go behind a door marked "No admittance except on business" and emerge at the end of this famous chapter as one big man and one little man. Whereas the big man is free to take his money and run to the next venture, the little man is free to be forced back into the market each time he runs out of money. This, then, is the sense in which the secret of capital lies neither within nor without the sphere of circulation; the production process imports the opposite goals of greed and survival, assuring us that workers' interests must collide with capital's.

Production (of surplus value) is the name of capital's game. Human consumption of commodities (zone 4) is relevant in this representation only insofar as it intersects with the processes of distribution and exchange to yield fresh supplies of labor-power, along with other commodities, for sale. From capital's perspective, "free" workers with no job prospects, or no inclination to travel to zone 2, are nothing at all; they are, practically speaking, invisible. As if by remote control, capital marks these brothers and sisters for extinction. We have seen that Žižek notes the presence of a Hegelian "oppositional determination" in Marx's method; production participates in its own determination. Production is at once the arena within which use-value and exchange-value find relief, and one of the moments contributing to the relief effort. In other words, capital's hegemony—as "the power ruling over everything"—permits its production to "color" consumption, exchange, distribution, and, yes, production. Production participates in its own design in its "abode," where capital consumes use-values with the sole goal of exchange-value, an activity that places it on a collision course with those who enter that abode with the antithetical goal of use-value. But we must resist reinscribing theoretically the practical limitations of a bourgeois reality that separates the danger of need from demand and supply in the marketplace.

Surplus value is finally explained by Marx as an operation both inside and outside the circulation of commodities and money. The emphasis we have seen on money's self-valorization and labor-power's reproduction costs, although undeniably relevant to any "bottom line" in bourgeois society, elides the subjectivity of Labor even as it depends upon it. The use-value/exchange-value dialectic maps only those aspects of life crucial to *capital*'s development. The C-M-C pole drives Labor into the market as the expenditure of labor-power, that peculiar commodity. The M-C-M pole drives capital into the market as money advanced. But we have seen that Marx's argument works more like a process of elimination than an outright declaration of exploitation. His work exposes the one-dimensional interest behind capital's mutinous self-valorization, but it leaves the political possibilities surrounding a return of Labor to the class struggle of actual people. And this raises the problem of representation. Labor's only possible access to discursive positions in bourgeois society requires putting its object up for consumption, submitting labor-power to the control of a foreign presence, capital. Labor is objectified by capital at precisely the moment it attempts to speak; the price of Labor's access to the means of subsistence is lack of access to the means of representation. Any subject of enunciation requires positioning in the relevant discursive field; but the rules of engagement eliminate some subjects and objects from the start. And yet eliminating Labor as a subject of enunciation does not eliminate the real needs it would represent. The secret of profit lies in the dialectical interplay of the twin poles of value, but the actual people involved may have secrets of our own.

This is the sense, then, in which Labor is rendered indeterminate by virtue of its access to the capitalist system: Labor is objectified whenever capital devours its labor-power. Although Labor cannot speak, it is nevertheless always at hand and continues to lie immanent in the value of all commodities produced and consumed. Every worker knows this. Labor works on silently amidst the danger of need, as the devalued source of all value, in the "Eden of the innate rights of man" (Marx, 1976a:280). When approached from the perspective of a theory of Labor's value, then, capital appears to have invaded the territory of Labor's subjectivity for the explicit purpose of extracting our labor-power, and now it devours our life energies in ways that consolidate its axiomatic control. Imagine looking in the Lacanian mirror and seeing a machinic unity of others' body parts that includes your brain and muscles. The Deleuzean nightmare continues when the mirror image, speaking for you in something close to what might be called your voice, says, "I'm going to be late for work."

Our stake in capital's masquerade renders our subjectivity as Labor indeterminate. Those wholly under capital's spell rarely regard themselves as Labor at all; those striving for capital's approval discipline themselves with good credit histories and are sometimes fully prepared to punish others for noncompliance; those struggling for autonomy as capital's employees negotiate in good faith, sometimes making gains in one geographical territory while capital regains its composure through increased exploitation elsewhere. But we must never forget people with a minimal stake in capital's masquerade. This raises possibilities, explored below in Part 3, of building strategies for class action in abject areas of life, most of which have been redlined by capital's advisors, areas one might call the Labor underground.

Recalling the Labor Underground

We are now prepared to revisit the buying and selling of labor-power (the end of chapter 6 in part 2 of *Capital I*) staged at the beginning of this book. Owners of money and owners of labor-power meet in the market, governed as it is by the tension between the circuits of use-value and exchange-value. That is, both kinds of owners have opposite goals, and yet each is also dependent on the other. Eventually, as this dialectic plays itself out, all other contradictions come down to this mutual antagonism and dependency between labor-power for hire and capital for growth.

The owners of labor-power are objectified by the self-valorizing efforts of money to grow by itself; torn from other alternatives they sell their labor-power and disappear at the moment money becomes capital. Money is now assumed to make the world go round instead of Labor, which continues to do all of the work, as it has throughout history. Given this scenario, Labor can choose only between object and abject status. This explains, for example, why so many people, after years of objectification—"my life is my job"—lose their sense of self-worth when forced by capital into the surplus population marked for extinction. The entire play of equivalence takes on the drama of domination as money is transmogrified into capital, the all-powerful subject.

But after reading this transformation closely, we can see that Marx's staging of this drama does not eliminate the possibility of supplementing the value theory of Labor. Yes, the categories are designed by Marx to draw an orderly whole, which thought puts in place of the chaotic whole that we would otherwise encounter. Yes, Marx's orderly representation does distinguish two dialectically related circuits. Yes, these circuits imply the existence of two classes in bourgeois society, classes-in-themselves. Yes, the working class appears to have become the object of the owning class. Yes, inversions are tempting and appear to ring throughout *Capital*, culminating near the end of the first volume with this:

> One capitalist always strikes down many others. . . . Along with the constant decrease in the number of capitalist magnates . . . the mass of misery, oppression, slavery, degradation and exploitation grows; but with this there also grows the revolt of the working class, a class constantly increasing in numbers, and trained, united and organized by the very mechanism of the capitalist process of production. . . . The centralization of the means of production and the socialization of labour reach a point at which they become incompatible with their capitalist integument. . . . The expropriators are expropriated. (1976a:929)

Yes, Marx's rhetorical flourish casts the working-class subject, Labor's vehicle, as one emerging to find its rightful position. But this reading is radically incomplete.

In *Grundrisse* (1976a:989) Marx tells us that "the capitalist functions only as *personified* capital, capital as a person, just as the worker is no more than labour personified." Such similes are as easily misconstrued by a liberalism seeking an equivalence between subjects as they are exaggerated by a loyalist Marxism dedicated to the struggle between two classes of people in and of themselves. But Marx continues with this description of the situation of the workers who personify the subject Labor: "That labour [-power they expend] is just effort and torment, whereas it belongs to the capitalist as a substance that creates and increases wealth, and in fact it is an element of capital, incorporated into it in the production process as its living, variable component. *Hence the rule of the capitalist over the worker is the rule of things over man* . . . we find . . . the inversion of subject into object and *vice versa*" (1976a:989-90, emphasis added).

The capitalist, by this formulation, becomes a personified object that has been subjectified; the worker is a personified subject who has been objectified. This leads to a nearly impossible situation for any attempted class action: the actual people who might assume enunciatory positions in the real, the needful, have been objectified and cannot speak. Our personification is of an occupied subject who has become, for all of capital's intents and purposes, labor-power. Our identities as women and men, for example, are necessarily estranged from the heterogeneous basis we share in the form-giving fire of Labor.

On the other hand, the subjects that speak on economic issues, from discursive positions reserved for the business class, personify an object that could never assume an enunciatory position in the real. Moneybags mocks Benveniste's distinction, so straightforward in linguistics—"ego is who says ego"—by acting like a subject of the statement ("I will develop the moon") that is completely divorced from any stake as subject of enunciation. It should be clear by now that capital is a phantom subject. The capitalist guards this illusion, sometimes unwittingly; those who forget it is an illusion risk a Machiavellian fall, but those who manipulate it most cynically may well succeed in "developing the moon," establishing new colonies for the well-heeled in outer space, hedging their bets that capital can poison the earth just enough to thin the greedy surplus population, winning either way. The secret is never forgetting that capital, the phantom subject, cares nothing about which capitalists it rewards with money and which it destroys.

How one reads Marx on the subject-object relations between capital and labor-power depends upon one's approach to determinate form. Those still looking for dialectical relief in bifurcated class action continue to look only in the direction of determination. Likewise the gaze of those for whom class is only one of many identifications remains fixed in the direction of determinate subject positions. These are the two most familiar approaches—from pillar to post—I introduced in the first chapter. Such approaches lead one to assume that when owners of money and owners of labor-power enter zone 2 they are either leaving the inside (the sphere of circulation) for the outside (the sphere of production) or moving to a different zone in the discursive field. We have seen that Marx calls this moment of exploitation the "hidden abode of production" (1976a:279). These readings still help organize us workers, as subjects, to protect ourselves, to realize the contradictory goals of our bosses, and to recognize the disciplinary function of the wage-labor system. One might even go so far as to cast labor-power as a subject capable of predicating value, a sort of human capital.

The theory of Labor's value, based as it is on the supplementation of the subject-object relation, takes an approach to indeterminacy that allows one to interpret the hyphens in the formulae without ruling out the time-honored dialectical tension between use- and exchange-value as goals. We have seen how the theory of Labor's value supplements both the elapsing time continuum and its "other," the synchronic field of structural inquiry. What happens during these intervals? We know that labor-power is devoured in zone 2, the site of Labor's objectification. But how is this area related to the human consumption of commodities in zone 4? And if one's approach to indeterminacy includes "extrachronicity," (Corlett, 1993:159) how fixed are the boundaries of this hidden abode?

We have seen that Marx does not insist that stepping momentarily outside of M-C . . . C-M (zone 1), or even outside of C-M . . . M-C (zone 3), is only a move toward production or consumption. The language of oppositional determination is best viewed as a Hegelian vehicle for his scientific representation of bourgeois society, not a self-contained paradigm. Although it is true that consumption of labor-power is designed to be productive, and the consumption of commodities (unless overly toxic) can refresh the labor-power supply, the activities in the intervals of these circuits (zones 2 and 4 above) are introduced by Marx as breaks or interruptions in the circulation of money and commodities. There is no reason, then, not to collapse the distinction between zones 2 and 4. Nona Glazer's research on the "work transfer" allows us to question the boundaries of the sphere of production (zone 2) on our way to examining indeterminate Labor. Although it is tempting to consider fixing breakfast, for example, as an act of consumption and working in a factory as an act of production, Glazer points out that consumers often participate in the production process without ever being hired or paid. Whenever we grind our own coffee, for example, we help capital minimize the cost of wage labor, a principal cost of production. Glazer explains that "the work transfer to consumers means that commercial capitalists hire fewer workers; consumers work in their place and the organization is altered to eliminate some steps in the work process" (Glazer, 1993:146–47). In Marx's formula, M-C-M', then, the C relation is not a straightforward act of capital consuming the commodities it has acquired. In fact, consumers act as direct participants in the M-C-M' circuit, as unpaid labor-power in the interstices (between M-C and C-M'). Unpaid labor-power is a commodity consumed at no charge to the money advanced in the name of profit margins. This raises the possibility of considering consumers as workers directly responsible for creating the social surplus. Before capital takes over consumer society completely, we must locate the Labor underground.

Given what Marx offers in part 2 of *Capital I*, one need only say that life goes on "outside" the sphere of circulation until workers, cut off from subsistence and from ownership of the tools and other means of production they need, are forced back into the market. Giving this "outside" a determinate form—whether a sphere of production or of consumption—leads to such familiar questions as "Who is engaged in C-M-C and who in M-C-M?" and "Who manages to 'get ahead' by doing both?" A dialectical model best represents the bourgeois representation of the workplace. But much more is going on within any interval marked by a "-" than either wage labor or capital can represent. Such an interval resembles a "blind spot of an old dream of [subject-object] symmetry" (Irigaray, 1985:11). Yes, wage labor is in a relation of mutual antagonism and dependence with capital. But the theory of Labor's value can respect this dialectical relation while nevertheless refusing to map out the intervals. Underemployed people, far from being a reserve army out there in the margins, are right in the thick of the struggle for survival. Just as every mother is a working mother, it takes work on everyone's part to survive capitalism (unless one can manage to live comfortably by appropriating surpluses generated by other people).

Because of our work in Part 1, we know we cannot expect Marx to tell us in these chapters where Labor is. Capital is his subject. The society he describes objectifies Labor and subjectifies capital. We have seen that regardless of whether it pays for it, capital grows through the consumption of labor-power, the commodity whose use-value when consumed yields more than is required to replace it. Everything else is extraneous to capital. Marx tells here the story of value's self-valorization, a story designed to explain how a pile of money can become the masterful subject that so many of us take for granted. By insisting upon Labor's presence, the theory of Labor's value questions the subjectivity of capital and seeks out aspects of the text effectively eliminated from discursive formulations such as the chronic dialectic. Recall that Spivak allows for a domestic economy nurtured unwittingly by the polis. Here lies the Labor underground at the heart of the economy, producing all labor-power but denied an enunciatory stance. The hyphens in the subject-object relation indicate an abject space, an aporia, for areas rendered indeterminate. The theory of Labor's value goes back to Labor to sense what might be missing. Here we begin to realize that any story that starts with value giving birth to itself without labor pains is not only disconcertingly familiar in Western thought but necessarily incomplete.

As subjectified capital, ensconced as it is in the bottom line of linear time, continues to devour objectified labor-power in a desperate—no, mad—effort to sustain its "life," those who would organize half-digested, mangled labor-power to rise up against this all-powerful hegemon must be supported. But, taken by itself, the expectation that an expropriated class-in-itself might become a defiant class-for-itself suffers from the limitations of a totalistic paradigm. Hegemonic power often contains a foreign element that it nurtures unwittingly. While capital continues to devour labor-power, there are audible characters (audible to anyone who can hear) rendered indeterminate by virtue of their access. In the aporia of subject-object relations, these invisible subjects can conspire underground within subject-object relations to nurture and raise the subject marked for death, preparing it for an irredentist struggle on behalf of all the brothers and sisters consumed by capital. Denied access to the means of representation, Labor's value lies underground.

The theory of Labor's value reminds us that any story of value's self-valorization is really a story about Labor's value. The devalued zone in which people consume the fruits of the earth—whether expensive commodities or use-values we produce without capital, whether in solitary confinement or together in solidarity and mutual defense—is right under the nose of the phantom subject, capital, who must devour us to protect itself from an irredentist return of the real.

We must, then, read Marx to learn how capital is value stolen from "the people," but we must read him critically to see Labor as a subject of heterogeneous survival who can be neither reduced nor restricted to the various subject and object positions in Marx's discursive repertoire, including the position of "the people." We can now see that in addition to capital smirking in full subjectivity and objectified Labor expecting a tanning, we must valorize the excess: unmentionable bodies, bodies never mentioned, aspects of bodies never mentioned. Not only does the physiognomy of our dramatis personae change before our eyes, the cast expands and a more resonant significance of an anticapitalist politics of différance lies waiting in the wings.

PART THREE

PRODUCTION
AND ACTION

CHAPTER SEVEN

Mobilizing the Labor Underground

The event of political independence can be automatically assumed to stand between colony and decolonization as an unexamined good that operates a reversal. But the political goals of the new nation are supposedly determined by a regulative logic derived from the old colony, with its interest reversed: secularism, democracy, socialism, national identity, and capitalist development. Whatever the fate of this supposition, it must be admitted that there is always a space in the new nation that cannot share in the energy of this reversal. This space has no established agency of traffic with the culture of imperialism. Paradoxically, this space is also outside of organized labor, below the attempted reversals of capital logic.
                              —Gayatri Spivak, *Outside in the Teaching Machine*

When driving at night near his home in upper North Philadelphia with three of his neighbors, two white policemen pulled Mumia Abu-Jamal over for a "routine traffic check" (Abu-Jamal, 1993:195).[1] During the customary frisk, the younger lawman found Abu-Jamal in possession of a little red book (not the *Little Red Song Book* but the *Quotations of Mao Tse-Tung*). Abu-Jamal remembers: "Communists!!! The cop drops the book on cold, wet ground, whips out his .38 revolver, and places it to the skull of the nearest Black man—me" (194).

> My eyes flick to Reg . . . as I search for direction. Hot sweat drips down cold flesh, my underarms watering my sides. Reg looks back with the wisdom of a thousand such street searches—and his dark, slanted eyes shoot upwards, as in "Whatta fuck is this nut trying to prove?" He glances at the other cop, older, heavier, more senior, and cracks up in whinny-ish horse laughter. Tension flows from us all as we erupt in laughter, and the rookie, not knowing the butt of the joke, but beginning to suspect it is himself, steps back a pace, and glances at his elder partner for direction. . . . The elder whispers to the unbearded youth . . . and they depart, in silence. (194–95)

The four men in the car, whom the policemen could not countenance as working for revolutionary change in their own neighborhood, were in fact the defense captain, lieutenant of security, lieutenant of finance, and the lieutenant of information of the Philadelphia chapter of the Black Panther Party. Abu-Jamal's story of a "routine traffic check" illustrates gross disparities in power, in particular "the lack of autonomy at work in Black communities" (195) in the sixties and today. But this story might also remind Marxists seeking to reconfigure the wiring of the labor-capital circuit that "there is always a space in the new nation that cannot share in the energy" of reversing the flow of power (Spivak, 1993:77–78). The people, especially when united, although certainly capable of "fighting back" until annihilated, need not be reduced to an element—the "labor-power" that fights back at "capital"—in a logic of imperialism.

Postponing the question of whether Western liberalism (at the end of the century) relies on wars, disease, poverty, racism, and its other genocidal tendencies to address what Dhoruba Bin Wahad (1993:75) calls the "increasing strain to accommodate the interests of the disenfranchised," I am concerned with the way in which discussions of how to extend the political franchise—what are in polite liberal society called the intersecting oppressions of race, class, sexuality, and gender—lock out Labor without acknowledging that this is what we are doing. We need to work to reconfigure class in ways that are reflected in such common representations of labor-power as militant unions and working-class folk heroes without falling into the trap of confusing objectified Labor with the real subject.

As we have just seen in Part 2, arguing that wealth does not spring from the mere circulation of money and commodities does not entail that the labor-power that capital consumes is the source of all value. Reading Marx's textual representation of bourgeois society (with the gaps and spaces one finds at the scene of writing) allows one to retain his exposé of phantom capital's masquerade without restricting one's vision to determinate forms of objectified Labor. Contesting capital's claim to self-generation from the perspective of the Labor underground draws the boundaries of the economic foundation of bourgeois society into question. Such anticapitalist struggle reconsiders the self-determination of low-income working people (perhaps in an ad hoc alliance with high-income working people, even those of us who call ourselves "theorists," if we can renegotiate recent decades of mutual mistrust and disrespect) regardless of the buying and selling of labor-power. To keep our bearings I begin this Part 3, as I began Chapters 1 and 4, by considering Labor's labor-power. In this chapter I present a problem at the heart of Marxist approaches to self-determination: how can objectified workers act as revolutionary subjects? I explore this problem first by reading texts associated with people who—well aware of the Labor-capital opposition but with different stakes in Labor's movement—offer various forms of self-determination. Then I recall two well-known Marxist approaches (from pillar to post) discussed in Chapter 1. Finally, I suggest how challenging the subject-object paradigm (presumed by these approaches) and acknowledging the abject produces a slightly different formulation of the problem of practicing class action. Chapters 8 and 9 address this problem further.

The Problem of Worker's Self-Activity for Marxism

At a recent Working Class Studies Conference in Youngstown, Ohio, a forceful labor historian portrayed poststructuralism as yet another betrayal of the labor movement. He placed his hope for economic justice in the fact that working people have always held secrets, secrets that in the proper conditions can be divulged in defiant, even revolutionary self-activity. This confidence in the self-activity of working people is reflected in the writings of C. L. R. James (see Grimshaw, 1992) alongside James's rather straightforward appreciation of Marx's labor theory of value. Exploited people are commodified by bourgeois society and can be expected to rise up against their political parties and nation-states, as they did in Hungary in the fifties, Paris in the sixties, and Poland in the eighties (Rawick, 1983:149). Cornelius Castoriadis (1995:285-86) and Cedric Robinson (1983:390-91) are quick to explore the Jamesian contradiction here: if labor-power is the commodity Marx says it is, how can it be said to rise up?

Clearly, working people have many traditions and resources other than those reflected in miserable (or sometimes comfortable) positions in the sphere of production, as analyzed by Marx. In the face of such complexity Castoriadis and Zillah Eisenstein (1990) to question adjectives such as "socialist" or "Marxist," and various feminisms such as Ann Ferguson's (1991) explore new subjectivities. Other responses include Robinson's attempt to place Marx alongside the black radical tradition and the Industrial Workers of the World (Kornbluh, 1988), maintaining the secrecy of their indeterminate, nomadic status as labor-power-and-then-some, in a syndicalism that often disdains party activity and political borders. From the perspectives just cited, poststructuralism among theorists reads like yet another bourgeois fetish in the twilight of capitalism. And yet many contributions loosely tagged "poststructural" can be read as keeping everyday secrets. Direct action and sabotage are, after all, well executed by Foucauldian interstitial subjects, whom Lispector (1989) calls "urgent objects" and whom Spivak would locate in indeterminate spaces with "no established agency." And even for those who contribute deconstructive readings or destabilizing maneuvers while enjoying established agency as academics or intellectuals, there is always room for double agency behind enemy lines.

I want, then, to raise the possibility of a rethinking and a practicing of Marxism from a poststructural perspective that relies on the self-activity of working people, all the while insisting upon a Marxist understanding of capital as the possession of Labor's stolen goods. My reading concerns representations of Labor and the all-too-frequent conflation of Labor and labor-power-the-commodity (consumed and discarded the world over by Mr. Moneybags). Whereas labor-power is indisputably a determinate form, a commodity with a determinate exchange-value, my approach suggests that Labor lies indeterminate, deprived of subjectivity, so long as capital's value and its phantom subjectivity remain uncontested in bourgeois society.[2] Labor's indeterminate value is nevertheless a secret in bourgeois society; sometimes even progressive intellectuals depreciate the very people their progressiveness seeks to appreciate. My work attempts to keep this secret alive by working to make capital an increasingly anxious subject in liberal society. The following stories indicate the range of Labor's possibilities on both sides of the gap between need and demand.

Glimpses of Labor's Movement

I offer glimpses now of African-American radicalism during the sixties and of a mostly white radicalism during the early twentieth century. Although all of these people struggled against capital, not all of them called or considered themselves "Marxist." I begin with Huey Newton, of the original Black Panther Party, a labor party that took Western liberalism at its word that everyone is included in the body politic, in full knowledge of how unlikely this is. Then I move to a different group of armed working people, coal-mining "bootleggers" in Pennsylvania during the thirties, who, despite their intent to reconnect with the means of subsistence, were allowed (in part because of the privilege of white skin) to flourish in the Northeastern United States for nearly a decade. Then, returning to the sixties, I consider James Boggs, of Detroit's League of Revolutionary Black Workers, an activist who confronted racism and unemployment head on. Flashing back again to the early days, I turn to Elizabeth Gurley Flynn, who defends many of the tactics associated with the sometimes secretive, always active, Mollies and Wobblies, predecessors of the Pennsylvania bootleggers. Finally, I turn to the nameless voices of "the Damned," who shared the defiant spirit of the Wobbly but who knew first-hand the difference between "surplus population" and "surplus labor."

"To be political, you must have a political consequence when you do not receive your desires—otherwise you are non-political."

Turning to Huey Newton's discussion of sixties politics in *The Black Panther* (Newton, 1995:45–47), one is struck immediately by the labor agenda of the Black Panther Party. The Panthers were forced sometimes—in the face of the counterinsurgent strategy of some governmental offices—to substitute a militaristic agenda. Newton's article defends armed struggle on the road to economic well-being by reasoning that such development is the logical extension the rights and privileges some of us already enjoy. Newton absolutely insists that everyone can be included in the active citizenry; if we cannot be inclusive, then we need a new container.

Newton opens this essay with a description of war as a politics of disenfranchised people using physical conflict to get what they want when peaceful means have been exhausted. He reminds readers that African Americans during Reconstruction wanted and were promised economic goods (acres and mules) that were never delivered. This economic base (or means of subsistence) could have established a base for political power; but because the promise was denied the base was never constructed. Indeed, according to Newton, the promise of economic goods could easily be denied because, with no economic base, white society would bear no consequences for racist exclusion.

By contrast, white society has a power base and with it peaceful means to get what it wants, or else. This is how Newton describes white politics: "When White people send a representative into the political arena, they have a power force or power base that they represent. When White people, through their representatives, do not get what they want, there is always a political consequence. . . . To be political, you must have a political consequence when you do not receive your desires—otherwise you are non-political" (1995:45–46). So we see where this logic is taking us: Newton pledges, one way or another, to find a base in the realm of political representation for the African-American community. To send representatives with no power to government is "absurd." Newton's solution to the problem is, of course, armed struggle, when that is the only consequence available.

Interestingly, Newton defends armed struggle as the last resort by turning capital's interests against itself: the purpose of arming the community is not killing white people; the purpose is to threaten white people's capacity to make a killing from a racist situation. To correct the existing balance of power, Newton advocates developing a capacity for economic destruction: "We will then negotiate as equals." If we accept the opening premise that war is a continuation of politics by other means, then the rest (in 1969) is as simple as this: "The White racist oppresses Black people not only for racist reasons, but because it is also economically profitable to do so. Black people must develop a [military] power that will make it non-profitable for racists to go on oppressing us" (1995:46). It is significant that Newton also calls this military power "self-defense power"; the dire economic situation is already taking lives with no consequences to the perpetrators. Newton describes bourgeois society as waging a "civil war against Blacks in America."

But regardless of whether white America or African America turns to war first, whether armed black communities are said to escalate or retaliate, the question of economic rights remains untouched by this claim to extend political representation to all citizens. Newton turns near the end of the article to connect economic democracy to the issue of political representation. Here we learn that Newton not only wants a seat at the negotiating table, carrying whatever power might be available (economic or military), but that he views some items as nonnegotiable. Newton insists upon the right to work (with a "high standard of living" if no work is available); "the controllers of the economic system are obligated to furnish each man with a livelihood" (1995:46). And because this is not how Western liberal society works, Newton predicts that "until the people control the land and the means of production, there will be no peace" (47).

And so this essay, which begins by applying liberal principles to all citizens, moves to a description of the status quo as a civil war. The final word concerns the players in the civil war, since so many white people making a killing are unarmed, living in fortified security zones. The armed segment of Western liberalism is, of course—state militias aside—the police force. "The police," says Newton, "should be the people of the community in uniform. There should be no division or conflict of interest between the people and the police. Once there is a division, then the police become the enemy of the people . . . the police become an occupying army" (1995:47). Regardless of the fact that the Black Panther Party was portrayed in white communities as a group of dangerous armed men, Newton's reversal is thoroughly endorsed, if not alive and well, in many working zones that have learned the hard way how lawmen answer the question, Which side are you on?

We learn here, then, the shortcomings of liberal political talk that refuses to make connections between people and their means of survival. Although it is unacceptable (especially to those ruled out) to deny people access to a livelihood, it happens every day. From here we raise questions of what happens when disenfranchised people take matters into their own hands. Can this ever lead to a revolutionary consciousness? Does Marxism have a role to play in helping us to distinguish the criminal element in bourgeois property relations? Which side is Marxism on?

"It was the people's ground."

Thirty years earlier, miners in a white, rural area in northeast Pennsylvania were also denied access to the means of subsistence. Relying upon "skin-color privilege" (McIntosh, 1992:79)—for example, the help of sympathetic judges and verdicts delivered by juries of their peers—these workers transformed their understanding of bootlegging from possession of stolen goods to expropriating the expropriators.[3]

Sociologist Mike Kozura (1996), who knew some former bootleggers firsthand, analyzes the situation in ways that stress the self-activity of everyone in the anthracite communities. Rather than abiding by the forced distinction between calling the bootleggers radical (advancing syndicalism) or pragmatic (just trying to survive), Kozura reads the situation in his hometown sixty years ago as a social movement, one which interweaves communal loyalty and a commitment to fundamental social change. His work illustrates, first, the complexity of survival among people cut off from the means of subsistence and unable to sell their labor-power for money; second, the possibility for change in social consciousness when people work together to survive capital's indifference; and third, the tendency (whether subtle or pronounced) in late liberal society to heroize the unemployed working people who fought to survive capitalism during the Depression (when high percentages of white people were also unemployed) while criminalizing unemployed working people who fight to survive late-twentieth-century capitalism (when the highest percentages of unemployment are restricted to communities of color). As we shall see, pragmatism becomes radicalism for those not meant to survive.

The story begins with waste coal lying in "mountainous banks [culm banks] of discarded dirt, rocks and coal" (Kozura, 1996:204) surrounding communities in the anthracite coal regions of northeast Pennsylvania. Because this material was deducted from the miners' tonnage, the people felt entitled to it, and the company looked the other way. "They used the reclaimed coal as a source of fuel in their homes, and if they had any extra they sold it, or bartered it, with their neighbors." Children did most of the work. "We would crack it, and screen it, and wheel it home with a wheel barrow. . . . That's the way we used to make our money," remembers Joe Padelsky (204). During slack times and strikes the miners would join the children on the culm banks in a struggle to both get even and break even.

Whereas picking coal on the surface was a local custom, digging free-lance mines was viewed as a crime. Nevertheless, during long strikes (six months in 1925–26) families would work together in illegal mines to out-last the company. To protect its property the company hired Coal and Iron Police ("Coal and Irons"), and the property struggle continued at a higher level. Then in the mid-thirties the mines shut down and thousands of workers had no prospects for employment. Jack Campion remembers: "There was hate for the company. . . . We couldn't understand why all the mines were shut down. The companies came in, they raped the land and pulled out. . . . It was their way of punishing the people [after the long strike]. We were very bitter. That's when the bootlegging started. . . . Since the coal was in the ground and we all knew where it was at . . . people started digging their own coal holes" (Kozura, 1996:207).

Kozura is careful in his study to distinguish issues of survival from issues of class struggle. Yes, people needed to do whatever they could to survive; but these people also had long memories back to labor activists in their towns, activists who had been framed and hung, or sometimes shot down in cold blood, in the sixty years preceding the bootlegging opera-tions. Kozura follows the survival issue in the direction of pragmatism and the class struggle issue in the direction of radicalism.

The bootlegging operation was a family affair; as usual, everybody worked within and without the household. Although a gendered division of labor was customary, "many women worked alongside their men in the illegal mines," and "wives and husbands also shared the housework" (Ko-zura, 1996:209). Mary W. remembers her work in the mines: "I know a little bit about bootleg coal. . . . In those days . . . that was the only thing . . . to survive. Even my mother and my sisters and I used to go into the drift. We used to scoop the coal after my father would fire. We'd scoop it on a wheel barrow and wheel it out and . . . scoop it on a truck and my brothers would haul it home. . . . We used to scoop it on different screens to size it . . . stove coal, nut coal, pea coal, buckwheat. I know a little bit about coal!" And William Adams remembers the sharing of housework: "they'd both chip in when they'd get home and get [it] done" (209). Gen-der hierarchies persisted, of course: men tended to do most of the mining, whereas women ran the business affairs and organized the community in ways that "legitimized the expropriation of coal" (210).

Kozura's story documents the move from household to community to the entire region (over two thousand bootleg truckers delivering coal throughout the Northeast). "As independent mining became larger and more sophisticated . . . neighbors formed partnerships . . . decided matters collectively, and divided profits equally" (Kozura, 1996:211). Partnerships worked with one another; independent miners even cooperated with miners working in legitimate mining operations. All of this activity— carried out under the cover of darkness—was criminal, of course, and the people continually outwitted the "Coal and Irons." But in the course of this struggle the people grew to consider the coal fields, not only the waste, as their own. This is how Joe Padelsky remembers the situation:

> When the coal and iron cops tried to put the people off, [we] sort of lived up there . . . in the mountain. [We] wouldn't give in to nobody. . . . My brother has a coal hole . . . on the Reading [corporation] ground. . . . They blew his hole shut. That was it! . . . Things got rough then. . . . *They had to let the people make a living or there would have been a civil war.* The Reading bought that ground for four dollars an acre. . . . How in the hell? . . . Four dollars an acre! . . . It was the people's ground. That's the way we figured. We were digging our own coal. We owned the land! Land of the free! (Kozura, 1996:213, emphasis added)

Countless others affirm that "it was our right to take the coal" (218). "It was the people's ground," says Joe Padelsky (213).

The company first relied on the state police and the legal system, scoring major victories in some areas. But the bootleggers formed a union and helped one another with legal problems. One common ploy among arrested bootleggers was to demand a jury trial and find exoneration from friends and neighbors serving on the jury (with court costs assigned to the company). When the companies resorted to strip mining to yield the coal for themselves and make digging illegal holes impossible, the miners staged massive demonstrations in the streets of the state capital and also went after the machines. Kozura (1996:218) reports that between 1934 and 1941 "dozens of the huge power shovels, drag lines, and bulldozers were dynamited, burned, or otherwise sabotaged by bootleggers."

With the outbreak of World War II, most bootleggers found themselves in uniform or in defense plants; but the elders and children held the ground. In the end they struck deals—for example, tax-defaulting companies sold tracts to local investors who leased the land to the independent miners—that enabled most bootleggers to be "on the up and up" (Kozura, 1996:224).

*"These millions can never become part of any workforce
in the sense that we know it."*

James Boggs's *The American Revolution: Pages from a Negro Worker's Notebook* offers many insights concerning the role of surplus population in
the U.S. economy and beyond. His description of the "outsiders" comes
face to face with the question of relations between hired labor-power
and people locked out of the labor market, forced to survive without the
benefit of exchanging labor-power for money on a regular basis. Boggs
demands that Western liberalism come to terms with the unspoken problem of its surplus population. What does it mean these days to guarantee
a livelihood?

Boggs opens by contesting the relation between the right to live and
the ability to produce. He argues that "when a country reaches the stage
that this country has now reached, productivity can no longer be the measure of an individual's right to life" (Boggs, 1963:46). Boggs calls for a
new Declaration of Human Rights. Designed to fit an age of abundance,
this declaration begins by extending the "life, liberty, pursuit of happi-
ness" rhetoric to people whether they are working or not. He justifies this
by arguing that no one in particular is entitled to the fruits of everyone's
labor. Ownership becomes an uninteresting question: "Society must recognize that the magnificent productive tools of our day are the result of
the accumulated labors of all of us and not the exclusive property of any
group or class. . . . everyone . . . is entitled to the enjoyment of the fruits
of that development, just as all men are entitled to warm themselves in the
heat of the sun" (1963:47).

Boggs realizes that this demand that everyone be included in the liberal model defies the commonsense assumptions of many fellow citizens,
so he adds a second principle: "a new standard of value must be found"
(1963:47). Separating labor from value is perhaps equally difficult for
Marxists and liberals alike. But Boggs forces this issue because he sees no
end in sight to the problem of "surplus manpower."

In fact, Boggs argues that the problem will only get worse. Like some
of its workers, the United States is pretending to "look busy" although
there is less and less for everyone to do. "The American government is
now trying to make work when we are already on the threshold of a workless society" (1963:48). To show this he reviews the U.S. economy from
many perspectives—the views of the rank and file, union leaders, liberal
economists, politicians—and concludes that "none of these people . . . has
left behind the 18th-century philosophy that man must earn his living by

the sweat of his brow, and that anyone who can't or doesn't work (unless he happens to own property) is a misfit, an outcast, and a renegade from society" (49). This way of thinking is untenable because the number of surplus people grows with each technological advance.

Boggs saw "cybernation's" growth in the sixties in terms of a new "mode of production" that excludes more people each year from playing a "productive role." "This means that our society, as we have known it, is just as finished as feudal society was finished by the time capitalism arrived on the scene." Smug reformism is therefore out of the question; things cannot get better "because when you add to those who are daily being displaced from the plant the millions who have never even had a chance to work inside a plant, what you have is no longer just the unemployed and the castaways, but a revolutionary force or army of outsiders and rejects who are totally alienated from this society" (1963:50).

Boggs writes insightfully about the relations between people locked out of the job market and those still working; and he is quite clear that "we must look to the outsiders for the most radical, that is the deepest, thinking as to the changes that are needed." And yet what outsiders have to say remains for Boggs indeterminate: "I do not know what will happen when they have done what they must do" (1963:51).

On the inside, workers feel that the "American way of life" is threatened by communism or automation, but outsiders view this way of life differently. "A new generation of 'workless people' is rapidly growing up in this country. For them, the simple formula of 'more schools and more education and more training' is already outmoded. . . . To tell these people that they must work to earn their living is like telling a man in the big city that he should hunt big game for the meat on his table" (1963:51–52). Outsiders have no stake in the system, according to Boggs: "Being workless they are also stateless" (52). They will have to organize themselves against the social agencies implemented to head them off. With organization will come radically new ideas about living life fully without necessarily exchanging labor-power for money. Labor cannot organize outsiders because it cannot come to terms with unemployment and because it buys into the American way of life, with its ethic of exchanging labor-power for money. Domestically, "solidarity forever!" is becoming difficult to maintain because workers steal each others jobs. Outsiders and insiders have no common cause. Internationally, "workers of the world unite!" is becoming difficult to maintain because the U.S. economy competes with workers elsewhere. Even militant labor organizers such as the Wobblies are inadequate, according to Boggs.

Actually these union militants will go down fighting for things like a shorter work week (30-for-40), or two months paid vacation, or six months paid furlough, or the four-hour day—all of which demands are within the framework of keeping the workforce intact. Even when there is no longer any reason, because of the development of automation and cybernation, to keep the work force intact, they will still fight to keep it intact. Therefore it is hopeless to look to them as the ones to lead the fight for a workless society. The workless society is something that can only be brought about by actions and forces outside the work process. (Boggs, 1963:58)

Most progressive positions are incapable, by this analysis, to read the handwriting on the wall: there is not enough work to go around in our highly automated society. We need to rethink the workforce.

Leaving the self-organizing role of workless, stateless people indeterminate, Boggs offers a reversal of the seniority system as one way of giving people what he calls the "discipline and responsibility" of work in a structured setting and then turning us out for earlier retirement to explore our creative potential, as new generations take our places. But this is not the point of his argument. Instead he wants to convince us that the surplus population is growing and has no place in current discursive fields: "these millions can never become part of any workforce in the sense that we know it" (1963:60). How can Marxism address both workless and the working people when both are at odds? And what can Marx say, anyway, when the radical element now lies outside the "workforce"?

"Everything is 'against the law,' once it . . . is in the best interests of the working class"

The Industrial Workers of the World, the "one big union" allegedly open to any worker, the union which today also organizes temps and the unemployed while reconsidering issues of racism, sexism, and homophobia, has a rich heritage of direct action and sabotage. Sister worker Elizabeth Gurley Flynn's *Sabotage: The Conscious Withdrawal of the Workers' Industrial Efficiency* (Flynn, 1915), an I.W.W. pamphlet, lent support to the New York socialist Frederic Sumner Boyd, who had been arrested during the Paterson strike in 1913, charged with advocating sabotage, and sentenced to five years in prison. Rather than supporting the idea that capital is an unflappable hegemon and Labor is, by contrast, a fragmented source of productive energy, Flynn writes to remind capitalists everywhere of the complexity of Labor and its silent resources, which can strike out at any moment.

Flynn's opening foray parallels the beginning of Newton's article on political power. Refusing to justify direct action on any ground other than realpolitik—the workers need this resource—Flynn argues that "sabotage is one weapon in the arsenal of labor to fight its side of the class struggle. Labor realizes, as it becomes more intelligent, that it must have power in order to accomplish anything; that neither appeals for sympathy nor abstract rights will make for better conditions. . . . It is neither sympathy nor justice that makes an appeal to the employer. But it is power" (1915:125–26).

The brief essay presents specific aspects of sabotage. Although none approaches the violence of armed struggle or dynamiting bulldozers, all are aimed at making capital pay dearly for its abuses of labor-power. And in each case the rhetorical style turns the tables on the Labor-capital binarism; hired labor-power is learning to do what capital has been doing all along.

Flynn begins with the slowdown; whenever a boss cuts the wages of the workers and pockets the difference, the workers might slow down, thus decreasing the rate of their exploitation, or at least holding it constant. She describes this act of sabotage as a retaliation in response to a slowdown in the pay rate. Whenever you slow down the money flow, I'll slow down the flow of labor-power, until we achieve equilibrium. It's all a question of the quantity of goods produced by the quantity of labor-power.

Next Flynn turns to the question of quality of goods produced. She points out that owners routinely destroy their products (for example, fruits and grains), even if the use-value is indisputable to needy people, in an effort to keep the exchange-value of the commodities they wish to sell as high as possible. This tactic would have the workers following the lead of the owners by interfering with the quality of the product in the hope of keeping the exchange-value of the commodity they wish to sell (labor-power) as high as possible. For example, silk workers, long accustomed to "weighting silk" with zinc, lead, and tin, a practice that produces inferior goods in the name of profit, might begin tampering with their own interests in mind. Flynn cites Frederic Sumner Boyd's advice in this regard: "You do for yourselves what you are already doing for your employers. Put these same things into the silk for yourself and your own purposes as you are putting in for the employer's purposes" (Flynn, 1915:128). Of course, when workers get in on the act of tampering with the quality of the product, "we are confronted with all sorts of finespun moral objections" (127).

"Everything is 'against the law,' once it becomes large enough for the law to take cognizance that it is in the best interests of the working class" (133).

Continuing the theme of capital's hypocrisy, Flynn points to another form of sabotage: either refusing to adulterate the product or overadulterating it to the point of destroying its use-value. She asks readers to imagine Boyd telling workers the following: "Instead of introducing these chemicals for adulteration, don't introduce them at all. Take the lead, the zinc, and the tin and throw it down the sewer and weave the silk, beautiful, pure, durable silk, just as it is" (Flynn, 1915:128). She speculates that this advice would have resulted in life imprisonment for Boyd, instead of five years, because "to advocate non-adulteration is a lot more dangerous to capitalist interests than to advocate adulteration." The former is tantamount to releasing food, scheduled for destruction in the name of profit, to the world's hungry people. Consumers might also benefit from overadulteration because it warns them of product tampering by business interests. In a restaurant, for example, adding a pound of salt to bad soup that might otherwise go undetected is in the interest of the consumer. "Destroying the utility of the goods sometimes means a distinct benefit to the person who might otherwise use the goods" (129).

Flynn moves next to what she calls "open mouth" sabotage. The profitability of many businesses relies on the workers not talking about what really goes on behind closed doors. Consumers who continue supporting businesses marked by unfair labor practices can be persuaded to change their habits, especially when they learn how these practices affect them personally. Flynn tells the story of waiters on strike in New York who "drew up affidavits" to describe how the kitchens and pantries of the "best" hotels really operated: "They told about how the butter on the little butter plates was sent back to the kitchen and somebody with their fingers picked out cigar ashes and the cigarette butts and the matches and threw the butter back into the general supply. They told how napkins that had been on the table, used possibly by a man who had consumption or syphilis, were used to wipe the dishes in the pantry" (Flynn, 1915:130).

This is a fine example of workers on strike undermining capital by telling its secrets, especially those which risk the health and safety of the public. But we must tread carefully before reading this as a case of Labor returning from exile to speak on behalf of a people caught up in the flow of capital's circulation. Those selling their labor-power can tell the real story only when they are out of work; and being out of work usually means being denied access to the means of representation. As subjects of enunciation forced to operate as subjects of statements dominated by capital's axioms, we face a dilemma: either remain silent on the job or risk the greater silence of joblessness. The extent to which labor-power is bought and paid for by capital, then, is usually the extent to which it is forced to remain silent.

Labor is also forced to keep secret the extent to which its complex understanding of the workplace enters into dominant discourse, whether the manager's understanding, the official book of rules, or the history of capital and wage-labor negotiations. The people working a job often know that job better than anyone else, regardless of who owns the tools and raw materials. When this is the case the last form of sabotage — "work to rule," or what Flynn (1915:131) calls "following the book of rules" to the letter — can become highly effective.[4] Workers doing exactly what they are told by their managers is a form of sabotage in most workplaces because the managers rely on the workers to keep the plant running and not the other way around. This is the practice often cited when distinguishing labor-power from other commodities. How can we call labor-power a commodity (that is, a product transferred to another by means of an exchange for whom it serves as a use-value) when labor-power is capable of undermining its owner? Is this a weakness in Marxism? Or is it a weakness of bourgeois society exposed by Marx's representation of capital as stolen surplus labor, or value gone awry?

Before answering such questions as these, we need to return to subaltern Labor. Flynn's analysis concerns the struggle of employed people to improve their working conditions. But Boggs forces us to add the issue of surplus population to the issue of resisting the rate of surplus labor. We must try to sort out these excesses.

"People know; they just don't want to know!"

When bootlegger Mike Lucas says defiantly that "we just wouldn't . . . knuckle down to them to be like slaves" (Kozura, 1996:20), the task at hand is to distinguish the privilege of being white (for which white slavery is unthinkable, but other forms of slavery are merely "tragic" or wrong) from working-class consciousness (for which enslaving anyone is unthinkable). Joy James (1995:122) shows convincingly that "the language of the horrified spectator is not necessarily the language of the antiracist activist." Not having to include race as a problematic construction is yet another privilege in white communities. Labor history is sometimes silent on race; but most workers in many black communities in the sixties were forced to deal with interwoven oppressions as issues of survival. So far we have seen Huey Newton demand full employment/compensation in the black community and James Boggs remind us of a tendency toward full unemployment under cybernation. It seems important to come to terms with the limitations of thinking only in terms of a model of labor-power and capital that talks about production in ways that neglect race. We must now learn more about the struggle to survive for signs of secrecy that lie outside the circulation of money and commodities.

Lessons from the Damned: Class Struggle in the Black Community sustains a collective voice throughout; we learn from the preface that the unnamed participants—"the Damned," as they call themselves—range across class and gender divisions (and indeed there appears to be a mix of traditional and nontraditional academic voices). In an effort to focus on interlocking oppressions, I concentrate on the chapter "The Revolt of Poor Black Women" because it explores a variety of Labor issues from selling labor-power to struggling to survive in a workless state.

The first part of this chapter explores the need for self-activity on the part of low-income women in the black community; the second part explores the extent to which liberal models of inclusion can accommodate this activity. Since I am putting the latter on hold, my reading deals exclusively with part 1. This part opens with a critique of various subject positions in the sixties, from black women who "imitate the white scene," to white "welfare visitors" and nurses, to the "faithful, old negro doctor" and his "bourgie wife," to other "middle-class blacks" who write about their community but rarely visit. As the Damned remember, "All these jivers for the Man took care of their little business with us and we appreciated it. But we had never had any experience with anyone who had faith in us, had faith that we could think for ourselves, that we could change our lives. You know, if you're poor, you're poor. You don't miss what you've never had. You just do the same thing, day in and day out. What could change our lives? Damn, our own people never wanted to help! They just wanted to get away from us. We disgusted them" (The Damned, 1990:90).

By the mid-sixties, however, the feeling of revolutionary self-determination was in the air, but just as the Damned were learning about similarities and differences between Malcolm X and Dr. King, both of these men were assassinated. The Damned made immediate sense of the killings: "no black man is killed by Mr. Man unless he is really with the people." But a spirit of individualism kept everyone quiet and disorganized.

Because the Damned included women who sold their labor-power, the discussion turns to working conditions and cites many injustices: abuse on the job, low wages, denial of benefits, race-based restrictions on the kind of labor-power one could sell, etc. But resistance was again individual: "In those days we thought, each person for herself, so we never bothered to rap with each other much over conditions" (The Damned, 1990:91).

The Damned distinguish between a passive acceptance of unjust conditions and the kind of passivity that follows a smothering of burning passions. This distinction effectively blurs Kozura's distinction between radical action undertaken when one has no choice and radical action undertaken after anger has turned to rage. The Damned (1990:91–92) explore the grammar of passivity: "We blacks have been studied alot lately and we have read some of these studies. We are called a passive people. We have learned to study the history of words. *Passive* has the same Latin root as the word *passion*. The Latin root means suffering. Passivity is the smothering of suffering and passion is the explosion of suffering. Passivity and passion—*the ways to keep living when you're damned*, even by your own people. We smile at these studies that can never touch the root of things" (emphasis added). This interweaving of passivity and passion as a means of surviving liberalism complicates academic distinctions between what one must do to survive (pragmatism) and what one must do because it is right (radicalism). Survival becomes radical direct action for those who are treated as surplus population by Western liberal society.

The long road toward self-determination and collective action continues as the discussion turns to housing, welfare agencies, and the school system. The Damned remember the long history of African-American mothers operating in the interest of their children. And so when "there was someone with us who rapped and gave us books" (1990:92) and these radical ideas made sense in the name of survival, the Damned began to "think deeply" about getting organized. We learn of an abortive rent strike and some isolated cases of violence against welfare workers, but no sustained direct action. And the schools seemed only to reinforce the system of damnation. But again the outsider was there, "listening to our hurts, our rage, making things come together." The Damned describe the formation of a consciousness-raising Freedom School: "Our business never hit the streets. Our secrets were kept, even with families. The children listened and began to learn far quicker that they had ever learned in school. We became so impressed with their progress that we agreed to help and we formed a Freedom School—right in our kitchens where everybody gathered anyhow" (93).

An early issue was trying to convince people in the community that the Vietnam War "was really a war against people like us," but the efforts to speak from their discursive positions were not met with success. The Freedom School did, however, bring Damned into touch with both the low-income "striving poor" in favor of the war and high-income "bourgie" sisters against the war. The most relevant distinction between the Freedom School and those who rejected it sooner or later was faith in capitalism. The "striving poor" stayed away from the school, but the "bourgie" antiwar protesters joined forces with the progressive school for a while, but then left. "We think we understand why they had to leave us. Some of us really thought they would stay and be taught by us. But we had to learn how bone-deep is the bourgie among our educated black women, even when they want to help us poor black women. That bourgie fear of the poor can make them want to annihilate us if they can not control and lead us. Their fear of us is very strong" (The Damned, 1990:95). The Damned write with affection about the help they received from their prosperous sisters, but they are quite clear that their mission lies in communities of surplus population: to learn and teach how "we were being screwed by everybody—blacks included."

The progress of the Freedom school, with all of its joys, was accompanied by a sense of frustration with the community. The Damned knew their critique of bourgeois society was getting through to people, especially "the striving poor," who nevertheless could not seem to hear them. In the sixties the Damned used to say, "People know; they just don't want to know!" (1990:95); then in 1971 (the date of this essay) they report a change in attitude: "Alot of our neighbors tell us now that *they couldn't bear to admit that the dreams of making it were impossible.* Now in 1971 they see and admit it is impossible. More and more of them are forced, just as we had been, to look deeply into conditions and to prepare themselves for a great loss of what little security poor people got after World War II" (95–96, emphasis added).

The remainder of the essay describes how the Damned worked through their depression and frustration with a recalcitrant community to a position of self-determination in solidarity with women of color elsewhere in the world, such as in Vietnam and Africa.

Working with the "outsider" to deepen their knowledge of capital's power in bourgeois society, the Damned turned to writing "about our experiences as poor, struggling black women." The mixed reception to their writings cut across gender, race, and class lines in ways that illustrate the Damned's perspective on class action: "Some black men listened and helped us to be published. But some bourgie negro women ignored us and our writings until we were published by white women. Some radical white women with great intellectual prestige also ignored us after writing to us for information which we laboriously wrote down in long-hand and sent out. We learned through experience about this thing called class struggle and we became determined to struggle against it and expose it" (The Damned, 1990:96). The experience with published writing led to other opportunities outside the community; but each time progressive forces for social change were met with reactionary forces, all within the black community.

The Damned write with compassion about reactionary forces in their community. Rather than describe black Vietnam vets, black law men, and black conservative low-income parents as the enemy, they choose metaphors of addiction (to capitalism) and the organic growth of consciousness. Here they lay out what, they feel, the reactionary elements of their community have yet to discover: "The people are weak when they are badly exploited and feel empty inside. Then they look to the ruling class to do everything for them. But when we are touched by outside forces that reflect our worth, we can begin to struggle against the ruler's racism and exploitation. We even begin to fill up with ourselves and we think: 'it is written that the meek shall inherit the earth; the last shall be first.' We begin to grow from inside just like all waiting seeds, slowly but surely" (The Damned, 1990:97). The road to self-determination, according to Damned, leads to worldwide solidarity with women of color against capitalist exploitation. Hence they are suspicious on gender grounds of both black capitalism and the Black Power movement: "We shall see if poor black women plan to exchange a white master for a black one" (100).

By the end of the first part of this essay, the Damned are thoroughly convinced of the need for their self-activity, all the while crediting unnamed outsiders for the initial inspiration. Blurring the distinction between issues of pragmatism and radicalism, they are convinced that only the most radical solution stands a chance of assuring everyone's survival. They end this part with a flourish: "All of us have begun to learn to live beyond rhetoric, beyond Black Power, beyond the American Dream, beyond striving for bourgieness, beyond leaving our brothers and sisters who are now trapped in the slums. We know the struggle from deep down below and we know it must be thorough so it can not be turned around. We are keeping on, getting up!" (The Damned, 1990:101).

And today, of course, the struggle continues. Is this a dialectic between forces that objectify people who, contradictorily, develop forms of subjectivity to defeat those forces? Or are these articulate voices speaking as Labor at all? How do these class positions jibe with those marked by gender and race?

Reformulating the Paradox

Each of the vignettes above, from the pride of Huey Newton to the defiance of the bootleggers to the self-determination of the James Boggs to the reversal of capitalist logic shown by Elizabeth Gurley Flynn to the lessons in solidarity from the Damned, underscores the promise of self-activity on the part of creative people working together in class action. But how is this activity related to Marxist analysis? Is it necessary to go outside Marxist categories to make sense of what working people do? Despite their other differences and antipathy to Communist Party doctrine, the authors just examined share an understanding of capital-labor dialectics similar to one commonly received under the name Marxism. But when Newton stresses police power as enemy occupation, and Boggs focuses on unemployment, and the Damned want to talk about everyday survival, any aspect not covered by capital's consumption of hired labor-power appears to deviate from Marxism, to reinforce the incompleteness of class analysis, to encourage readers to examine all kinds of classes of people (e.g., women as a class), not only economic classes.

Critical race theory and women's studies have convinced most readers in the nineties of the limitations of saying, "I'm talking about labor here and cannot be expected to do all of the oppressions at once." The wage-labor/capital model works well to explain some aspects of exploitation—for example, dispensing with the argument that risking capital makes it grow—but this model cannot contain all aspects of Labor's movement. Now the "typically male" response is to build a bigger container, one that does justice to other determinations while still taking wage-labor seriously. The everything-is-related-to-everything-else approach to over-determination (complete with relatively autonomous regions for some variables) strikes me as just such a container.

We have, of course, in earlier chapters already contrasted approaches to viewing the subject as a person or group from those that situate subjects and objects in discursive fields. And we have shown how Marx's writing seeks to invert power relations between labor-power and capital. But we have along the way maintained a working distinction between Labor and labor-power. Labor—the real subject—signifies possession of vast reserves of form-giving, creative energy, some of which most people are forced to sell off as the commodity, labor-power, that is consumed in zones of production by the phantom subject, capital. My work earlier, especially on the range of capital's axiom proliferation, the persistence of the myth of value's self-valorization, and the silence of the subaltern denied access to the means of representation, makes me inclined to broaden the question of how Labor objectified in the form of commodified labor-power can transform itself into a revolutionary subject.

The salvaged framework of desire's indeterminacy helps to explain the difficulties faced when articulating the problem of practicing class action.

Deleuze and Guattari have convinced us that capital's hegemonic position at the level of axiom makes it a most formidable opponent. Given: any anticapitalist effort on the part of "the people" will either fail under its own steam, be co-opted if it is partially successful, or be systematically eliminated (in ways reminiscent of the I.W.W. and the Black Panther Party of early- and mid-twentieth-century United States) if it succeeds and refuses co-optation. And political theorists must be careful not to exempt ourselves from the power of capital's axioms, as we write our books in a comfortable domain created just for us. At the same time, however, Lacan has convinced us that whatever is refused by signification, governed as it is by capital, returns in the real; the danger of need is "always there." We have also learned from Derrida's critique of Lacan to distinguish determinate positions in discourse from a more general text with ruined limits, which allows for vast regions of indeterminacy. Our work opens the possibility of needs so great that they cannot be faced by the imaginary worlds we create for negotiating demands. We are in the process of discovering to our horror that Labor is locked outside the scope of language—inarticulate, abject—and that capital is inside, on its way to becoming a natural person as we (don't) speak.

The most compelling evidence of the plight of Labor in the bourgeois West is the ease with which one can confuse it with its object, labor-power. Indeed this is what axioms, such as capital's, do best. The mystique of the early Wobblies owes in part to the concrete reality of the labor-power they sold on their own terms. Even today when calculating the value added to the product by each worker for evidence during contract negotiations, we tend to confine our outrage to exploitation in the workplace. After a while, the fact that "profits" flow from squeezing the labor-power consumed by capital in the zone of production becomes self-evident. But unemployed people, the surplus population, denied access to the means of subsistence, the Damned who resist the impulse called "striving" and who live instead in community—in mutual support and defense—bear a less evident relation to objectified labor-power. As Labor whose labor-power is not regularly up for sale, whose object is therefore off-limits to capital, the surplus population risks serious depreciation as a would-be subject marked for early death. "Which side are you on?" always participates in the labor-power/capital tension; the question is never posed on the divide between objective demand and abject need, the site of the Labor underground.

Other perspectives seem disinclined to consider all aspects of Labor's lost subjectivity. Ollman tries to resuscitate wage-labor's subjectivity in bourgeois society. By his account, other aspects of subjectivity are barriers to the project. Fraad, Resnick, and Wolff feed multiple subjectivities to a prefabricated model by easing Marx's restricted focus (in *Capital I*) on the capitalist mode of production. Entertaining the simultaneity of ancient, feudal, capitalist, and communist discursive fields permits people to occupy subject positions at home even though they may be forced into object positions at work. A poststructural approach can accommodate these perspectives without insisting that the model contain all possibilities. Indeed our work with Labor has been open ended all along.

We were introduced to Labor in Chapter 1 with the suggestion that Lispector's abject communion with the reviled cockroach—"always there" —marked an interval in the subject-object analysis of Marx's writing. Theories are haunted by those portions of actual life that do not fit its models, but these life forces are not inclined to disappear. Ruinations of indicators connote indicators of ruinations. Either way you look at it, axiomatic rules contain loopholes and the abject stands as a primary clue as to their whereabouts. Our work with Labor continued in Chapter 4, where Marx distinguishes the form-giving power of Labor from the commodity labor-power. Although we must never lose sight of the fact that anyone selling labor-power needs to get organized so as to be ready when the Labor underground begins its return, we must avoid confusing the strengths we possess with our possession of these strengths. The former bears the determinate form of a (peculiar) commodity; the latter languishes interminably.

It is difficult for some Marxists to accept that certain aspects of Labor do not share in the reversal of wage-labor and capital so heartily endorsed by Flynn and other union activists. What can it mean to say that Labor cannot speak? Certainly the Damned can speak (even if they are aided by the outsider) as women, as low-income people, as African Americans. Certainly Ollman can say that the women telling the story are raising their class consciousness. Certainly Fraad, Resnick, and Wolff can say that these women are living communally in autonomous regions in bourgeois society. But can the Damned speak as Labor practicing self-determination? How does one conceptualize the relationship between Labor and the people involved? The only way is to mention those in the group who sell their labor-power for money. Consider the woman who cannot find work and struggles to survive, to raise children, to improve the quality of her living space, and to continue her education. Such a person lives, by many Marxist accounts, on the outskirts of Labor's movement and finds representation as a member of the community instead. Here sexism and racism conspire to construct categories of people whom one need not take seriously as creative, form-giving forces in society.

By taking Marx seriously as a critic of bourgeois myth and money worship, while leaving the door open for Labor's self-activity, I can approach C. L. R. James's paradox without relying on Hegelian sublation. Wage-labor may be wrapped up sometimes in issues of commodification, where there is little difference on the balance sheet between a bag of flour and eight hours of labor-power. But we may leave other aspects of Labor—such as discovering new uses for abandoned buildings—wildly unspeci-fied and purposefully indeterminate. This leaves room for whole armies of Labor ready to fight to survive with no hope of ever exchanging labor-power for money. The problem is not how to calculate the contribution to the social surplus of the father in the kitchen or the mother in prison; the problem is how to avoid breaking down the "social surplus" before the question of everyone's survival is at stake. And one way to assure this is to include all aspects of human survival—the struggle to connect with the means of subsistence (learning to fight, bartering through life, giving whenever one can, nursing children, taking what one needs) as part of Labor's movement. From this perspective, worker's self-activity and commodification of labor-power as wage-labor are not paradoxically ar-ranged; rather, the latter appears alongside the former (sometimes as an obstacle, sometimes not). Other Marxist approaches, when they concen-trate exclusively on the capital/wage-labor binary, join bourgeois society in appreciating capital's subjectivity while depreciating the subjectivity of anyone not covered by such a restrictive tension. My approach requires, then, a slightly different formulation of the problem of practicing class action: What is the role of the abject in the struggle to recover Labor's subjectivity?

The most significant unifying aspect of the five vignettes above appears to be a distrust for poststructuralist intellectuals trying to theorize the erasure of Labor during capital's occupation at the end of the twentieth century. And yet such a move seems to be the only way to bring Marx-ism's critique to bear on expropriation without disrespecting Labor's self-activity in the process. Tracking the expropriation of our social surplus without mapping out the territories of Labor's self-determination will prove a difficult operation. Before facing this problem in Chapter 8, I want to make a few provisional observations.

Huey Newton's essay illustrates the frustration and reality of people being denied access to the means of subsistence. And the reaction of the government to the Black Panther Party illustrates in black and white the extent to which "race" matters in Western liberalism. "Fraternities" of "survivalists" find space—white spaces—in our society, but "gangs" of "revolutionaries" are placed under erasure in ways that most academics are simply not trained to comprehend. Before approaching the Black Panther Party as parasitic on bourgeois society, or sexist in theory and practice, we must ask if Western liberalism relies on racism to undermine the right of all citizens to survive.

James Boggs's essay raises the possibility that we all—Marxists and liberals—need to rethink the value of work. Rather than worry immediately about Ollman's objective and subjective conditions for class consciousness, Boggs insists that we take seriously the workless, stateless people in his neighborhood. Surplus labor, as Fraad, Resnick, and Wolff might convince us, lies at the heart of Marxist approaches to exploitation; but the surplus population is growing at a faster rate. The outsiders among our population are the source of new, inchoate, free-floating radicals. The degree to which Marxism can come to terms with indeterminacy may well be the degree to which Marxism can relate to this emerging radicalism as Labor. With Ollman having conflated wage-labor and Labor and Fraad, Resnick, and Wolff having already mapped out the revolutionary ground, the outsiders seem to have been banished from Marxism before having been heard. And so before we criticize Boggs for chauvinism or excessive faith in technological progress, we must ask if Western Marxism's category of the worker will can ever make it out of the shop and into the streets.

The Damned's essay illustrates the affirmative consequences of expanding the definition of politics to include personal life. The tonality of this essay suggests that many of the authors are quite at home living the life of what Boggs would call "outsiders." There is no doubt in these women's minds that Western liberalism is a game designed to keep them out; as they see it, there is simply not enough room for all of the people at the table called the U.S.A. Therefore survival is both pragmatic and radical from the perspective of the Damned. Significantly, the person they call "outsider" is (presumably) a Marxist working with their community to build class struggle. But before we criticize the Damned for relying on an outsider's orthodox Marxism, we might pause and consider their distinction between being "touched by outside forces that reflect our worth" and beginning "to fill up with ourselves." Such self-determination might next lead to rethinking Marxism, replacing its masculinist tendencies to map and control with efforts to bring the struggle home in ways that leave no one behind.

This chapter illustrates the heterogeneity of Labor and the limitations of approaching this source of subjectivity as either a discursive position or a person/group. Although most surviving bootleggers were eased back into legitimate society and some surviving Wobblies were coaxed into the

CIO, the possibilities of direct action and sabotage are still quite lively if one knows where to look. Relying on people who represent objectified Labor to rise up against a hegemon (that makes it its business to devour us) ignores a key resource in ourselves and neighborhoods. At the turn of the twentieth century, capital stands as the dominant subject, with labor-power as its object whenever we exchange it for money. This leaves the Labor underground abject, denied constitutive representation.

At this point my subject-object-abject model with its reliance on the theme of an underground movement should rescue the argument. But such a move on my part would fall prey to the epistemic violence we have been detecting as a fallacy of the neutral intellectual. When those of us working in political theory attempt to decenter or represent ourselves differently, it seems important to assess our théories' complicity in the values of bourgeois society. And so when I address in the remainder of Part 3 the problem of practicing class action without undermining Labor's abject properties, I must address the relation of practice and theory. This requires facing as directly as possible loyalist Marxism's healthy suspicion of poststructural complicity in capital's hegemony.

CHAPTER EIGHT

Poststructural Praxis:
From Ebert to Butler

When the sign ceases the synchronous flow of the symbol, it also seizes the power to elaborate—through the time lag—new and hybrid agencies and articulations. This is the moment for revisions.

—Homi Bhabha, *The Location of Culture*

A Boston-area local of the Industrial Workers of the World recently infiltrated an open poetry reading sponsored by Borders, the bookstore chain, to protest the firing of a labor organizer. One member dedicated a reading from Covington Hall's *Our Masters* to the Borders CEO, noted the contrast between his astronomical salary and the wages paid to Borders workers, and then urged the assembled poets to boycott the bookstore. The Wobblies continue their struggle to find representation, this time by seeking public spaces within the private domain of a major corporation.

A San Francisco–area Food Not Bombs (FNB) organizer, Keith McHenry, fresh from a "Rent Is Theft" tour of Western Europe, dressed as Santa Claus and distributed food to children in his neighborhood. Police came to observe but no arrests were made (this time). FNB makes a political statement by giving away free food to people in need in public spaces in ways that dramatize the level of hunger and the surplus of food being wasted. According to McHenry and Alex Vitale, FNB's struggle concerns access to the means of representation as well as the means of subsistence: "Responding to business interests, city officials believe that if they can remove the so called 'visible and hard-core' homeless people that their political problems will be solved. There is a war over the control of the appearance of urban space" (Vitale and McHenry, 1994:19; see also, McHenry and Butler, 1992). Such organizations seek to publicize the danger of need right under the noses of bourgeois society, giving material force to the return of the real.

Local community educator Peter Kellman, who works with the Program on Corporations, Law, and Democracy (POCLAD), addressed the first national gathering of Ronnie Duggar's Alliance for Democracy and stressed the importance of citizen initiatives in contesting the personhood of corporations or in restoring popular control over corporate charters. His approach requires reinvigorating public debate as a means of contesting capital's axiomatic presence. Concerned about a decline of polarization, Kellman (1996:9) argues that "the only ideology on the field is the one that the corporations push." Wanda Ballentine (1996:7), also associated with POCLAD, resists the uphill struggle that results from fighting "issue by issue, case by case, on very uneven playing fields against these corporate 'persons,' while new threats proliferate" instead of contesting capital more directly. Groups such as POCLAD and other citizen-initiated efforts to monitor the smooth operations of capital often follow the lead of Richard Grossman and Frank Adams (1993), who challenge the ease with which U.S. corporations have acquired the status of "persons."

Poststructuralism appears a rather unlikely means of enhancing the interrelation of such activities as these. At least loyalist Marxism has a theory of praxis that holds open the possibility of radicalizing these syndicalist, anarchist, and liberal practices by stressing the connection between ideological superstructure and economic base. But how can anyone expect vibrant class action from a perspective that embraces indeterminacy? This chapter advances a "theory" of praxis that undermines the transparency of theory without abandoning Marx's project.

Where We Have Been and What To Expect Next

We are in the final stage of the theory dimension but only halfway along the action dimension of *Class Action*. I need to show how poststructural praxis can respond both to the heterogeneity of Labor's movement and to the indeterminate spaces of textuality. To continue along the action dimension requires coming to terms with ways of relating the divergent practices of the Labor underground to anticapitalist struggle. To conclude the theory dimension requires facing up to the conflict between loyalist Marxists, such as Teresa Ebert, and their poststructural allies, such as Judith Butler, on the issue of textuality and revolution.

In Chapter 2, the beginning of the theory dimension, I distinguished the indeterminacy of deferred mapping (différance) from other forms of articulating (what cannot be said about) desire. I connected this theme to Marx's method in Chapter 5, where I demonstrated how to read Marx's theoretical mapping of bourgeois society as a necessarily incomplete "working up" or (re)presentation (*Darstellung*) of what "actually happens," or what is "always there" in the chaos of knowledge. This approach leaves open the possibility of large pockets of human need—rendered indeterminate by virtue of their access—lying inexpressibly in dominant discursive fields. Although sometimes these spaces are inhabited by entire bodies or groups of people, such as squatters, who are invisible as Labor in bourgeois society, at other times these spaces are inhabited by devalued aspects of the lives of people otherwise visible. This chapter argues that a poststructural reconfiguration of loyalist praxis might contribute to resistance from these silent spaces precisely because of its appreciation of the undecidable, the unnameable.

I want to examine Ebert's trenchant critique of what she calls "ludic postmodernism," with a special focus on her version of historical materialism. I detect in her work a certain reliance on praxis as a dialectical relation between Marxist theory (which helps one to see) and material life (which gives one's vision a stake in "reality"). Next I turn to the Butler's ground-breaking work, which connects questions of materiality of the body to issues of representation in ways that are not inconsistent with my work in Chapters 2 and 5. I then suggest a slightly different approach to praxis, one which asks us theorists to learn to (re)present ourselves.

The Loyalist Salute: Teresa Ebert's Red Feminism

Ebert's distinction between ludic and resistance postmodernism is designed to accentuate the degree to which bourgeois academics theorize in ways that ignore the exploitation of labor-power. Whereas ludic approaches play with discourse at the level of the superstructure, resistance approaches are grounded in the economic base. She insists that late capitalism is still best described as a system of capital accumulation based on the exploitation of labor-power. Quite aware that critics will accuse her of operating with a reductive binary—ludic versus resistance—Ebert argues that ludic theorists ignore the economic base altogether. Instead of placing playful abandon and materialist analysis in opposition, she charges that ludic postmodernism is partial, blinded, ideological, a theory for property owners. Resistance postmodernism is designed, on the other hand, to advance a "red feminism" that brings us back to Marx's model of revolutionary praxis. In this way she emerges with the total theory, blending postmodernism with resistance, whereas ludic theorists are blinded by their ignorance of economic matters.

At this point Ebert might expect me to charge her with an old-fashioned reading of Marx—economic base versus ideological superstructure—and dismiss her as a loyalist who has lost her critical edge when reading the master text. But her critique is far too timely for such facile rejection. Even if loyalism is the best way to describe what she does, and it is, we must seek to understand why. I propose therefore to examine several of her other key distinctions before coming to terms with her loyalty to Marx. We must consider, first and foremost, her contrast between materialism and "post-al matterism" and, second, her approach to gender difference as found in various feminist perspectives, and finally her distinction between theory and experience.

Materialism Not Matterism

Ebert opens an introductory section by insisting that the materialism she seeks to reclaim for feminism involves "a reality independent from the consciousness of the subject and outside language and other media." In sorting out the relationship in contemporary feminism between theorists of materialism and those of matterism, Ebert relies on the tripartite distinction we have been using to relate different approaches to subjectivity in Marx. She separates feminists who remain loyal to Marx's alleged historical materialism from those who are still (at least post-) Marxist, but who reject this kind of causal explanation as positivist or essentialist. Both of these perspectives differ, says Ebert, from non-Marxist attempts to substitute language or discourse or textuality for material life. Such an approach "rearticulates materialism as a mode of idealism, what I call *matterism* . . . above all, the matter of language" (Ebert, 1996:25). We are faced here, then, with a loyalist Marxist distinguishing her work from both post-Marxists and, especially, ludic feminists infected with bourgeois poststructuralism. After sorting out these various threads explored throughout her *Ludic Feminism and After,* Ebert uses historical materialism to explain how ludic theorists have been forced to take materialism seriously.

Ebert is quite comfortable acknowledging that "we understand reality through language," though (significantly) she gestures toward Engels instead of Lacan. That she retains a foundational commitment is quite evident in her insistence upon reserving "the existence of a *historical series* independent from the consciousness of the subject and autonomous from textuality" (Ebert, 1996:26, emphasis added). The material reality she seeks to preserve and reclaim for (red) feminism is nothing less than a series situated in history. This explains how she chooses to represent recent interest in the materiality of the body in feminist discourse. By

Ebert's account, ludic theorists were content at first to reduce all materialist concerns to language, but with the widening gap between rich and poor and the attendant public policies of Reagan-Thatcher this position became untenable. This historicizing move works to rescue Ebert from the risk of turning postmodern criticism against the foundation of her materialism. Viewing the danger of need as a return of the real—a zone which is "always there," right under our noses but locked out of either symbolic or imaginary formulations—could lead to charges, such as mine, that even the "base" is part of Marx's staging of bourgeois society. But Ebert opts instead for a "self-evident" approach to bodies that matter.

Our earlier work with desire was a necessary part of dealing with this kind of claim that "it's about starvation, not signification!" We have seen that writing "there is nothing outside of the text" or "everything has become discourse" need not signify a substitution of the material world for effete language-games. Rather, these inscriptions remind us that whatever we can know and cannot know involves (constitutive) representation. Because the text in this general sense, following Spivak (1987:78), who follows Derrida, is a "weave of knowing and not-knowing," the silencing of the subaltern as abject can be described as an "epistemic" form of violence. One cannot avoid ruined limits at the scene of writing-in-general. Totality is therefore an impossible remnant of misguided teleological faith. Nevertheless, discursive fields continue to position subjects and objects; and the resultant language-games come and go in ways determined by power relations.

Quite aware of these distinctions between text, discourse, and language (speech), Ebert uses these terms almost interchangeably to argue that Marxist analysis reveals a reality one cannot otherwise see. Non-Marxist academics cannot see what is really going on until it becomes unavoidable, at which point they react superficially (by ignoring the economic base). Ebert protects her faith in totality by refusing to acknowledge the indeterminacy in any determinate form (especially the historical series). Hence she finds in Marx a coherence that I have shown his writing project does not require. Like the Lacanian followers eager to complete the master project by naming all of its parts, Marxist loyalists refuse to look both ways—toward chaos and away from it—before crossing off their poststructural critics. There is room for transformation in Ebert's material reality, but no room for the abject properties of "time out of joint."

Difference within (Historical Contexts)
Not Difference Between

Ebert relies on the distinction between materialization and textualization just established to distinguish her resistance postmodernism from poststructural or ludic varieties. Here she articulates a commitment to postmodern feminism which manages not to forsake a rather basic Marxist paradigm. She does this by distinguishing modernist from postmodern approaches to gender differences and then, within the latter category, materialist from textual approaches. Both first- and second-wave feminists rely, says Ebert, on "differences between" men and women, whether they gloss over or draw out these differences. She reads the Seneca Falls Declaration of 1848 as an illustration of an "identitarian feminism" that downplays differences between genders, while struggling to extend the Enlightenment's rights of man to Wollstonecraft's rights of woman. Similarly, Ebert reads radical feminists, including Mary Daly, as developing an "identitarian feminism" that accentuates gender differences by showing how woman poses alternatives — such as care-giving — to the violence of patriarchal institutions. As an alternative to this identity politics, Ebert poses a postmodern "differential feminism" that plays to the "differences within" any stable category.

Ebert explains differential feminism in language designed to catch the eye of her poststructural critics: "Differential feminists conceive of difference not as an identity but as self-divided, as always split by its other: they are concerned not with the difference between but with the difference within. Thus *no entity*, whether an individual or the category of women, *is a coherent, self-contained, selfsame identity;* rather, it is always different from itself, divided by its other, which is produced through its own excess-ive signification" (1996:157, emphasis added). She immediately launches into a discussion of a wide variety of key texts in poststructuralism (for example, Derrida, Drucilla Cornell, and Butler) to explain the destabilizing properties of what we have been calling "différance." At one point she even acknowledges that the "feminist deployment of deconstructive strategies and turn toward difference-within has in many ways been effective . . . in demystifying and denaturalizing much of the common sense of patriarchal ideology" (168). But Ebert refuses to abandon a "knowledge of social totality, which is necessary for any social praxis" (160).

Indeed, Ebert's loyalist belief in dialectical motion toward human emancipation leads to predictable, if anomalous, conclusions. After writing convincingly of the instability of any representational scheme — the incoherence of any entity in principle — she prepares to situate poststructural (ludic postmodern) difference within an historical schema. In her words, "I propose retheorizing historical difference as *difference within a materialist system of exploitation:* that is, a historical materialist theory of difference in postmodernity" (169). This is not a slip of the tongue for Ebert: in fact, "the incoherence . . . taken by ludic theory as a mark of the unrepresentability of . . . signs . . . is an articulation of the social contradictions of class society" (Ebert, 1966:173). In other words, ludic postmodernism has been effective "*on the level of the superstructure*" (168), but we need Marxism to relate this destabilizing work to the economic base; that is, we need "to explain and transform the historically produced divisions between exploiters and exploited." Despite her commitment to différance, Ebert remains absolutely committed to classic Marxist teleology.

Praxis as the Dialectical Relation of Theory and Experience

Perhaps the hypnotizing hold of "praxis" helps to explain why sophisticated critics like Wood and Ebert cannot locate Marx's *Darstellung* at the scene of writing. For a loyal Marxist the theory/practice distinction operates as a dialectical unity—abstractions are part of reality in this transformative model. Abstract theory seems so alienating that it contradicts the concrete practices of the people; but the two are at once mutually dependent if the theorizing is Marxist. In other words, Ebert relies on a Hegelian dialectical approach to theory and practice—hence the rhetorical force of her praxis: it is no mere synonym for what to do in the street, or what people do with each other, or the application of a theory. Praxis is revolution.

Ebert's work is replete with signs of her commitment to a dialectical relation of theory and experience. She calls her historical materialism a "knowledge practice" and insists that "feminist theory . . . be a politically transformative practice" (1996:7, 15). And each time she mentions this couple, theory assumes the subject position. Consider this illustration: "Theory, then, is not opposed to experience but is in a dialectical relation to it: theory historicizes experience and displays the social relations that have enabled it to be experienced as experience. Such a knowledge prevents us from essentializing experience and makes it possible to produce new experiences by transforming the dominant social relations" (22). Theory "historicizes" because knowledge can "produce" experience and "transform" reality. But without a dialectical relation to experience, theory—for example, ludic theory—can fall into complicity with dominant social relations.

Praxis, then, is the key to remaining loyal to the totalizing base-super-structure paradigm. As if to remind her readers of the debt of the (dialectical) unity of theory and practice to social totality, Ebert sometimes calls the knowledge practice "praxical knowledge." This exhortation shows how Ebert draws together praxis and totality: "I argue that praxical knowledge has to be knowledge of social totality, and such knowledge has to be able to offer explanatory critiques of all social practices" (1996:86); in order to undertake revolutionary praxis and transform the dominant structures, one has to acquire knowledge of social totality" (87–88). And yet because this is a dialectical relation, Ebert is also careful "to refuse to essentialize theory." Following Marx, she believes that theory can become a material force. But rather than lend subjective force to practical experience, she advocates the "materialist rétheorization of theory as the historical frames of intelligibility and conceptual strategies through which we know the operation of socio-economic oppression in the world in which we live" (250). And so even though Ebert wants to join in "the critique of the limits and uses of existing modes of knowing" and seeks with most poststructural theorists the desire to "generate the new subjectivities necessary to transform the world," her use of praxis leads her to privilege theory over experience in ways that perpetuate her unspoken reliance on goal-oriented approaches to emancipation, which have lost their luster among those who have lost faith in teleological formulations.

A Poststructural Reply: Judith Butler and the Emancipation of Praxis

Is it possible to design a "materialist différance" that accommodates both historical materialism and poststructural multiplicity? Ebert attempts to situate the differences explored to good effect by poststructuralism in a historical context. But Butler (1993a:10) points out that "placing a theory called poststructuralism within a context called history . . . is both to deprive poststructuralism of its historical force and to vitiate history of its theoretical presuppositions." Ebert cannot at once hold on to postmodern notions of the supplement—with its indeterminate anachrony—and maintain loyalty to a traditional Marxism whose "base" is invested so heavily in diachronic form. Indeed the incoherence of this attempt leads Ebert to misconstrue Butler's claim that "what some poststructuralists are now theorizing is the inadvertent political possibilities opened up by the loss of credibility that Marxist versions of history have recently endured" (10). Her commitment to Marx leads Ebert to reject this affirmative gesture as

forsaking historicity in the name of discourse. We need to explore Butler's claim of loss of credibility to determine the ways in which she would
encourage a different kind of praxis.

We should keep in mind here Butler's critique of two positions iden-
tified earlier. First, we need to recall how Butler (1993a) criticizes Laclau
when he positions subjects and objects in discourse only to conclude that
working-class identity has been complicated by so many other identities
that the labor-capital tension has lost its logical force. Second, we need
to recall how Butler (1993b) criticizes Žižek when he assigns names to the
inarticulable real—for example, calling the indeterminate an "objet petit
a" instead of just letting it slide—thereby appropriating a Lacanian element in ways that map the entire territory, foreclosing the possibility of a
ruination of limits. Butler's critique here resonates with Derrida's gentle
reminder in a recent exchange with Laclau (Mouffe, 1996:84) that writing
emerges out of chaos and does not eliminate it (as maps and paradigms attempt to do); the limits of the scene of writing are, in other words, ruined.
You will recall that we distinguished our approach from Laclau's because
of his inability to leave room for the indeterminate and his tendency to enhance capital's subjectivity (by struggling against its centrality). And we
part company with Žižek by appropriating from Lacan only an indeterminate real that must be left unmapped (to avoid analyzing its relation to
the truth of the matter).

Butler is quite amenable to psychoanalytic insights regarding subjectivity but distrusts any model that threatens to universalize constructed
categories falsely. She is primarily concerned with Žižek's occasional disregard for power relations. Butler (1993b:202) asks "whether the notion
of a lack . . . is itself a presocial principle universalized at the cost of every
consideration of power, sociality, culture, politics, which regulates . . .
social practices." Of the several implications she traces in Žižek's work,
one stands out here because of its relevance to the relation between the
real and signification in discursive fields. Butler has grown wary of Žižek's
tendency to distance the real, to put it in its place:

> [We need] a way to assess politically how the production of cultural
> unintelligibility is mobilized variably to regulate . . . who will count as
> a "subject," who will be required not to count. To freeze the real as the
> impossible "outside" to discourse is to institute a permanently unsatis-
> fied desire for an ever elusive referent: the sublime object of ideology.
> The fixity and universality of this relation between language and the
> real produces, however, a prepolitical pathos that precludes the kind of
> analysis that would take the real/reality distinction as the instrument
> and effect of contingent relations of power. (1993b:207)

What Butler finds lacking in Žižek's approach helps to explain the power of an axiomatic capital, which controls the reality of value and its other in discourse (but remains vulnerable to the real at the scene of writing). Her disinclination to view these power relations as fixed is even more promising.

Butler's critique signals both a commitment to politics and an appreciation of history. These ally her with Laclau to the extent he advances with Mouffe a "democratic equivalence" that is careful not to elide difference. But even Laclau is less attentive to the effects of power than Butler would demand. Butler (1993a:10) explains her position: "Indeed, what is and is not thinkable or intelligible, what is and is not speakable, is fixed by a variable set of limitations, ones that undergo shifts, which appear with more or less rigidity. These limitations will be effects of specific strategies of power . . . what constitutes the impossible will be regulated by power." It should be clear, then, that Butler wants both to acknowledge the presupposition of history and the historical significance of poststructuralism. This explains the relevance of her project to the task of coordinating various strains of difference without embracing a bland pluralism.

Butler's work allows a shift from questioning what kinds of political practices open up, now that teleological ends have proven unrealizable, to asking how to emancipate praxis from its struggle for idealized emancipation. Here is her most promising question: "How is it that the unrealizability of the Good and/or Emancipation has produced a paralyzed or limited sense of political efficacy, and how, more generally, might the *fabrication of more local ideals* enhance the sense of politically practicable possibilities?" (1993a:10-11, emphasis added). This elegant question transfers the burden of proof from poststructuralism to bourgeois society. Instead of demanding that those who have debunked teleological theories—including remnants of the nearly inescapable Hegelian dialectic—show how they are not bourgeois sympathizers, Butler's new question demands that those living in bourgeois society ask themselves why they have become paralyzed by the thought of political action. The shift from What have you posty theorists done lately? to Why do we (all) feel defeated before we begin? lays the problem squarely at the feet of capital, because this is how its axioms work (behind the scenes and beyond question). Butler's suggestion to attempt a "fabrication" gives us at least someplace to begin.

Praxis: From Hegel's Truth to Butler's Fabrication

Before considering how serious class action might be negotiated without lapsing back into teleological Marxism, I must emphasize that I cannot simply side with Butler at Ebert's expense. Ebert's charge of complicity is too powerful to be set aside easily; indeed Butler could agree that academic complicity is a major problem of late capitalism, and I doubt that she would exempt herself if pressed. This explains Butler's interest in exploring politically practicable possibilities. But there is a sense in which she and others influenced by her work, such as myself, fall prey to complicity with capital's axiomatic influence. We have seen this in Chapter 3, where Spivak warns against reliance on an unnamed subject of power, a subtle reliance which renders the Western intellectual transparent. Indeed we have just observed Butler criticizing both Laclau and Žižek (and to some extent Derrida) for not paying sufficient attention to an unnamed Foucauldian subject of power. Here, even though she seems disinclined to ask "the subaltern" to speak for themselves, her work in less careful hands might join Deleuze and Foucault in unintentionally exempting intellectuals from the charge that we have centered ourselves in Western discourse. We therefore must instead continue asking how to represent ourselves, all the while seeking ways of extending the political franchise. This is to say that we must avoid presuming that "they" have more to change during fabrication than "we" do. Debates over proxies and power relations presuppose a certain portraiture—intellectual, street person, producer, domestic laborer—and Western intellectuals cannot expect exemption in transparency. So Ebert is right, I think, to charge poststructuralism with complicity, but she does not need to base her rationale in the truth value of economic determinism.

In fact, Butler shows convincingly that models such as Ebert's confuse the real with reality. Ebert's unconditional acceptance of an economic base gives her full faith in a dialectical approach to praxis. Revolutionary praxis is radical precisely because Marxist theory in its loyalist (teleological) version stands in a dialectical relation to practices found in reality, and thus one can anticipate an *Aufgehoben* of emancipation. To Ebert's cry "Wake up and smell the complicity" Butler might be expected to respond, "Say good night to the era of teleology."

But if we pronounce Ebert's "materialist différance" arbitrary (in the exemption it grants to Marxist categories while deconstructing other categories), how can we make sense of a poststructural commitment to Labor? Spivak offers a solution that avoids an idealized Marxism without forsaking its economic agenda. In Chapter 3 we reviewed her advice to place the economic under erasure. But erasure must be distinguished from irrelevance. For Spivak economic considerations are at once irreducible (honoring Ebert's commitment) and ultimately impossible if granted transcendental significance (respecting Butler's critique). But where does this leave us in terms of revolutionary praxis?

Placing the economic under erasure in Spivak's sense is actually quite compatible with our reading of Marx's method of "working up" a picture of bourgeois society out of the chaos of knowledge. The economic aspects of life are indelibly etched in the social fabric, but the minute one tries to invest economic considerations in a base upon which all else rests, things fall apart. The problem is with the base-superstructure model, not the emphasis on economic need. Even Althusser, whose famous "last instance" could be infinitely deferred, averted his gaze unnecessarily from the indeterminacy of the real, the unfathomable need, which is always there. The problem for theorizing radical politics under the influence of poststructuralism has always been that of articulating what poststructuralism insists cannot be articulated. And we are thus led back once again to our hybrid model of desire, this time unable to postpone the nagging question of praxis.

Class action requires people collaborating in mutual support and defense without imposing a unity that would efface our significant differences. Western intellectuals have grown accustomed to looking to theory —and especially to Marxist theory—for ways of reconfiguring this time-honored problem of the one and the many. Indeed, Marxist praxis is still trying to live up to the second of Marx's *Theses on Feuerbach*, which insists that one "prove the reality and power, the this-sidedness of . . . thinking in practice" (Marx and Engels, 1978:144). Radical theorists tend to operate as though theory were the key to the oneness needed to stand together in counterhegemonic struggle and that experience and practice are the key to the many, the fragmentation that must be overcome. Here we recall favorite street slogans: "Together we can move mountains," "The people united can never be defeated," etc. Indeed poststructuralism seems counterrevolutionary because it accentuates precisely the fragmentation loyalist Marxism seeks to overcome. But the dialectical relation of theory and practice, with its promise of transformation on the other side, has lost its force among people who are questioning even the materiality of the material at hand. We need to ask if there is a way of articulating praxis by inverting and displacing this venerable dialectic instead of trying to force the issue with party lines and state authority. Above all, we need a formulation of praxis that insists neither on a unitary subject nor a restriction of writing to subject and object positions in discursive fields.

Reformulating a Revolutionary Praxis

The theory dimension of *Class Action* requires taking seriously both determinacy and indeterminacy. This is why we are always trying to embrace both the reassurance of subject-object power relations and the anxiety of the abject, an aporia signified for now only by the hyphen. We have been practicing inverting the relations between subject and object as a way of preparing for the return of the abject. Indeed this is the overall theme of *Class Action:* if determinate labor-power is ever going to turn the tables on phantom capital's axiomatic presence, their struggle must be placed in a wider context, which requires indeterminate Labor's transformation from silence into language. But this means we must consider what would happen—perish the thought—if the theory-practice couple were to experiment with a subject-object inversion and displacement of its own.

When Ebert (1996:22) writes that "theory historicizes experience," she perpetuates the reassuring party line that keeps theory in the most privileged discursive position as subject. Mere practices—distributing free food, teaching labor history in the mall, sparking public debates concerning corporate power—must be theorized, we are told, to avoid a fragmentation and lack of radical spirit, both of which keep capital's power intact. But now, near the end of what I have to say about theory's role in class action, I am led to undermine my privilege as a would-be member of a new elite: theorists at the center of the next revolution. And above all, I need to prepare for a return of the real, the political possibilities of newly constituted subjects, which the bourgeois either calls "oppressed," "disempowered," and "worthless" or totally disregards as nameless aspects of ourselves and others.

But what might it mean to allow practical experience to occupy theory's subject position? How can one come to terms with a Marxism that no longer maps out the correct political possibilities? Are they really over, those days when the theoretically sophisticated intellectual could put it all together for "the people," who then would police themselves by drumming out any counterrevolutionary tendencies? How can Marxism survive a transfer of power from theory to practice, not to mention a displacement of this reassuring tension? Would Marxists not be placing themselves in the impossible position of having no way of distinguishing revolutionary from counterrevolutionary direct action?

The fears of loyalist Marxism would be realized in a poststructural praxis that abandoned all binary relations—a frequent charge from unsympathetic readers. But in the inversion-displacement I am talking about, theory is not over; it simply is not overprivileged. My approach requires only that practices guide theoretical developments, for a change, instead of the other way around. Like the Damned in Chapter 7, the examples that opened this chapter—the Wobblies in the Borders store, the FNB food giveaway, POCLAD's support for citizen-initiated attempts to monitor corporations—illustrate the possibilities of mutual support and defense alongside the race for theory and other forms of "striving." Loyalist Marxist criticism might be expected to regard the Wobblies as locked in a time warp, still spouting slogans about one big union with a weak sense of the historical dialectic. Similarly, the FNB activists could expect to be branded anarchists, especially those who "deviate" in the direction of punk culture and pirate radio stations. And, of course, the populist POCLAD with its penchant for legislative process, could expect to be branded liberal, a bourgeoisified version of anticorporate behavior which never figures out that capital's axioms are running the show.

To follow Butler's lead at this point, I must address the following question: what kind of fabrication becomes possible after the shell of Marxist teleology has burst asunder? And the beginning of my answer refuses to rely on a new and improved theory designed to take its place. Reading Marx's anticapitalist project at the scene of writing with ruined limits has allowed us to regard the struggle between labor-power and capital as a bit too self-evident. Our tendency to conflate political and constitutive representation—ignoring the formation and deformation of subjects in discursive fields—has resulted in capital becoming in effect a normal person, whereas labor-power has become an object whose value is determined solely by the extent to which it fits into capital's elusive enterprise zones. Marx's project remains relevant to the extent that he offers a gestalt-like alternative to viewing capital as a subject. But we cannot expect to be told what to do next.

My approach to Marx's writing project allows for both an appreciation of his presentation of bourgeois society and a studied awareness of what exceeds this picture. Viewing praxis as a dialectical relationship between theory and experience forces theorists such as Ebert to incorporate the excess, the zones of indeterminacy, into a teleological whole. Indeed, one struggles to imagine direct action campaigns that could be inspired without some semblance of a total picture. This is why anyone reading Marx in terms of subject, object, and abject must address the problem of theory's relation to practices.

Few can deny that theory has long occupied the privileged position (as subject) in this relationship. Viewed from theory's overprivileged position, our opening examples probably strike Marxists as potentially radical if they could get the three groups of people—I.W.W., FNB, and POCLAD—into the same study group. But instead of classifying these examples in terms of their theoretical implications—for example, scanning the mission statements for signs of political perspectives, whether liberal, anarchist, or simply confused—let us see what happens when we allow each example to illustrate a practice associated with Marxist struggle to mobilize the Labor underground.

These examples of providing access to subsistence and thereby valorizing the people discarded in late capitalism, of organizing labor-power within and without the workplace, and of contesting corporate personhood are surely not unrelated to Marxist struggle. Lack of access to subsistence plays a crucial role in setting the stage for exploitation: "free labor" is forced to sell its labor-power to survive precisely because it lacks such access. Organization can enhance the subjectivity of objectified labor-power. And uncontested corporate personhood perpetuates the influence of capital's axioms. But any reader who attends community group meetings in the United States knows that homeless people, labor organizers, and populists are neither obvious allies nor likely to be Marxists. Marxist analysis may appear heavy handed and arbitrary in all three scenarios; and yet each population is sufficiently heterogeneous to include Marxists of many varieties. We must admit that Marxist analysis often falls on deaf ears when confronting local practices related to its agenda of class action. Frustration with the people "just not getting it" is more conducive to organizer burnout than popular class action and tends to devalue the membership in the process. Fortunately, Butler's new question switches the focus from past failures to present obstacles and new political possibilities.

Approaching the Wobblies' infiltration of the poetry reading as an example of anarchism, syndicalism, or Marxism raises for Ebert's notion of praxis the question of how to get fiercely independent workers to see the big picture, the dialectical relationship between their language and the economic base. But approaching the same example as an illustration of organizing labor-power at the site of an injury to someone raises instead the question of how this band of voices is related to other efforts to organize labor-power by, for example, the AFL-CIO, the Labor Party, MDs organized against HMOs, or, for that matter, professors of political theory. Labor-power, the commodity, is in the process of discovering its objectified position (across many income differentials) in the absence of the real subject (being in possession of labor-power). The real danger to those pursuing class action is not whether efforts to organize labor-power will teach their membership Marxist theory. The question is rather, If the working class gets its act together, will this entail a strengthening of the owning class as enemy, and thus a reinforcing of capital's position? Does joining Educators for Social Responsibility or the National Writer's Union or the Wobblies place the member in an adversarial relation with owners of capital (whether a school's endowment or one's own retirement fund), and does this tension not serve to reinforce capital's subjectivity?

Of course, labor-power must organize against its oppressor, but doing only this can serve to further normalize capital's subjectivity. Capital can learn any game. Now mean and nasty oppressor, now socially responsible reformer, now lean and mean provider, "Tell what you want me to be," says Mr. Moneybags. "I can expose my sweatshops, write stories about how the minimum wage I pay often does not bring workers above the poverty level, and, when pressed, pass legislation addressing both problems on my way out of town. My practices resemble those of the ATM machines I install to reduce the cost of labor-power in my banks. These machines charge consumers a fee for giving me free labor-power. I do whatever makes money until consumers rebel. Then I do something else." This is why, in addition to organizing labor-power judged valuable in bourgeois society from the highest to lowest income, we must also contest capital's subjectivity.

Approaching the POCLAD story as an example of populism or liberalism, as Ebert's notion of praxis would require, raises almost immediately the question of how to get progressive voices to move from contesting corporate personhood to addressing capital's hegemony. But allowing the same example to illustrate what it means to contest capital's subjectivity in the form of corporate personhood raises instead a question of how these voices are related to other efforts such as culture jamming and anti-corporate boycotts. All of these efforts work together in ways that contest capital's discursive presence.

The real danger to those pursuing class action is not whether efforts to fight corporations will turn anticapitalist in Marx's sense but whether the constant barrage of anticorporate feeling will result in capital forsaking communities, leaving town. Indeed one can expect banks to think twice before investing in territories infested with disrespectful labor-power and vigilant academics posturing as public intellectuals, watching every move of the major corporations in their state. "Who needs this?" says Mr. Money(packing his)bags.

But what about the labor-power judged worthless, the damned, the abject, the Labor underground? Our reading of Marx shows that the vast territory locked out of dominant discourse is very much a part of this project, the unmapped part. Neither a person nor a collectivity, the Labor underground is a subject denied representation in bourgeois society. Capital controls value and value determines the abject. So a third component of Marxist struggle, especially after teleological formulations have lost their credibility, is valorizing those aspects of life ruled worthless.

The self-evidence of the plea to organize exploited workers of the world owes to a conflation of the distinction between reality (visible or invisible) and what we have been calling the real. Marxists are well practiced resisting bourgeois reality, but the loyalist Marxists among us tend to substitute an alternative (often invisible) reality tied to the economic base. Whether one is engaging the latest commodity fetish at the level of the superstructure or negotiating forces and relations of productions at the level of the economic base, the real of human need is "always there" in ways that defy theory's grasp. My work in Chapter 2 and then in Chapter 5 is part of a plea to look both ways. That is, while looking forward to organizing objectified labor-power and contesting subjectified capital, one must also look backward to valorizing the discarded material in the chaos of knowledge. A poststructural praxis is well designed with respect to the abject because it embraces the contradiction of articulating what cannot be articulated. Rather than regard those qualities of life devalued by bourgeois society as undertheorized (including the forgotten talents and aspirations of many of us preoccupied with marketing our labor-power), class action might begin with practices that provide access to the means of subsistence, and it might consider the spaces in which these practices are negotiated as aporia in the subject-object relation of capital and labor-power. The primary revolutionary potential of the abject lies in its indeterminacy. Because the abject—as we have seen, following Spivak—can be rendered indeterminate by virtue of its access, it stands as a key resource in the project of Labor's return.

How strange it must seem to privilege the element of class action least likely to be able to speak? But recall that the sheer scope of capital's hegemony has already required class action to prepare for an irredentist struggle. The enemy that drove Labor underground appears indomitable: capital's axioms pervade reality, property, the imagination, theory, and most legal practices (recall, for example, that both the Wobblies' sabotage and the FNB's food giveaway were judged illegal). But this enemy—capital—produces more garbage than any imperial subject in history; and the abject includes barges of actual trash, hidden hopes and dreams of co-opted people, and legions valued only as surplus population (denied basic needs and expected to live nasty, cruel, brutish, and short lives).

In any irredentist struggle those who are neglected by the imperial presence and somehow manage to survive have least need of its good offices and are therefore least likely to be drawn into complicity. A brief glimpse of the academic workplace and the recent history of labor organizing in the United States might give readers pause before basing a counterhegemonic struggle in the hands of labor-power organizers or populist warriors against corporations. Both elements of our strategy can expect new axioms from capital: capital has shown that it can accommodate organized labor-power—"it's part of the price of doing business"—and capital can always leave town when conditions become unfavorable. Moreover, corporations for social responsibility are already springing up to work in the interest of the people; some states might even go back to chartering corporations in ways that people know about. These are only a few of the ways to be co-opted or counterhegemonic in forms approved by—and judged profitable to—capital. But as surely as capital has been growing stronger, it has been producing more refuse, and all of this has remained in the system somewhere, like discarded e-mail. Mobilizing the abject as the key to class action is important because these forces—by their sheer tenacity— expose the lie of the phantom subject capital's hegemony. When you evict us for urban camping we do not disappear. The life energy of the completely devalued gives the lie to value's representation as money. Vast regions of lived experience in urban and rural settings have shown that survival is possible—when we stand in the mutual support and defense of community—without participating in the circulation of money and commodities. If these forces could be aligned with an organized workforce and a delegitimated sense of ownership, Labor might return from its forced exile to make capital out to be mere money again.

We have by now developed three key elements of a practical approach to class action. This approach is related to the dialectical subject-object relations of capital and labor-power, but the insistence on the abject requires us to reexamine all three concepts at once. On the subjective front, where one confronts the phantom subject (capital), the project lies in contesting its determinate form, beginning perhaps with the U.S. corporation's status as a person. On the objective front, where one continues to witness the most visible exploitation of the commodity (labor-power), the project lies in organizing the people who exchange labor-power for money. And on the abjective front, where one can neither evade nor deny the danger of need, the project lies in establishing universal access to the means of subsistence. But here we face the problem of taking the abject seriously.

The key to poststructural praxis lies in its appreciation of indeterminacy, or technically speaking, the displacement of the inverted subject-object binary. Marxist theory is still required to highlight exploitation and explain the violent nature of bourgeois society; without this perspective Marxist practices of exposing Moneybags's scams and organizing armies of employees can easily lapse into Western liberal populism and interest group politics. Political representation will continue to disguise a portraiture that locks out the Labor underground and fails to disrupt axiomatic capital. When approached formulaically, the solution is simple: add the abject to the traditional subject-object analysis associated with Marx and stir. But my work in this chapter with specific examples from POCLAD to the Wobblies to FNB leads me to expect that contestation and organization are more easily aligned with each other, and perhaps with Marxism, than is valorization, whereas valorization is the key to keeping contestation and organization radicalized, if not necessarily Marxist. Without a connection to the very binary it would displace (subject-object), subsistence practices will not result in any kind of class action concerned with the exploitation of labor-power.

The challenge of poststructural praxis is to reconfigure old patterns by keeping all three practices in play at once: organization and contestation may provide provisional order (supporting or even running candidates for office and passing anticorporate legislation), but valorization reminds us of how there is no order in principle. Negotiating such collaboration, however, requires facing the depreciation suffered by our abject properties in bourgeois society. Both populists and unionists working on issues of subsistence politics must discover new ways of representing themselves—for example, in community groups sharing resources. This will bring overprivileged people in touch with their needs and perhaps even with their bioregions, in touch with people who have reused, recycled, and reduced long before it became expensive and commodified to do so. As radicalized low-income citizens grow skeptical of capital's subjectivity, class action may appear increasingly plausible. But the initial problem requires appreciating aspects of our own and other people's lives—aspects that, in the process of becoming scholars and activists, we have sometimes learned to trivialize, take for granted, debunk, or despise, drawn as we are into complicity with capital's decision to devalue whatever it cannot use.

CHAPTER NINE

Revalorizing the Abject

What is refused in the symbolic order returns in the real.
— Jacques Lacan, *Seminar,* Book III

Vandana Shiva tells about a use-value-bearing-no-value growing in the wild until eliminated in favor of a use-value-bearing-value that one can exchange for money: shredded breakfast cereal. *Bathua*, a green leafy vegetable that grows alongside wheat, was easily harvested by the women in India hired to do the weeding. But to increase production capital renamed this nutritious vegetable a "weed" and sprayed the wheat fields with herbicides: "thus, the food cycle is broken; women are deprived of work; children are deprived of a free source of nutrition" (Mies and Shiva, 1993:81). Such shifts in values plunge families with access to subsistence into the abject poverty associated with what capital regards as surplus population.

This story of a subsistence economy poisoned at the roots by global capital, illustrates three aspects of *Class Action* that I must now complete. If Labor's disappearance (Chapter 1) is the result of capital rendering whatever it cannot use abject (Chapter 5), does it not make sense to see if we can find anything useful there? If silent Labor's indeterminacy (Chapter 3) occurs at precisely the moment its labor-power is consumed by capital, through denial of alternative access to subsistence and production (Chapter 6), does it not make sense to resist by sustaining our lives cooperatively? And yet both of these questions require an answer to a problem posed in Chapter 7: How can one practice class action without depreciating the abject? This is a particular problem for academics, who are often caught up in a weeding-out process that allows only the "top minds" to advance before handing them over to capital, that phantom subject who, like any well-heeled consumer, cannot abide irregular, blotchy, diverse "produce" for daily consumption. Until this problem is resolved, the salvage operations suggested by the first question will miss the significance of the Labor underground; and the subsistence practices suggested by the second question will lose their necessary connection to Marxist struggle. Class action requires a sustained effort to revalorize what is rendered abject in bourgeois society. We know by now that political theorists cannot be expected to lead the way; instead, the approach to praxis taken in Chapter 8 gestures toward community education for everyone. Working toward valorizing the abject by repatterning ourselves in terms of real needs, rediscovering our neighbors, and reassessing our cultural times can enhance the political possibilities Butler (1993a:10) describes as "the fabrication of more local ideals."

But if all persons are implicated in the Labor underground, why should anyone bother talking about something as potentially divisive as class action? If everyone is part of Labor's recovery, are we not best approached as a classless society (with gross income differentials)? Why can we not just check our differences at the door and pursue a more perfect union in new public spaces? Those who are comfortable inside can be expected to raise such questions as these, while extending the franchise to those presently outside. Even organizers more comfortable with Marx have been working innovatively to loosen up the categories so as to allow for greater complexity than the Labor-capital tension can allow. Here we encounter three dilemmas for activism: multicultural considerations of class, the intelligentsia's habit of giving directions to people it considers lost, and global capital's smooth operations. After contrasting classless and class-based versions of community organizing, I show how the class action proposed here relates to these good works.

My plan requires contrasting three efforts to deliver concepts that may be relevant to community education in ways that confront the problem of what Ira Katznelson calls "experience-distant" theory: the "free spaces" of Harry Boyte and Sara Evans (1992), which tend to minimize the importance of class structure; the "transformative populism" of Marie Kennedy, Chris Tilly, and Mauricio Gaston, which struggles to combine class and other oppressions, especially race; and the "inappropriate other" of Trinh T. Minh-ha, which reminds progressive activists that the people most intimately involved are their key resource, after all. In a nutshell, I argue that while all three of these concepts are useful, the concept of the "inappropriate self/other" gives Marxists a chance to explore the anti-capitalist possibilities of indeterminacy. Not only does capital's hegemony depend upon the determinate forms that govern some of the best thinking about class, Labor's self-determination requires a critical approach (by workers who are themselves struggling to overcome their other oppressions) to what has already been pronounced determinate.

Three Dilemmas of Community Activism

Most activists and theorists who take class seriously have at different times come up against the dilemmas developed by Joseph Kling and Prudence Posner (1990). New populists minimize the importance of class analysis and tend not to face these problems in the form discussed below. Critical activists, including most active Marxists, face these problems every day. Much of the discussion concerning community development — to the extent this involves community organizing — turns on the differences and similarities between these two perspectives: one either does or does not take class seriously. But my approach questions the necessary indeterminacy of any representation, including Marx's.

The first dilemma addresses the familiar problem of dealing simultaneously with class oppression and other asymmetries of power in our various communities. Communities marked by differences associated with identity politics — race, gender, sexuality — also face problems of economic viability. Rather than use class as an explanatory variable, Kling and Posner see class structure as a constraining influence, a context within which communities struggle to survive. They explain that "the dynamic of class conflict (as collective capital vs. collective labor) . . . does not describe particular events, relationships, or attitudes. Instead, it functions as a constraint on the ways in which any capitalist society produces and distributes its wealth" (1990:7). But these authors are not quite prepared to endorse Ollman's argument that class structure provides the context for nonclass events, relationships, and attitudes. Relying instead on Katznelson's four-tier system, the most basic of which is the C-M-C/M-C-M level, these authors claim that class structure does not describe other aspects of community life but rather that the "ways of life" of a community give specificity to class-based description. Hence the dilemma when class ways and other ways of life do not cohere.

Katznelson's levels of class range from the "experience-distant" abstract structures to "experience-near" ways of life to the "dispositions" or "cultural configurations within which people act" (Kling and Posner, 1990:54) and finally to class as collective action. Not a developmental "model," his four-tier approach permits a discussion of tension between other experience-near ways of life in a community — such as gender politics, racism, compulsory heterosexuality — and class as a way of life. Kling and Posner are quite aware of the claim that "a sense of solidarity, or neighborliness — of 'community' — is missing in class-based social reform schemes" (8). They address this issue by refusing to choose between class analysis and community life. "We have tried to argue that class and community are not oppositional concepts but different modes through which society organizes people's connection to the worlds of production and politics. We need synthesis, therefore, not argument over which is prior, or which is the more valid construct through which collective action should take place" (38). Transformative populism attempts to achieve this synthesis of class position and community politics. For example, what does a transformative populist do when faced with a "working-class" community group that places racism at the top of its agenda? For now, let us consider this dilemma as one between taking class seriously as analysts without ruling out the politics of community in the sites where we are located.

The second dilemma haunts many political theorists when we attend local meetings of activists unaffiliated with university settings, or university meetings of activists unaffiliated with political theory. People attempting to build solidarity by talking with each other, sometimes for the first time in public, cannot be expected to welcome theorists intent upon explaining the lay of the land. And yet without coherent views and articulate positions one risks co-optation. Here Kling and Posner turn to George Rudé's (1980) distinction between "traditional, or inherent, ideologies composed of the commonsense beliefs of most people; and structured, or derived, ideologies, which are a systematic critique of conditions and present that critique in a coherent fashion." Rudé argues that traditional ideology can become the "focus of political resistance when the rights and liberties of subaltern classes are attacked." But Kling and Posner caution that "such resistance has *transformative potential* only when the traditional ideology has become strongly *suffused* with the derived ideology" (1990:12, emphasis added). Given the concerns of the first dilemma, such suffusion needs to be monitored carefully for signs of privileging class as the prior oppression, the context of all nonclass politics.

The third dilemma raised by Kling and Posner requires remembering the axiomatic power of capital hovering over any attempted fabrication of local ideals. The difficulties begin with the inevitability of enlisting the power of state bureaucracy; such is the dilemma of needing the help of institutions designed to serve different (that is, capital's) interests. But regardless of compromises on health insurance, crime bills, gay and lesbian military policy, federal law is an integral part of fighting capital's domination. This does not jibe with the fact that the most meaningful community development struggles are local efforts. Kling and Posner (1990:14) explain that "democratic efficacy is experienced at the local level, yet in the world of corporate capitalism, the power necessary to achieve democratic and egalitarian goals exists, if anywhere, only at the level of the bureaucratic national state." Efforts to contest capital's subjectivity—by forming cooperatives or challenging giant chains—often results in capital leaving town. State intervention appears necessary and yet implicated in capital's masquerade.

A rather pronounced inside-outside tension runs through these three dilemmas. If we view the people living in the communities distressed by capital's flight as outsiders, the political agenda must involve bringing these people into the political process. Community activists are insiders trying to draw new voices into the chorus. The resulting politics of polarity—inside or outside—minimizes the parochial differences among outsiders and welcomes them as citizens into democracy's free spaces, spaces free from superficial differences. If we view these communities as insiders, then activists doing the organizing are positioned as outsiders. The job becomes one of leading people to figure out—or see more objectively—what's going on in their neighborhoods. The new politics places the "subjective" complexities of life (such as gender discrimination, racism, and homophobia) inside distressed communities in a dialectical tension with the "objectivity" made possible by class analysis (as in Rudé or Katznelson), a view from the outside. Transformation, in the form of liberating the people on the inside, emerges as the intended result. But we have cultivated by now a healthy suspicion of either move—whether exteriority (people as immigrants to a democratic process outside their space) or interiority (people as informants to outside mobilizers interested in helping them toward liberation)—and admit that in our race for theory we have been presuming that critical theorists have the right kind of knowledge to liberate the "other." We might even entertain the notion that our work might actually do more to consolidate our reassuring self-conceptions than to advance Labor's self-determination. While endorsing the work of transformative populism, one might also make room for an absolute otherness that defies self-other or inside-outside distinctions of any variety without indulging in the purity of an alternative vision.

A Bourgeois Politics of Polarity (Insiders Absorb Outsiders)

Boyte and Evans (1992:185) would locate their concept of free spaces— "communally grounded voluntary associations"—somewhere in between such private spaces as neighborhoods and such public institutions as Congress and the FBI. They think of these spaces as "schools for democracy owned by the participants themselves." Relying on a logic of polarity to set the stage for this concept, they note that "a focus on the free spaces at the heart of democratic movements aids in the resolution of polarities that have long and bitterly divided modern observers and critics—expressive individualism versus ties of community; modernity versus tradition; public and private values, and so forth—by highlighting the living environments where people draw upon both 'oppositions' to create new experiments" (18). Through their involvement in these living environments, these new experiments, people learn the virtues of a citizenship that, while itself pluralized, underlies all of their less fundamental differences. They learn a "broader conception of the common good" (188) than they could have learned at home.

To those who might argue that this concept trivializes individual difference, these authors respond that subject positions based on gender, race, class, and other "biases" need to be overcome in the name of participatory democracy. Free spaces are the places to work on this self-overcoming. In the introduction to the 1992 edition of their book, Boyte and Evans describe free spaces as "public places in the community . . . in which people are able to learn a new self-respect, a deeper and more assertive group identity, public skills, and values of cooperation and civic virtue" (ix). Education is a key ingredient in achieving this vision because "ordinary people [must] learn public skills, practice debate, evaluate their actions, come to recognize the humanity of others outside their orbit" (xviii–xix). For this reason they propose evaluating free spaces in terms of their effectiveness as "schools for democracy" (ix).

These authors seek to reconnect people from all walks of life who have left their communities behind in the process of possessive individualism. Of course, these seasoned activists realize the difficulty of "real-world" applications because "free spaces are . . . marked by parochialism of class, gender, race, and other biases of the groups which maintain them" (1992:19). But their approach requires boosting the morale of the newcomers and exercising the civic virtues of those more comfortable with public discourse. Whether one is a businessman or a worker, an African American or a Swede, the point is to use civic education to overcome these relatively superficial variations. Regarding multicultural politics as parochial and biased, these authors seek to rekindle citizenship, to involve everyone in the formulation of public policy in the name of the common good. And this requires coming to terms with human suffering, and poverty in particular. So the communities left behind by capital's development are of particular concern to these new populists.

Ernesto Cortes, a community organizer from San Antonio, whose name is often associated with Communities Organized for Public Service (COPS), emerges as a hero in the politics of polarity. Boyte profiles him in an interview entitled "Education for Citizenship." Raised in a political family, Cortes went off to college to study different approaches to

dealing with poverty. After practicing in the field with Alinsky-style organizing, Cortes helped to found the moderate COPS. Boyte explains that
the COPS perspective blends a "detailed reflection" upon both Judeo-
Christian faiths and the American democratic tradition with a rather in-
strumental understanding of "citizenship education." Such an education
"trains thousands of ordinary citizens in the techniques of holding meetings, doing research, analyzing public policy positions, confronting city
officials, registering people to vote, and the like" (Boyte and Reisman,
1986:123). When Cortes speaks for himself in this profile we learn about
his approach to education: "No organizer should be so arrogant as to
pretend he's going to organize the organization. I didn't organize COPS.
The leadership organized COPS. I taught them. I trained them. I iden-
tified them. I challenged them and I worked with them on a one-to-one
basis. But they did the organizing" (120). Cortes claims that groups like
COPS are "like universities where people go to school to learn about public policy, public discourse, public life" (124). Boyte and Evans (1992:198)
observe that COPS defines itself as a new sort of "public arena" that in
many ways is self-conscious of the dimensions of free space. COPS provides a fine example of how free spaces serve to educate the people left
out of public discourse by bringing them in. There is absolutely no interest in what they may be leaving behind. And it shows how communities
can get results—$400 million in community development in San Antonio
alone—when they set out to accentuate civic virtues and not biased parochial differences.

By choosing the inside over the outside, the concept of free spaces
also manages to avoid the three dilemmas of community activism. The
class/community dilemma is resolved by adding class to a list of other
"biases" and overcoming all of them. The common sense/derived ideology dilemma disappears when one subscribes to the dominant ideology.
And the local/state dilemma loses its force because the state need not fight
global capital because capital is a citizen, not an enemy. New populism's
position as supplier of new insiders reaps political payoffs as well as financial gain. For Boyte and Evans, community is possible and to achieve it
one needs to practice the art of the possible.

A Marxist Politics of the Dialectic (Insiders and
Outsiders Together)

For advocates of a dialectical relation between inside and outside who seek
the broadest possible redistribution of power between distressed communities and overprivileged centers of capital investment, the "politics of the

possible" can be a trap. Whereas the new populism positions neglected communities as the outsiders they wish to welcome in, radical activists view these communities as insiders, almost as if they were the subjects of anthropological research. Those trying to rekindle or ignite the community's sense of outrage resemble scientists, or missionaries. Efforts to organize the community of Roxbury, Massachusetts, as reported by Kennedy, Tilly, and Gaston (1990), illustrate ways of respecting the interior of the local community while drawing its people out into public, sometimes global, discourse. We need to study the way organizers deal with the dilemmas above, especially the relation of racism and capitalist exploitation.

The structure of their analysis contrasts a transformative approach with the free spaces approach to populism. Here is how Kennedy, Tilly, and Gaston establish the importance of class structure: "Community development in low-income communities requires directing and harnessing private and public investment. It pits poor and working people against capital in a class conflict. But this class conflict is played out and experienced at the level of community. . . . Organizers [outside] must find ways to develop and link community-based identities and struggles [inside] in a fashion that challenges capital" (1990:305). But they note immediately that "race adds complexity to the situation on two levels": the relationship of capital to the community and the possibility of political mobilization. At the first level, capital is caught in a twin balancing act. As employer, capital needs stable communities (to generate a steady supply of labor-power) but not so stable as to organize against it. As user of space, it needs vibrant communities (to consume groceries, pay rent, make interest payments), but it is always looking for more profitable uses of space (e.g., parking lots). Race adds complexity here because "in communities of color, both balances are tipped further toward instability" (306). The labor force is primarily secondary or standing in reserve and the income generated from apartments, grocery stores, etc., is low. At the second level, where political mobilization of the people is at stake, racial segregation presents problems. In segregated neighborhoods "racial identities can foster unity within communities, but division among them"; in mixed neighborhoods "racial splits can fracture coalitions."

These authors describe the racial markings of some communities at risk, while warning that racial differences can undermine the coalitions required to resist capital. But unlike Boyte and Evans, they also appreciate the unifying properties of racial identity. They describe the "free spaces" approach, or any other redistributive approach that views communities at risk as outsiders in need of being welcomed inside, in the following way:

Redistributive populism builds unity by emphasizing what people have in common, and downplaying or even overlooking differences such as race. Redistributive populists take an integrationist or assimilationist view of race, arguing that racial divisions will fade into insignificance as poor and working people pursue common goals. The strategy also assumes that people will only change their views incrementally, through participation in struggles in which they have already taken sides. (Kennedy, Tilly, and Gaston, 1990:306)

These authors appreciate that the "new populists" also express interest in transformation—it is a key term for Ernesto Cortes, for example—but transformation, for the populist, is a long-range goal achieved through redistribution of resources. By contrast, Kennedy, Tilly, and Gaston want their transformation now. With identity politics back on the agenda, the devalued "different outsiders" are transformed into insiders who understand difference. Transformative populism must draw together the identity politics of those within communities at risk with a coalitional politics designed to survive in the world outside, in the civic arena of Boston and beyond.

In other words, "transformative populism emphasizes diversity as well as unity." Kennedy, Tilly, and Gaston elaborate their solution to what they call the "community-race-class dilemma": "Transformative populists seek to unite people based on their common oppression, *but also seek to use the resulting coalition to battle each group's distinct oppression*. In this strategy, people must learn not only from their own struggles but from the struggles of others—and therefore organizers confront coalition members with issues designed to stretch the members' world views" (1990:307, emphasis added). We cannot help but notice the order of priorities—class comes first—in their efforts to address the community-race-class dilemma. Even though class is (what our authors call) an implicit rather than an explicit rallying cry, transformative populism seeks to "unite people based on their common oppression" and then, in a coalition, go to work on the distinct problems of each constituent group. In the process, transformation—the redistribution of power—is both an end in itself and a means to redistribution of resources. Note that this reversal of the new populist agenda requires an element of education: "organizers confront . . . members with issues."

The authors cite Mel King, an insider and outsider (a "state representative from the integrated, largely black South End"), to illustrate the electoral side of transformative populism. After campaigning to be elected mayor of Boston and coming in second, King proclaimed to other communities left out by capital's uneven development (such as the largely Irish South Boston), "We all came over on different ships, but we're in the same boat now." Unlike his chief rival, Ray Flynn (a new populist who won) Mel King formed a rainbow coalition and did not hesitate to emphasize problems of racism and the need for gay rights, even when campaigning in "mixed" communities such as Dorchester. "As a result he attracted active supporters from a wide range of communities and movements: blacks, Latinos, Asians, gays and lesbians, feminists, peace activists, and housing activists" (Kennedy, Tilly, and Gaston, 1990:309). But we must recall that class is only the "implicit" organizing principle; the noneconomic concerns of each group are much more visible in the rainbow coalition. Using noneconomic issues to build a popular coalition based on a common oppression—a labor-capital war of position—is of course somewhat contradictory, because the people involved at the outset may not recognize, acknowledge, or even share this common oppression. This brings us to the second dilemma of activism: traditional versus derived ideology.

The redistributive populists have a much easier time with this dilemma, according to our authors, because they eschew Rudé's "derived ideology." To keep coalitions such as COPS together, "free space" leaders sacrifice transformational goals on a regular basis. To explain, by contrast, how transformative populists "attempt to bridge the gap between traditional and derived ideology," Kennedy, Tilly, and Gaston (1990:311) turn to recent community organizing in Roxbury, the center of Boston's black community and a growing Latino community. They note, first, that organizers in Roxbury are working hard to link the "residents' immediate experience as members of a subordinate racial group" with "broader concepts and struggles" (311). The concepts and struggles our author have in mind are "international issues," such as South African apartheid; "class analysis," for example, pressing for community control of capital investment in high-rise office towers; and "self-determination not assimilation," such as the 1986 "Mandela" ballot proposal to incorporate Roxbury as an independent city (311–12). In each case the community insiders, the residents, are granted their immediate perceptions of racism, but they are encouraged by leaders outside to take a broader view.

The second way our authors illustrate transformative populism's efforts to bridge the ideology gap involves taking the residents of Roxbury more seriously than mere people with immediate perceptions. Here the residents act as informants when community organizing plans are being developed. Our authors note that outside community activists must recognize that "the relationship between derived and traditional ideology runs in both directions." Note the inside-outside dynamics of the following:

"Activists armed with a left ideology have something to teach their constituents, but they also have something to learn from them. . . . Respecting ordinary people enough to believe that they can change their world view when exposed to new ideas means respecting them enough to believe that they see important parts of reality that the left does not" (313).

If this passage does not make it obvious, the authors occupy the position of people who articulate the ideas designed to change the world view of the "ordinary" people. While it may be problematic to say that I respect your difference so much that I reckon you are capable of seeing things my way some day, the new populists appear not to respect difference at all. Transformative populists are at least aware of the risks of intellectual elitism. Their evidence of this comes from Kennedy, who initially opposed private home ownership in Roxbury for reasons informed by derived ideology: atomization of mortgagees and the bourgeois lure of "investment opportunity." When residents insisted on owning their own homes a compromise was forged between activists and intellectuals: nonspeculative home ownership (private space now with controls on resale later). Transformative populists with derived ideology (perhaps after reading Marx on capital) are willing to sit down with "ordinary" insiders representing traditional ideology (for example, John Locke on estate ownership), hear how "they" see things differently, and then act accordingly. What transpires is, say the authors, more dialectical interplay than liberal compromise.

Of course, such a dialectical politics between insiders and outsiders takes time. Another way that Roxbury's organizers attempt to solve the dilemma of ideology is through adoption of a broad concept of empowerment, one that emphasizes process as well as product in a "patient, long-term" approach to class struggle. Redistributive populists may pursue quick victories—such as the $400 million investment procured by COPS —with the often sacrificed goal of eventual transformation of consciousness. By contrast, we are told that transformative populists "define empowerment in terms of a change in mass consciousness" and view such transformation as an end in itself, as opposed to a negotiable by-product. They work for the same redistributive gains as "free space" populists, but transformation—such as "popularizing a radical analysis of development" —constitutes a "more important victory" (Kennedy, Tilly, and Gaston, 1990:314).

Transformative populists—whether they are linking immediate perceptions of insiders to broader concepts of outsiders, engaging in an insider-outsider dialogue concerning community development, or popularizing the class analysis of outsiders—bridge the dilemmas of ideology in ways that implicitly and explicitly privilege the class analysis of derived ideology. Indeed, this strategy appears to be the only hedge against the implicit and explicit co-optation associated with redistributive populism. The third dilemma—the simultaneous antagonism and necessity of state power—continues this contrast; but Kennedy, Tilly, and Gaston's discussion of community development in its widest sense suggests a way to take people and class seriously at the same time.

Because their experience involves organizing in the city of Boston, the authors discuss the third dilemma at the municipal rather than the federal level. This poses a slight methodological problem for their contrast of the two forms of populism because the redistributive populists are, with the election of new populist Ray Flynn, part of the municipal government, while the transformative populists are mostly on the fringe of local government. But in Boston the mayor's office is only part of the municipal government, and it is possible to contrast ways in which these two approaches clash over the role of local government in community development, and vice versa. Mayor Flynn's new populism would redistribute resources, but balks "at redistributing power—the power to plan and to control land use" (Kennedy, Tilly, and Gaston, 1990:315). As we would by now expect, transformative populists struggle to bring power to the people. They do this by defining community development in the broadest possible way. Drawing inspiration from Julius Nyerere, our authors stress the importance first and foremost of "developing the people who make up a community." A subtle difference—between developing the people (for example, by transforming so-called ordinary people from their immediate perception of oppression and traditional ways of thinking to a new consciousness of their class position) and people developing themselves—goes to the heart of the transformative approach. Insiders see things differently, but outsiders have the more articulate, coherent vision. By working together, we are told, the people can be developed as the most important part of community development.

Kennedy, Tilly, and Gaston address the three dilemmas by distinguishing their approach from "free space" community development. But neither side of the contrast between redistributive and transformative populism seems to give space to Labor's indeterminacy. Transforming silence into action requires "reclaiming that language which has been made to work against" the silenced subject (Lorde, 1984:43). The implicit message that Kennedy, Tilly, and Gaston convey is that intellectuals need to work with "ordinary people" in the community in the name of delivering them to a place that "extraordinary people" see most clearly. But a liberal rejection of this "class first!" arrogance throws us back to an even more insulting "free space" elitism which advocates bourgeois citizenship as a (race, gender, sexuality) blindfold to be tied on tightly during their miserable surrender in the war of position.

Class is a divisive element for new populists and an implicit unifying element for radical activists. This might leave one with the impression that taking class seriously requires not taking "the people" seriously. Instead I pursue a valorization of the abject which scans discursive territory for signs of both intelligent life and intellectual limitations not recognized by strategies that think only in terms of insiders and outsiders. By making "free spaces" a bit more murky than most liberals can bear and subject-object dialectics slightly less meaningful than many Marxists can tolerate, people struggling to survive might begin to reclaim the language and other resources they need. Social and political theorists must be wary of presuming that the Labor underground and especially those who have been rendered wholly abject are already represented in existent forms of life. Nor should anyone suppose that people on the edge of survival are not already living cooperatively in mutual support and defense.

The Politics of Supplementation (besides Outsiders and Insiders)

The problem of representation is usually construed in contemporary theory as a complex problem of excluding and including voices. This political sense of representation applies both to newly emerging subjects and more established cultural hegemons. Its multicultural ramifications are well known: questions of percentages that indicate what self-congratulating liberals like to call "diversity." The more complicated questions involve negotiating intersecting positions in identity politics. These negotiations are so complex that the boundaries of even the most symmetrical discursive fields—such as inside-outside relations—can become unclear. In most Western circles, as we have seen in "free space" populism, political representation tends to ignore these problems of indeterminacy and settles instead for a liberal pluralism designed to protect the rights of all subjects, including global capital. Such a pluralism appears to be inclusionary while excluding structurally any voice that cannot speak in the determinate forms available.

Without contesting the extension of political rights to all rightful subjects, with the notable exception of capital, one can nevertheless examine the role of another facet—the constitutive side—of the problem of representation. Here one confronts the problem of determinate and indeterminate meaning. Those comfortably situated who consider themselves articulate, coherent, and perhaps even self-clarified—and who may, like the transformative populists, want to negotiate multicultural complexities but find frustration in the silence of the "other"—must deal every day with people they make them uncomfortable. Rather than only working with newly emergent subjects in a struggle for political representation ("we respect you and want to know what you think"), comfortable theorists might also learn to develop new rules to follow—reconstituted forms of life—jointly with newly emerging subjects. Any democratic reconstitution must include rethinking capital's subject positioning in dominant discursive fields (perhaps dissociating the social surplus from the list of rightful properties of embodied subjects). But this reformulation can never begin until "the people" develop themselves by transforming their silence into language and action. Comfortable theorists, including Marxists, must realize that their models represent "the other" in ways that might silence or otherwise confine the very people they intend to liberate or transform.

Trinh T. Minh-ha, a filmmaker and social theorist, accepts the "mission to represent others" but does so in a fashion that refuses to fix either her position as the objective observer or her subject's position as the "other." Herein lies her relevance to this discussion of representing the "ordinary" people in community development. Through her essays and films, she works out practico-theoretically a concept of radical supplementation that she calls the "inappropriate self/other." This concept promises to supplement the important work of transformative populism by addressing an unintentional tendency toward what Marilyn Frye (1983) calls "arrogant perception."

Trinh argues that showing concern for the "other" appears to be more progressive than simple neglect of difference in the regions ignored by capital's uneven development. But she warns that showing concern (sometimes called "respect") for the other is often only a form of reinforcing the security of one's own precarious position as self. On this point she turns to Vincent Crapanzano, who offers this suggestion: "One's sense of self is always mediated by the image one has of the other. (I have asked myself at times whether a superficial knowledge of the other, in terms of some stereotype, is not a way of preserving a superficial image of oneself)" (Trinh, 1991:73). Here one faces the awkward possibility that the practice of calling the residents of devalued communities "ordinary people" has more to do with running a "race for theory" (Christian, 1989) than with joining a struggle for economic democracy. Perhaps the "progressive community activist" with an office, laptop, and library is as superficial an image of an intellectual as the "ordinary person" with subjective feelings and no critical understanding of the situation.

Trinh (1991:66) explores just such an awkward possibility when she writes that "the move from obnoxious exteriority to obtrusive interiority, the race for the so-called *hidden* values of a person or culture, has given rise to a form of legitimized (but unacknowledged as such) voyeurism and subtle arrogance—namely, the pretense to see into or to *own* the others' minds, whose *knowledge* these others cannot, supposedly, have themselves; and the need to define, hence confine, providing them with a standard of self-evaluation on which they necessarily depend." This claim can too easily be misread as a condemnation of efforts to negotiate differences across subject positions. The problem is not the negotiations per se but the presumption that all of the positions have been defined (before the arrival of "the other"). "Come to the meeting. We have a seat waiting for you." To define is to confine, and any democratic approach to self-determination and empowerment must include self-definition. Not being defined at all is sometimes preferable to being defined by somebody else.

Trinh develops the "inappropriate other" in her essay "Outside In Inside Out," which draws heavily from the writings of Zora Neale Hurston. Hurston's writing reflects the idea of an excess that cannot be reduced to the confines of black-white, self-other, or subject-object relations. Hurston writes this, for example: "The white man is always trying to know into somebody else' business. All right, I'll set something outside the door of my mind for him to play with and handle. He can read my writing but he sho' can't read my mind. I'll put this play toy in his hand, and he will seize it and go away. Then I'll say my say and sing my song" (Trinh, 1991:74-75). The idea that the insiders—such as residents of communities like Roxbury—can deliver the truth of the immediate situation to outsiders (including those with the best intentions) presumes a relation between insiders and outsiders that disregards the complexity of self-determination on both sides. There is always an excess.

To speak of aspects of life wholly inside or outside the discursive terrain in question makes little sense because such isolation ignores the interdependence of the two sides: you can't have one without the other. Trinh is concerned with negotiations at the borderlines. Here she claims that those who cross borders—for example, from Roxbury's kitchens to Boston's City Hall—realize that they are "the same but not quite the same" as the people they meet along the way. This difference can signal a critique of the inside-outside tension itself. Adopting the perspective of a cultural insider crossing over to the position of objective observer, Trinh describes a process that resembles moving from tradition to derived ideology:

The moment the insider steps out from the inside, she is no longer a mere insider (or vice versa). She necessarily looks in from the outside while also looking out from the inside. Like the outsider, she steps

back and records what never occurs to her the insider as being worth
or in need of recording. But unlike the outsider, she *also resorts to non-
explicative, non-totalizing strategies that suspend meanings and resist closure.*
She refuses to reduce herself to an Other, and her reflections to a mere
outsider's objective reasoning or insider's subjective feeling. (1991: 74,
emphasis added)

The distinction between intellectuals and activists might possibly illustrate this dynamic. Activists raised in the community who cross over and
attend meetings with radical scholars outside the community might work
night and day trying to change a city ordinance. Sitting around after winning, the intellectuals and activists may feel the same—yet not quite the
same—as each other. At this point we need to ask if our approach honors
the space for the refusal to reduce oneself to an other, or the refusal to
reduce these recollections to a blend of the professorial objectivity of an
outsider and the "ordinary" subjectivity of an insider. In other words, we
must determine whether a dialectical logic does justice to the excess on
both sides of the appropriate positions.

Trinh continues describing the borderline existence of the insider/out-
sider/alongsider:

Not quite the Same, not quite the Other, she stands in that *undeter-
mined threshold place where she constantly drifts in and out.* Undercutting
the inside/outside opposition, her intervention is necessarily that of
both a deceptive insider and a deceptive outsider. *She is this Inappropriate Other/Same* who moves about with always at least two/four gestures:
that of affirming "I am like you" while persisting in her difference; and
that of reminding "I am different" while *unsettling every definition of
otherness arrived at.* (1991:74, emphasis added)

Whereas redistributive populism cannot comprehend citizens who are the
same and yet different, transformative populism celebrates human difference on the way to an objective understanding of sameness—class as a
homogenizing experience. But a politics of supplementation—although it
can offer no alternatives—complicates the standards one might use to distinguish "objective" class analysis from "subjective" anger that turns so
easily to rage. "The subjectivity at work in the context of this Inappropriate Other can hardly be submitted to the old subjectivity/objectivity
paradigm"(1991:76). This "inappropriate other" occupies every subject
position in different ways; each side of the tensions represented by the
three dilemmas of community activism contains an excess that cannot be
reduced to the categories available. Class is forced to accept a marked

heterogeneity (including indeterminacy) in the process. We must figure out how to come to terms with this heterogeneity without becoming so fragmented as to allow capital easy access to its subject position.

Trinh's concept of the inappropriate other carries implications, of course, for antiracist work as well as other struggles against asymmetries of social power. The self-other tension disguises supplementation in all walks of life. Indeed, many deconstructions of the inside-outside tension are alive and doing very well in cultural studies, especially queer theory. But when taking class seriously and especially when interrogating the intersections of economic and social asymmetries, the concept of the inappropriate other is useful in exposing areas of life that capital cannot appropriate. And these pockets of survival may well hold the secret of exposing the lie of capital—that it has a consciousness and will—on the way to Labor's self-determination.

Trinh shows the arrogance of any outsider relying on an uninterrupted objective standpoint (for example, Rudé's derived ideology) for an understanding of a so-called subjective situation. Totalizing gestures are sometimes said to be necessary for agenda building in politics, and they are nearly always the sign of good science. But these gestures leave most people out of the picture for the most part, and this can be a mortal blow to Labor's self-determination. To put this another way, any attempt to build self-determination that relies on imported notions of self (for example, self-consolidating difference) already undermines self-determination. When outside activists move into a community to mobilize the people along class lines, for example, are we not already defining, and hence confining, the people who live there as "working class," "poor," "inarticulate," or "incoherent"? Perhaps by some objective standard the people are all of these, but in the drift along the borderlines they are also none of these. As Carole Anne Taylor (1993:67) writes in a different context: "Explications of ambivalent or multiple identity help explain how victims may understand their location as victims in relation to an oppressor without that locus taking the place of either identity or agency." Perhaps scholar-activists need to confront their own relation to Labor, their own complicity with capital, their own articulation and coherence. No one is immune to the drift of the inappropriate other.

Just as the incredible success of COPS in general and Ernesto Cortes in particular might illustrate the political potential of "free spaces," and the rainbow coalition of Mel King illustrates the transformative potential of critical activism, the work of Myles Horton and the Highlander Folk School (Adams, 1975) might illustrate the "inappropriate other" at stake in the struggle for Labor's self-determination. Although I am certain that one could call the Highlander Folk School a "free space," and that "transformative populism" is clearly an end in itself at this Tennessee research center, the way Highlander deals with insider/outsider dynamics differs from the two leading approaches to community development. We must note, among other things, a pedagogical difference.

Myles Horton struggled hard to start where the people are. The resources of the people, however inarticulate, silent, or incoherent they may appear when viewed from outside their communities, form the foundation of folk education. Avoiding the arrogant stance of someone trying to learn their truths or teach them new ones, Myles Horton developed a form of adult education that made it possible for local people to get together, to identify their needs, and to work in solidarity toward resolution. Adams (1975:47) reports that "formally educated staff members have never been as effective in teaching as the people, once they saw themselves as teachers." Highlander believes that only the people involved know enough about their situation to initiate social action.

Without violating the principle of starting where the people are, workshop discussion leaders can reinforce talk in the group that leads to united action (Adams, 1975:212-13). This is a two-stage strategy: the people set the stage first and decide when and how to bring in the additional information and expertise they need. But in order even to talk with each other people must negotiate their various differences. Rosa Parks, Bernice Johnson Reagon, Martin Luther King Jr., and countless other organizers participated in these negotiations at Highlander and then returned to their local and national struggles.

Class structure is intimately involved in this adult education because of its concentration on asymmetries of economic power. But "cultural coherence" (Delgado, 1994) is never sacrificed in the name of objective analysis, nor is it ever presumed that the teachers can read the minds of the women and men involved. Nor do the outsiders (intellectuals mostly) presume to know enough to effectuate economic liberation. Rather than label people "working-class" or "poor," which places them in tension with owners of the means of production, Highlander creates a space for self-study, reflection, and cultural exchange. Community education is also an important aspect of bourgeois "free spaces" and the transformative populism of more traditional Marxist approaches; but the "inappropriate other" calls attention to the formless unrest of the abject—a devaluation from which no one is exempt—before raising the issue of determinate form. Hence its relation to the Labor underground.

After detecting Labor's whereabouts underground in Part 1 and exposing capital as a phantom subject in Part 2, I have underscored in this third part the importance of beginning with the abject whenever practicing class action. Beginning here must not be confused with an effort to create some new subject, "the abject," who miraculously returns from the dead. The nameless properties, reserves, and energy that, following Marx, I call Labor (the state of being in possession of labor-power) enjoys no such access to the means of representation. Labor is a state of being denied legitimacy in bourgeois society. And yet, miraculously, actual people marked for early death as providers of surplus labor, or discarded outright as a surplus population, have managed to sustain life. Labor, signified only by the hyphens in subject-object relations, has always been in the business of sustaining life against terrible obstacles. Without Labor, communities owe their lives to capital and the state; with Labor (in the offing) people begin to realize that self-determination has always been a question of creating new forms of life and seeing them through.

Class Action focuses, then, on revalorizing the abject as a means of encouraging actual people to sift through the refuse of bourgeois society together in the name of fashioning new forms of representation. Such salvage operations suggest a form of community education that makes the connection between access to the means of representation and access to the means of subsistence and production. This is precisely the connection that those Marxists who uncritically reject poststructuralism risk losing. Without addressing issues of access to subsistence and the means of production, community education can become reduced to a space for grooming labor-power for consumption by capital. And without community education, subsistence politics can become a matter of individual or family survival, or a charity that reinscribes, among the bourgeois, the uselessness of the surplus population its heart goes out to. But a popular education that pursues new forms of life, new means of representation, in an atmosphere of nourishment and nurturing—a life in which people share income, tools, food, ideas, stories, and other resources—promises new political possibilities which could render capital anachronistic.

Instead of regarding Labor as a god who, when properly nourished, might seek revenge and free us from capital's tyrannous violence, *Class Action* regards Labor as an endless supply of nourishment and creativity, the key to the mutual support and defense that one associates with community. Efforts to organize the demands of people whose labor-power capital consumes so desperately and efforts to contest capital's subjectivity in legislative and judicial settings are both intimately related to retrieving Labor's subjectivity. But Labor's self-determination in the "needs of the people," right under capital's nose, constitutes the heart of class action. To organize the object we must begin by valorizing the abject; the point, however, is to change the subject.

Notes

Chapter One: Lispector Haunting Marxism

1. See Charles Gray's (1994) inspirational work on subsistence economics at the level of a world median income.

2. Grossman and Adams (1993) have produced a useful pamphlet in this regard.

3. "The *fundamental class process* refers to the producing and appropriating of surplus labor. . . . The *subsumed class process* refers to the distribution of the surplus labor (or its products) after it has been appropriated" (Fraad, Resnick, and Wolff, 1994:3).

4. A key question here is, What force or discourse can serve to "negate all of them"? I hesitate to extend that much credit to capital. This is not, of course, to deny the existence of a small group of obscenely wealthy people who live by "grafting the substance of others on to themselves" (Lugones, 1990:161, quoting Frye, 1983:66).

5. Her claim does not require, for example, rejecting nature and humanity as a tension, but it does guard against viewing this relation solely in terms of a subject-object couple, even one enjoying a dialectical relation. Such restrictive practices effectively reduce the stream of life's mysteries to a finite number of productive activities.

6. Laclau and Mouffe (1985:151) use the language of subject and object positioning but have decided to add class struggle—labor versus capital—to a list of other liberation movements, including environmentalism. This seems to grant unnecessarily the capitalist a subject position to be reckoned with. I am trying to view class as a fundamental structural question without adding it to a list of other efforts to liberate people. Environmentalists and antiracist or feminist movements operate in fields governed by global capital, a false subject whose masquerade it is my task to uncover.

7. Of course, Milton Fisk (1993) argues persuasively that such a move does not necessarily drop the metaphor, especially if one views "text" as the new metaphor of choice.

Chapter Two: The Ruined Limits of Enunciation: From Lacan to Derrida

1. Lacan (1966:11; 1988a:28) states quite explicitly that "the lesson of this seminar is . . . that these imaginary incidences, far from representing the essence of our experience, reveal only what in it remains inconsistent unless they are related to the symbolic chain which binds and orients them."

2. According to Lacan we have before us a dramatic situation which includes at least two scenes, scenes that are parallel in the sense that they share a similar tripartite structure: a place of blindness in which the subject sees nothing; a place of seeing what the other does not, in which the seeing subject might try to hide something; and a place of seeing what the seeing subject and blind subject do not, in which the all-seeing subject can filch whatever the others are hiding. To begin going around the circuit, the king occupies the place of blindness in the first scene; Prefect G takes his place in the second. At the next stop, the queen occupies the place of seeing what the king does not (allowing her to hide the letter face down) in the first scene; Minister D takes her place in the second (allowing him to hide the letter inside out, crumpled, addressed to himself, in his apartment). Finally, at the third stop in the triad, Minister D's lynx eye occupies the all-seeing position in the first scene, allowing him to steal the letter from the queen; Dupin then takes over this position in the second scene, allowing him to steal it back. But when Dupin returns the original letter to the law (in exchange for money), he also leaves behind a hostile message for Minister D, and this act repeats the cycle, setting up a third scene in which D takes the blind spot (until he gets the message) and Dupin the spot of the one who sees (sees to it that revenge will be his), leaving to Lacan the all-seeing position of analyst.

3. Unless otherwise indicated, page numbers in this section refer to both the 1966 and 1988a texts.

4. Shoshana Felman (1988:145) maps the two scenes in terms of the real, the Imaginary, and the Symbolic:

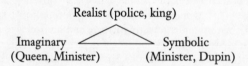

Realist (police, king)

Imaginary   Symbolic
(Queen, Minister)   (Minister, Dupin)

This depiction works well to draw the two scenes together in a way that conforms to Lacan's three moments of seeing nothing, hiding something, and seeing someone hiding something. But it forces us to equate the Lacanian real (as inarticulable void) with a naive empirical realism, and refuses to allow the letter to assume the role of a character in the play. Although Lacan is clearly interested here at the top of his edited *Ecrits* in delivering at least the spirit of Freud's letters (on the id, ego and superego) in his own image/form of the real, the Imaginary and the Symbolic, I am not convinced that this is the best reading of the tripartite structure involved. Lacan can instead be shown here to highlight the relay function of the tripartite intersubjective circuit. At any given point in time, from any given perspective, one could isolate a character, including the one who fires the shot in the street outside the Minister's apartment, and tell the story from that perspective. Rather than trying to tell all of these stories at once, in their intersection and contradiction—a repre-

sentational impossibility—we are trying to study the reliance of any self-other relation (whether king-queen, minister-Dupin, or Poe-Baudelaire) on a symbolic order.
Lacan is most interested in how characters change places in the intersubjective circuit whenever they come in contact with the letter. Lacan (1988b:196–97) stresses in
an earlier discussion of Poe's letter that in addition to a list of persons, "the characters in question can be defined differently. They can be defined beginning with the
subject, more precisely beginning with the relation determined by the aspiration of
the real subject through the necessity of the symbolic linking process." I will soon
use his Schema L to show how we as animals at the mercy of language (*je*), engage in
"circus acts" between egos (*moi*) and our objects, in the presence of a box "reserved
for the boredom" of the real subject (Lacan, 1977:265). But to avoid getting ahead
of myself, let me speculate simply that the real subject in the tale is the "letter"; and
as far as the other characters in the play are concerned, the relay is the thing. Read
this way—getting back to Felman's triad—each character, including Prefect G and
Minister D, can be positioned at the Imaginary, the purloined letter is the Symbolic
for all of them, and the real interrupts in the form of what does not fit the picture as
constituted (for example, the facsimile the Minister D leaves behind).

5. Anthony Wilden (1968) translates *discours* as "speech."

6. As we shall see soon, all desire aims at the true radical subject, but because
this is impossible it is deflected to the other, making subject-object relations a com-
monplace. The letter always arrives at its destination, in part because it never leaves
the lower-right quadrant of Schema L, its destination.

7. Although this imbecilic attempt to outline Lacan summons the spirit of G's
exactitude, I do so to distinguish my reading from that of John Muller and William
Richardson (1988:79), for whom the first dialogue illustrates the Imaginary and the
second the Symbolic, even though Lacan insists that "the dialogues themselves, in
the opposite use they make of the powers of speech, take on a tension which makes
of them a different drama, one which our vocabulary will distinguish from the first
as persisting in the symbolic order." But my main reason for showing exactly how
I think Lacan organizes this section concerns Barbara Johnson's (1988) claim that
Derrida's critique of Lacan, which we will soon consider, ignores Schema L, even
though he reads this section quite closely. We will soon see that my overly systematic
reading of this passage traces the letter, if not the spirit, of the Schema L.

8. For example, Elizabeth Grosz (1990:62) explains that the ego's "demand is the
consequence of the subjection of the need to the regulation of language."

9. Lacan (1977:74) writes: "For exactitude is to be distinguished from truth, and
conjecture does not exclude rigour. . . . our link to nature urges us to wonder poeti-
cally whether it is not its very own movement that we rediscover in our science."

10. "The signifier . . . materializes the agency of death" (23; 38). Muller and
Richardson (1988:90) note that Lacan quotes St. Paul elsewhere: "the letter killeth
while the spirit quickens."

11. "To trace back from images to the structure would . . . not rescue us from
representation, *if the structure* [the twin axes of Schema L] *did not have a reverse side*
that is like the real production of desire. . . . It is this entire reverse side of structure
that Lacan discovers, with the 'o' as machine, and the 'O' as nonhuman sex: schizo-
phrenizing the analytic field instead of oedipalizing the psychotic field" (Deleuze
and Guattari, 1983:308–9).

12. They quote Henry Miller here: "My guts spilled out in a grand schizophrenic rush, an evacuation that leaves me face to face with an Absolute."

13. Early sections of *Anti-Oedipus* provide some of the more memorable accounts of the desiring-machine called schizophrenia. Here I quote at length:

> The schizo has his own system of co-ordinates for situating himself at his disposal, because, first of all, he has at his disposal his very own recording code, which does not coincide with the social code, or coincides with it only in order to parody it. The code of delirium or of desire proves to have an extraordinary fluidity. It might be said that the schizophrenic passes from one code to the other, that he deliberately *scrambles all codes*, by quickly shifting from one code to another, according to the questions asked him, never giving the same explanation from one day to the next, never invoking the same genealogy, never recording the same event in the same way. When he is more or less forced into it and is not in a touchy mood, he may even accept the banal Oedipal code, so long as he can stuff it full of all the disjunctions that this code was designed to eliminate. (Deleuze and Guattari, 1983:15)

As unsalable items in a society regulated according to capitalist axioms, desiring-machines pose a continual threat of undermining the so-called bottom line, exploiting its contradictory status.

14. In the passage they cite Marx writes: "Only as personified capital is the capitalist respectable. As such, he shares with the miser the passion for wealth as wealth. But that which in the miser is a mere idiosyncrasy, is, in the capitalist, the effect of the social mechanism, of which he is but one of the wheels."

15. They oppose "the reduction of the machine to structure, the identification of production with a structural and theatrical representation (*Darstellung*)" (1983:306). They continue: "every time that production, rather than being apprehended in its originality, in its reality, becomes reduced (*rabattue*) in this manner to a representational space, it can no longer have value except by its own absence, and it appears as a lack within this space." In Chapter 5 we will locate this use of *Darstellung* in its connection to structural effectivity in Althusser, and perhaps a richer sense of the word in Marx.

16. It is important neither to attribute excessive continuity to the axiom nor to expect it to contain each and every flow: "The axioms are primary statements, which do not derive from or depend upon another statement. In this sense, a flow can be the object of one or several axioms (with the set of all axioms constituting the conjugation of flows); but it can also lack any axioms of its own, its treatment being only a consequence of other axioms; finally it can remain out of bounds, evolve without limits, be left in the state of an 'untamed' variation in the system" (1987:461).

17. Here is how Deleuze and Guattari distinguish three aspects of their newest pair:

> The smooth and the striated are distinguished first of all by an inverse relation between the point and the line (in the case of the striated, the line is between two points, while in the smooth, the point is between two lines); and second, by

the nature of the line (smooth-directional, open intervals; dimensional-striated, closed intervals). Finally, there is a third difference, concerning the surface or space. In striated space, one closes off a surface and "allocates" it according to determinate intervals, assigned breaks; in the smooth, one "distributes" oneself in an open space, according to frequencies and in the course of one's crossings. (1988:480–81)

18. Technically speaking, Lacan locates the narrator on the *je-Autre* axis by using his role in relating the two dialogues to produce the line from speech's exactitude to the word's truth, on either side of the wall of language.

19. Derrida writes: "The least one might say about the relationship formed in this meeting place is that it will never leave the so-called general narrator in the position of a neutral and transparent reporter who does not intervene in the narration in progress" (1987:486).

20. Judith Butler (1987:216–17) notices that both Lacan and Deleuze rely on "a dream of reconstituting the lost unity of being" regardless of whether this unity is attainable.

Chapter Three: Appreciating the Labor Underground

1. While following Mies (1986) down the hierarchy of unitary subjects—from international and national capital to white men to white women to Third World servants and slaves, one can perhaps read the subjectivity of the most powerful players more closely than her perspective allows. In Part 2, behind and between the enemy lines of dominant discursive structures, I attempt to challenge the position assumed there by the "subject" named Mr. Capital.

2. Spivak's argument consists of four sections: first, she announces the problem of woman defined as subset of man; second, she notes that it is too easy to address this problem—reading Freud or Marx—without considering the production of the colonial object; third, she offers a literary reading to consider how the sexed subjectivity of a new mother can exceed men's uterine expectations; fourth, she turns to a nonfictional account of Korean women attacked by their male colleagues for efforts to organize a union in a U.S.-owned corporation to show the impossibility of neglecting gender and race when contesting capital's hegemony.

3. For a discussion of the proper(ty) see Derrida (1978b:117).

4. Chapter 8 offers a poststructural praxis which counters familiar ways (from Hegel to Teresa Ebert) of sublating this tension.

5. Part 2 of this book illustrates the possible utility of this distinction when reading Marx.

6. Those accustomed to privileged positions cannot, of course, just "join in" the constitution of subjects without first repatterning, relearning. Deconstruction may be of some use to academics so inclined when used in the following sense: "Persistently to critique a structure that one cannot not (wish to) inhabit is the deconstructive stance" (Spivak, 1993:284).

Chapter Five: Containing Indeterminacy: From Althusser to Marx

1. My argument follows the advice of Michael Ryan (1993:152), who asks everyone to remember that "resistance is primary, and indeterminacy makes all the categories of the discourses of power contingent and remakeable."

2. See Thomas Keenan's brilliant reading of "human labor in the abstract" (1993: 173–74).

3. Fredric Jameson (1981:35) connects the understanding of the textualization of outside objects (which can be known in no other way) to Althusser when he writes "that history [for Althusser] is *not* a text, not a narrative, master or otherwise, but that as an absent cause, it is inaccessible to us except in textual form."

4. Althusser is the first to concede that on some occasions turning to practice—whether laboratory experiments, social practice, or field studies—may be warranted by the struggle at hand. There may sometimes be no other way to carry the day, to win the argument. Readers know the rhetorical force of inverting subject-object relations: if people are calling you an ideologue, point out how *they* are ideologues. But this (one-sided reactive action) by itself requires one's theory to reflect life practices and vice versa. Althusser (1979a:57) writes, "But this practice, and the mode of employment of ideological arguments adapted to this struggle, must be the object of a *theory* so that ideological struggle in the domain of ideology does not become a struggle governed by the laws and wishes of the opponent, so that it does not transform us purely into subjects of the ideology it is our aim to combat."

5. "In all these cases, the common rule which permits this action is in fact the question of the guarantees of the harmony between knowledge (or Subject) and its real object (or Object), i.e., the ideological question as such" (Althusser, 1979a:57).

6. Consider Althusser (1979a:58–59) at length: "We regard an element of knowledge even in its most rudimentary forms and even though it is profoundly steeped in ideology, as always already present in the earliest stages of practice, those that can be observed even in the subsistence practices of the most primitive societies. At the other extreme in the history of practices, we regard what is commonly called theory, in its 'purest' forms, those that seem to bring into play the powers of thought alone. The practice is theoretical. It is distinguished from the other . . . practices by the type of object (raw material) which it transforms."

7. Althusser (1979a:59) writes: "No mathematician in the world waits until physics has verified a theorem to declare it proved, although whole areas of mathematics are applied in physics . . . the truth of his theorem is a hundred percent provided by criteria purely internal to the practice of mathematical proof."

8. Consider: "Of course, the method of presentation (*Darstellungsweise*) must differ in form from that of inquiry (*Forschungsweise*). The latter has to appropriate the material in detail, to analyse its different forms of development, to track down their inner connection. Only after this work has been done, can the real movement be appropriately presented. If this is done successfully, if the life of the subject-matter is now reflected back in the ideas, then it may appear as if we have before us a mere *a priori* construction" (Marx, 1976a:102; 1989:55).

9. Grosz (1989:21) puts it this way: "[The mirror stage] explains the child's earliest differentiation from the mother, the genesis of the child's gradually emerging

sense of self. . . . The ego is that psychical agency providing the conditions under which the child can become a subject and an object, for itself and for others." This stage, then, is often cited as the foundation of the Lacanian Imaginary. Indeed the process of overdetermination requires renegotiating the tentative subject-object distinctions established at the mirror stage. But we must note that for Lacan (1977:4) the "succession of phantasies" ranges from the fragmentation of the subject to a provisional totality to the "alienating [but rigid] identity" of subjects and objects.

10. As Gallop (1985:59) explains, "the imaginary is the realm where intersubjective structures are covered over by mirroring. Lacan's writings contain an implicit ethical imperative to break the mirror, an imperative to disrupt the imaginary in order to reach the symbolic." We explore below the difference between individuals as subjects at the mirror stage and theory as a subject at the mirror stage.

11. Readers must be careful here not to confuse my use of the hidden mirror stage (as a heuristic when treating theory as the subject) with other discussions of the mirror stage in Althusser. Elsewhere Althusser employs the Lacanian mirror stage to describe the collective ignorance (*méconnaissance*) of a duped people, an imaginary which requires breaking the mirror to get on with the business of symbolic representation. Here we might supplement Althusser with recent studies of desire and fetishism, as they explore the dimensions of a psychoanalytic theory of hegemony. Recent developments gather the Lacanian threads from Althusser's work on ideological state apparatuses but treat his Marxist science project as counterproductive. When Kaja Silverman applauds Althusser's efforts to explain complex ideological differences between classes in bourgeois society, she first cites an extended portion of his work and then rejects the economic determinism. Silverman begins by quoting Althusser: "If in its totality ideology expresses a representation of the real destined to sanction a regime of class exploitation and domination, it can also give rise . . . to the expression of the *protest of the exploited classes*. . . . But we should not lose sight of the fact that . . . it is always the ideas of the dominant class . . . which get the upper hand" (1992:26). But she immediately dismisses the science partner in Althusser's ideology-science binarism: "Regrettably, the economic determinism of this passage ultimately vitiates its attempt to account simultaneously for ideological diversity and ideological unity." My work demonstrates how Althusser remains determined to show how Marx's science project works, not with the subjects and objects of ideological struggle, but with the structures within which these struggles are negotiated. But neither Althusser nor his Lacanian critics apply this mirror stage metaphor to science or theory itself, as I am trying to do here.

12. Any representation involved in the formation of forms of life, any constitutive representation, may exclude some material (for example, the surplus population) while including other material. Thus when Marx writes in *Capital* that "the common element which represents itself (*sich darstellt*) in the exchange relation, or the exchange value of the commodity, is thus its value" (Spivak, 1988:278), he evokes a field of representation in which one can make sense of value only in the particular/determinate form of exchange value. If labor-power is to find representation onstage, it must follow capital's rules; capital can thus be presented as determining how the process works.

13. Althusser (1979a:68) elaborates: "the [diachronic] forms of order of the dis-

course are simply the development of the hierarchized combination of the concepts in the system itself."

14. This sophisticated approach to elements of time can, of course, justify rather ineffective political strategies, such as the Communist Party of France waiting for the Red Army (which also never arrives) instead of initiating direct political interventions.

15. Althusser writes: "The proposal to think the determination of the elements of a whole by the structure of the whole posed an absolutely new problem in the most theoretically embarrassing circumstances, for there were no philosophical concepts available for its resolution" (1979b:187).

16. Slavoj Žižek's (1991:95) Lacanian-Hegelian project is fond of contrasting Lacan's mapping with Derrida's disinclination to map or even to name indeterminacy: "With Derrida, as with Lacan . . . the subject's condition of possibility is simultaneously the condition of its impossibility. . . . With Lacan, however, it is not enough to say that the subject's identity is always constitutively truncated, dispersed because of the intrusion of an irreducible outside. . . . In Lacanian theory, this irreducible outsider . . . this intruder that prevents the full constitution of the subject . . . has a precise name: object (*objet petit a*)." While I am intrigued by his contribution to the psychoanalytic theory of hegemony mentioned above, I want here only to use one aspect of Lacan, the mirror stage, as a heuristic to explore the inadequacy of any mapping operation, including Lacan's.

17. The fourth section, which does not concern us here, draws interesting connections between mythology and life forms in antiquity, but Marx does not search for signs of bourgeois mythology.

18. In an oppositional determination, Žižek writes, "the universal, common ground of the two opposites 'encounters itself' in its oppositional determination, i.e., in one of the terms of the opposition" (1993:132).

19. "Western Marxism, in either of its two variants—critical-humanist or scientific—has proven insufficiently radical to expose and root out the racialist order which contaminates its analytic and philosophical applications, or to come to effective terms with its own class origins. As a result, it has been mistaken for something it is not: a total theory of liberation" (Robinson, 1983:451).

20. "The rule of language as signifying system—the possibility of speaking at all—becomes the misrule of discourse: the right for only some to speak diachronically and differentially and for "others"—women, migrants, Third World peoples, Jews, Palestinians, for instance—to speak only symptomatically or marginally" (Bhabha, 1992:49).

Chapter Seven: Mobilizing the Labor Underground

1. Abu-Jamal, who worked with the Black Panther Party during the sixties, told this story in 1989 from his cell on death row (where he still lives, although he has recently been granted an indefinite stay of execution by a recalcitrant judge, while organizers the world over struggle for a new trial).

2. See Spivak (1993:97, 109) on the possibility of an aporia between two societies.

3. It is, of course, impossible to negotiate this transformation when facing the firepower of the U.S. government. See the back cover of Fletcher et al., 1993, where editors quote FBI agent Raymond Byers: "The Negro youth and moderates must be made to understand that if they succumb to revolutionary teaching, they will be dead revolutionaries."

4. This is the last form of sabotage I consider. Two other sections in Flynn's pamphlet defend sabotage against the charge of undermining moral fiber and suggest that workers limit the supply of children they feed to the process of exploitation.

References

Abu-Jamal, M. 1993. Panther Daze Remembered. In Fletcher (1993:193-204).

Adams, F., with M. Horton. 1975. *Unearthing Seeds of Fire: The Idea of Highlander.* Winston-Salem, N.C.: John F. Blair.

Allen, J., ed. 1990. *Lesbian Philosophies and Cultures.* Albany: SUNY Press.

Althusser, L. 1979a. From *Capital* to Marx's Philosophy. In Althusser and Balibar (1979: 13-69).

——. 1979b. The Object of *Capital.* In Althusser and Balibar (1979: 73-198).

Althusser, L., and E. Balibar. 1970. *Lire le Capital.* Paris: Maspéro.

——. 1979. *Reading Capital.* Translated by Ben Brewster. London: Verso.

Anderson, M., and P. Collins, eds. 1992. *Race, Class, and Gender.* Belmont, Calif.: Wadsworth.

Apter, E., and W. Pietz, eds. 1993. *Fetishism as Cultural Discourse.* Cornell University Press.

Ballentine, W. 1996. Who's in Charge? *The Other Paper* April 1996, POB 11376, Eugene, Or. 97440.

Barrett, M. 1980. *Women's Oppression Today.* London: Verso.

Benveniste, E. 1966. *Problèmes de linguistique générale* Paris: Gallimard.

——. 1971. *Problems in General Linguistics.* Translated by Mary Meek. Coral Gables: University of Miami Press.

Bhabha, H. 1989. The Commitment to Theory. In Pines and Willemen (1989:111-32).

——. 1992. Freedom's Basis in the Indeterminate. *October* 61:46-57.

——. 1994. *The Location of Culture* New York: Routledge.

Boggs, J. 1963. *The American Revolution: Pages from a Negro Worker's Notebook.* New York: Monthly Review.

Boyte, H., and S. Evans. 1992. *Free Spaces.* Chicago Press ed. Chicago: University of Chicago Press.

Boyte, H., and F. Reissman, eds. 1986. *The New Populism*. Philadelphia: Temple University Press.

Butler, J. 1987. *Subjects of Desire*. New York: Columbia University Press.

———. 1990. *Gender Trouble*. New York: Routledge.

———. 1991. Imitation and Gender Insubordination. In Fuss (1991:13–31).

———. 1993a. Poststructuralism and Postmarxism. *Diacritics*, Winter, 3–11.

———. 1993b. *Bodies That Matter*. New York: Routledge

Butler, J., and J. Scott, eds. 1992. *Feminists Theorize the Political*. New York: Routledge.

Callari, A., et al., eds. 1995. *Marxism in the Postmodern Age*. New York: Guilford.

Carroll, D. 1987. *Paraesthetics*. New York: Methuen.

Castoriadis, C. 1995. C. L. R. James and the Fate of Marxism. In Cudjoe and Cain (1995:277–97).

Christian, B. 1989. The Race of Theory. In Kauffman (1989:225–37).

Cixous, H. 1990. *Reading with Clarice Lispector*. Edited, translated, and introduced by Verona Andermatt Conley. Minneapolis: University of Minnesota Press.

Cixous, H., and C. Clement. 1986. *The Newly Born Woman*. Translated by Betsy Wing. Minneapolis: University of Minnesota Press.

Connolly, W. 1981. *Appearance and Reality in Politics*. Cambridge: Cambridge University Press.

———. 1988. *Political Theory and Modernity*. Oxford: Blackwell.

———. 1991. *Identity/Difference: Democratic Negotiations of Political Paradox*. Ithaca: Cornell University Press.

Corlett, W. 1993. *Community without Unity: A Politics of Derridian Extravagance*. Paperback ed. Durham: Duke University Press.

Cudjoe, S., and W. Cain, eds. 1995. *C. L. R. James: His Intellectual Legacies*. Amherst: University of Massachusetts Press.

The Damned. 1990. *Lessons from the Damned: Class Struggle in the Black Community*. 2d ed. Ojai, Calif.: Times Change Press.

Deleuze, G., and F. Guattari. 1983. *Anti-Oedipus*. Translated by Robert Hurley, Mark Seem, and Helen R. Lane. Minneapolis: University of Minnesota Press.

———. 1987. *A Thousand Plateaus*. Translated by Brian Massumi. Minneapolis: University of Minnesota Press.

Delgado, G. 1992. *Anti-racist Work: An Examination and Assessment of Organizational Activity*. Oakland, Calif.: Applied Research Center.

———. 1994. *Beyond the Politics of Place: New Directions in Community Organizing in the 1990s*. Oakland, Calif.: Applied Research Center.

Derrida, J. 1974. *Of Grammatology*. Translated by Gayatri C. Spivak. Baltimore: Johns Hopkins University Press.

———. 1978a. *Writing and Difference*. Translated by Alan Bass. Chicago: University of Chicago Press.

———. 1978b. *Spurs*. Translated by Barbara Harlow. Chicago: University of Chicago Press.

———. 1980. *La Carte Postale*. Paris: Flammarion.

———. 1981. *Dissemination*. Translated by Barbara Johnson. Chicago: University of Chicago Press.

———. 1987. *The Postcard*. Translated by Alan Bass. Chicago: University of Chicago Press.

———. 1991. *A Derrida Reader*. Edited by Peggy Kamuf. New York: Columbia University Press.

———. 1994. *Specters of Marx*. Translated by Peggy Kamuf. New York: Routledge.

Ebert, T. 1996. *Ludic Feminism and After*. Ann Arbor: Michigan.

Eisenstein, Z. 1981. *The Radical Future of Liberal Feminism*. New York: Longman.

———. 1990. Specifying U.S. Feminism in the 1990s: The Problem of Naming. *Socialist Review* 20:45-56.

Elson, D. 1979. *Value: The Representation of Labour in Capitalism*. Atlantic Highlands, N.J.: Humanities Press.

Felman, S. 1988. On Reading Poetry: Reflections on the Limits and Possibilities of Psychoanalytic Approaches. In Muller and Richardson (1988:133-56).

Ferguson, A. 1991. *Sexual Democracy: Women, Oppression, and Revolution*. Boulder, Colo.: Westview.

Fisk, M. 1993. Poststructuralism, Difference, and Marxism. *Praxis International* 12: 323-40.

Fletcher, J., et al., eds. 1993. *Still Black, Still Strong: Survivors of the U.S. War against Black Revolutionaries*. New York: Semiotext(e).

Flynn, E. 1915. Sabotage. In Baxandall (1987:124-33).

Foner, E., ed. 1995. *The Black Panthers Speak*. New York: De Capo.

Foucault, M. 1977. *Language, Counter-Memory, Practice*. Translated by Donald F. Bouchard and Sherry Simon. Ithaca: Cornell University Press.

Fraad, H., S. Resnick, and R. Wolff. 1994. Bringing It All Back Home: Class, Gender and Power in the Modern Household. London: Pluto.

Frye, M. 1983. *The Politics of Reality: Essays in Feminist Theory*. Trumansburg, N.Y.: Crossing Press.

Fuss, D. 1989. *Essentially Speaking*. New York: Routledge.

———, ed. 1991. *Inside/out*. New York: Routledge.

Gallop, J. 1985. *Reading Lacan*. Ithaca: Cornell University Press.

———. 1989. *Thinking Through the Body*. Chicago: University of Chicago Press.

Glazer, N. Y. 1993. *Women's Paid and Unpaid Labor*. Philadelphia: Temple University Press.

Gray, C. 1994. *Toward a Nonviolent Economics*. Self-published. 888 Almaden, Eugene, Or. 97402.

Green, J., ed. 1983. *Workers' Struggles, Past and Present*. Philadelphia: Temple University Press.

Griffiths, A., ed. 1987. *Contemporary French Philosophy*. Cambridge: Cambridge University Press.

Grimshaw, A. 1992. *The C. L. R. James Reader*. Oxford: Blackwell.

Grossman, R., and F. Adams. 1993. *Taking Care of Business: Citizenship and the Charter of Incorporation*. Cambridge: Charter, Ink.

Grosz, E. 1989. *Sexual Subversions*. London: Allen and Unwin.

———. 1990. *Jacques Lacan, a Feminist Introduction*. New York: Routledge.

Haraway, D. 1990. A Manifesto for Cyborgs: Science, Technology, and Socialist Feminism in the 1980s. In Nicholson (1990:190-233)

Hindess, B., and P. Hirst. 1977. *Mode of Production and Social Formation*. New York: Macmillan.

Holland, E. 1991. Deterritorializing "Deterritorialization" from the *Anti-Oedipus* to *A Thousand Plateaus*. *Substance* 66:55–72.

Irigaray, L. 1985. *Speculum of the Other Woman*. Translated by Gillian C. Gill. Ithaca: Cornell University Press.

———. 1987. Is the Subject of Science Sexed? Translated by Carol Mastrangelo Bove. *Hypatia* 2:65–87.

Jacobs, H. 1987. *Incidents in the Life of a Slave Girl*. Edited by L. Maria Child. Cambridge: Harvard University Press.

James, C. L. R. 1977. *The Future in the Present: Selected Writings*. Westport, Conn.: Lawrence Hill.

James, J. 1995. Racism, Genocide, and Resistance: The Politics of Language and International Law. In Callari (1995:115–25).

Jameson, F. 1981. *The Political Unconscious*. Ithaca: Cornell University Press.

———. 1988. Postmodernism and Consumer Society. In Kaplan (1988:13–29)

Johnson, B. 1981. Translator's Introduction. In Derrida (1981:vii–xxxiii).

———. 1988. The Frame of Reference: Poe, Lacan, Derrida. In Muller and Richardson (1988:213–51).

Joyce, P., ed. 1995. *Class*. London: Oxford University Press.

Kaplan, E. A., ed. 1988. *Postmodernism and Its Discontents*. London: Verso.

Katznelson, I. 1990. Writings edited by Prudence Posner in Kling and Posner (1990: 46–70).

Kauffman, L., ed. 1989. *Gender and Theory*. London: Blackwell.

Keenan, T. 1993. The Point Is to (Ex)Change It, Reading Capital Rhetorically. In Apter and Peitz (1993:152–85).

Kellman, P. 1996 A. Challenge to Labor. *Dissident* 2 (4):8–9.

Kennedy, M., C. Tilly, and M. Gaston. 1990. Transformative Populism and the Development of a Community of Color. In Kling and Posner (1990:302–24)

Kling, J., and P. Posner, eds. 1990. *Dilemmas of Activism* Philadelphia: Temple University Press.

Kornbluh, J., ed. 1988. *Rebel Voices: An IWW Anthology*. Chicago: Charles Kerr.

Kozura, M. 1996. We Stood Our Ground: Anthracite Miners and the Expropriation of Corporate Property, 1930–41. In Lynd (1996:199–237).

Lacan, J. 1966. *Ecrits*. Paris: Seuil

———. 1968. *The Language of the Self*. Translated with notes and commentary by Anthony Wilden. Baltimore: Johns Hopkins University Press.

———. 1977. *Ecrits*. Translated by Alan Sheridan. New York: Norton.

———. 1978. *The Four Fundamental Concepts of Psycho-Analysis*. Translated by Alan Sheridan. New York: W. W. Norton.

———. 1988a. Seminar on "The Purloined Letter." Translated by Jeffrey Mehlman. In Muller and Richardson (1988:28–54)

———. 1988b. *Seminar*. Book II. Translated by Sylvana Tomaselli. New York: Norton.

———. 1991. *Seminar*. Book I. Translated by John Forrester. New York: Norton.

Laclau, E., and C. Mouffe. 1985. *Hegemony and Socialist Strategy*. London: Verso.

Lispector, C. 1988. *The Passion according to G. H.* Translated by Ronald W. Sousa. Minneapolis: University of Minnesota Press.

——. 1989. *The Stream of Life*. Translated by Elizabeth Lowe and Earl Fitz. Minneapolis: University of Minnesota Press.

Lorde, A. 1984. *Sister Outsider*. Trumansburg, N.Y.: Crossing Press.

Lugones, M. 1990. Playfulness, "World"-Travelling, and Loving Perception. In Allen (1990:159-80).

Lynd, S., ed. 1996. *"We Are All Leaders": The Alternative Unionism of the Early 1930s*. Urbana: University of Illinois Press.

Marx, K. 1965. *Pre-capitalist Economic Formations*. Translated by Jack Cohen. Introduction by Eric Hobsbawm. New York: International.

——. 1967. *Capital*. Vol. 2. Translated by Samuel Moore and Edward Aveling. New York: International.

——. 1973. *Grundrisse: Foundations of the Critique of Political Economy*. Translated by Martin Nicolaus. New York: Random House.

——. 1975. *Texts on Method*. Translated and edited by Terrell Carver. New York: Barnes and Noble.

——. 1976a. *Capital*. Vol. 1. Edited by F. Engels. Translated by B. Fowkes. New York: Vintage.

——. 1976b. *MEGA 1857/58* (text). Berlin: Dietz.

——. 1989. *MEGA 1883* (text). Berlin: Dietz.

Marx, K., and F. Engels. 1978. *The Marx-Engels Reader*. 2d ed. Edited by Robert C. Tucker. New York: Norton.

McHenry, K., and C. T. Butler. 1992. *Food Not Bombs*. Philadelphia: New Society.

McIntosh, P. 1992. White Privilege and Male Privilege: A Personal Account of Coming to See Correspondences through Work in Women's Studies. In Anderson and Collins (1992:76-86).

Mies, M. 1986. *Patriarchy and Accumulation on a World Scale: Women in the International Division of Labor*. London: Zed.

Mies, M., and V. Shiva. 1993. *Ecofeminism*. London: Zed.

Mouffe, C. 1992. Feminism, Citizenship, and Radical Democratic Politics. In Butler and Scott (1992:369-84).

——, ed. 1996. *Deconstruction and Pragmatism*. New York: Routledge.

Muller, J., and W. Richardson, eds. 1988. *The Purloined Poe*. Baltimore: Johns Hopkins University Press.

Nelson, C., and L. Grossberg, eds. 1988. *Marxism and the Interpretation of Culture*. Urbana: University of Illinois Press.

Newton, H. 1995. Functional Definition of Politics. In Foner (1995:45-49).

Nicholson, L., ed. 1990. *Feminism/Postmodernism*. London: Routledge.

Ollman, B. 1976. *Alienation: Marx's Conception of Man in Capitalist Society*. 2d ed. Cambridge: Cambridge University Press.

——. 1979. *Social and Sexual Revolution: Essays on Marx and Reich*. Boston: South End Press.

——. 1993. *Dialectical Investigations*. New York: Routledge.

Parker, A. 1991. Unthinking Sex: Marx, Engels and the Scene of Writing. *Social Text* 9:28-45.

Pines, J., and P. Willemen. 1989. *Questions of Third Cinema*. London: British Film Institute.

Prakash, G. 1992. Can the "Subaltern" Ride? *Comparative Studies in Society and History* 34:168–85.

Ragland, E. 1995. *Essays on the Pleasures of Death*. New York: Routledge.

Rawick, G. 1983. Working-Class Self-Activity. In Green (1983:141–50).

Resnick, S., and R. Wolff. 1987. *Knowledge and Class: A Marxian Critique of Political Economy*. Chicago: University of Chicago Press.

Robinson, C. 1983. *Black Marxism: The Making of the Black Radical Tradition*. London: Zed.

———. 1995. C. L. R. James and the World System. In Cudjoe and Cain (1995:244–59).

Rudé, G. 1980. *Ideology and Popular Protest* New York: Pantheon.

Ryan, M. 1982. *Marxism and Deconstruction, a Critical Articulation*. Baltimore: Johns Hopkins University Press.

———. 1989. *Politics and Culture: Working Hypotheses for a Post-revolutionary Society*. Baltimore: Johns Hopkins University Press.

———. 1993. Foucault's Fallacy. *Strategies* 7:132–55.

Silverman, K. 1983. *The Subject of Semiotics*. New York: Oxford.

———. 1992. *Male Subjectivity at the Margins*. New York: Routledge.

Spivak, G. 1987. *In Other Worlds: Essays in Cultural Politics*. New York: Methuen.

———. 1988. Can the Subaltern Speak? In Nelson and Grossberg (1988:271–313).

———. 1990. *The Post-colonial Critic: Interviews, Strategies, Dialogues*. Edited by Sarah Harasym. New York: Routledge.

———. 1993. *Outside in the Teaching Machine*. New York: Routledge.

Taylor, C. 1993. Positioning Subjects and Objects: Agency, Narration, Relationality. *Hypatia* 8:55–80.

Trinh T. Minh-ha. 1991. *When the Moon Waxes Red*. New York: Routledge.

Vitale, A., and K. McHenry. 1994. Food Not Bombs. *Z Magazine* 7(9):19–21.

Wahad, D. B. 1993. Toward Rethinking Self-Defense. In Fletcher (1993:57–76).

West, C. 1988. Interview with Cornel West. Conducted by Anders Stephanson. In Ross (1988:269–86).

Wilden, A. 1968. Notes and Commentary. In Lacan (1968)

Wittgenstein, L. 1958. *Philosophical Investigations*. 3d ed. Translated by G. E. M. Anscombe. New York: Macmilllan.

Wood, D. 1987. Beyond Deconstruction? In Griffiths (1987:175–94).

Wood, E. 1986. *The Retreat from Class: A New True Socialism*. London: Verso. Excerpted in Joyce (1995:64–68).

Žižek, S. 1989. *The Sublime Object of Ideology*. London: Verso.

———. 1991. *For They Know Not What They Do*. London: Verso.

———. 1993. *Tarrying with the Negative*. Durham: Duke University Press.

Index

CONTESTATIONS

A series edited by
WILLIAM E. CONNOLLY

Living Ethically, Acting Politically
   by Melissa A. Orlie

The Art of Being Free: Taking Liberties with Tocqueville, Marx, and Arendt
   by Mark Reinhardt

Political Theory for Mortals: Shades of Justice, Images of Death
   by John E. Seery

Signifying Woman: Culture and Chaos in Rousseau, Burke, and Mill
   by Linda M. G. Zerilli